A Han[illegible]
English
Pronunciation

A Handbook of English Pronunciation

Robert Hooke and Judith Rowell

Italian notes by David Hart
Portuguese and Spanish notes by Roger Jones
French notes by Che Viccars
Greek notes by Irene Warburton
German notes by Margaret and David Wright

Cartoons by Pamela Winterton

Edward Arnold

First published 1982
by Edward Arnold (Publishers) Ltd
41 Bedford Square, London WC1B 3DQ

British Library Cataloguing in Publication Data
Hooke, Robert
A handbook of English pronunciation.
1. English language – Text-books for foreigners
2. English language – Pronunciation
I. Title
428′.1 PE1128

ISBN 0-7131-8022-6

Filmset by Willmer Brothers Limited
Birkenhead, Merseyside
and printed in Hong Kong by
Wing King Tong Co Ltd

Contents

Introduction

A Handbook of English Pronunciation is for students of any nationality learning English as a second or foreign language. It is clearly and simply written for students from early intermediate level upwards. It concentrates on the sounds of English, and also gives help with stress and intonation. The lessons can be used in the classroom, in the language laboratory or for private study.
Foreign Language Notes. For speakers of the major European languages, there are notes in their mother tongues to explain similarities and differences between sounds in these languages and in English. The notes help students move from their native sounds to the English sounds. These foreign notes should be used together with the English descriptions of sounds in each lesson.
Received Pronunciation. The descriptions of the sounds in this book are based on Received Pronunciation, the educated speech of the south east of England. Learners of English may well be exposed to other regional accents, and should learn to understand them. However RP has been chosen as the model for production because it is the most widely understood and is the most common accent in standard course books.
Phonetics. The phonetic alphabet used in this book is the International Phonetic Alphabet as used by Professor Gimson in his "Introduction to the Pronunciation of English" 3rd Edition. However, this handbook is intended to be a practical guide to students of all levels – some simplification is therefore inevitable.

How to Use this Book

This book is divided into three sections – consonants, vowels, diphthongs. Before you begin each section, you should read the introduction to that particular section. If you do not do this, you may not understand all the words used in the lessons.

Pre-tests

At the beginning of each section, there are pre-tests on the sounds in that section: two on consonants, one on vowels and one on diphthongs. You should do these tests before you begin the sections, because they will tell you which sounds are most difficult for you, and therefore which lessons you should concentrate on.

Format of the lessons

1. In each lesson there is a detailed description of how the sound is made, with diagrams and sometimes photographs to help you. There are also notes on the spelling of the sound because in English one sound can often be spelt in many ways.
2. The first exercises in each lesson are just for you to listen to. They will help you get used to the sound and hear the difference between two or more similar sounds.
3. In the next exercises you will be asked to listen to words and repeat them. Often these will be words which sound almost the same but are different, such as 'pet' and 'pat'. You will probably not know the meanings of all the words in these exercises and the listening exercises, but that is not important. In fact it may be easier to concentrate on the sound if you do not know the meaning.
4. In each lesson there is a short dialogue. Some of the words in the dialogue contain the sound you have been practising in the lesson. These dialogues will help you use the sound in ordinary speech. For each dialogue, there are some questions on stress and intonation. These are not connected with the particular sound you are practising, but they will help you notice the rhythm of English. The answers to all the

questions are on page 204. (See page xii for more on stress and intonation.)

5. The group activities at the end of each lesson are to give you an opportunity to use the sound freely. Most of these are for class use, but you can do many of the activities even if you are using the book alone.

6. Many of the lessons have a "silly sentence". These are just for fun – don't take them too seriously!

Phonetic symbols

When we use phonetic symbols we use lines like this / /, for example /t/.

When we are talking about the letters you use to write a word, we will use ' ', for example 'd'.

In these lessons we will be using phonetic symbols to show you the sounds instead of the letters of the alphabet. Each phonetic symbol is used for one sound of English. The sounds may be spelt in a lot of different ways, for example the /s/ sound (as in 'sing') can also be spelt certain, science, or psychiatry, but all of these words have the same *sound* at the beginning of them.

Some of the symbols may be the same as the letters of the alphabet e.g. /t/ /d/, but others are not, for example: /ʒ/ /ŋ/. Remember that when we use the symbols, we are thinking about how the word sounds and not how it is spelt.

The cassette

The symbol is used in the book to tell you what is on the cassette. In all the exercises the words are spoken once, with space for you to repeat them. If you want to hear the words again, you should rewind the cassette. The dialogues are recorded once only at normal speed with no space. You should use the pause button on your cassette recorder when you repeat the parts of the dialogues.

A word of advice

The importance of listening

If possible, use another tape recorder and record yourself when you do these exercises. You may think you have made a sound correctly but you cannot be sure until you hear it. If you are not pleased with the way you did an exercise do it again and listen to the new recording. Keep doing it until you *are* pleased. This is very important for the exercises where you repeat phrases or words.

It is also very important that you rely on your teacher or an English

speaking friend to guide you. You may not hear some mistakes that you make, but an English speaker will hear them very quickly and be able to help you.
Some English sounds will be easier for you to pronounce than others; that is because there may be the same sound in your own language. Other sounds that you do not have in your language will be more difficult. You should be very careful if your language has a sound *almost* the same as the English sound. These sounds may be the most difficult.

Stress and Intonation

Before we move on to each sound in detail there are two important things to think about when we put words and sentences together. These two things are stress and intonation. Stress and intonation are very important ways of making your English *sound* English.

Word stress

In words which have more than one part (syllable), one of these parts sounds more important than the others. This is the stressed syllable. Every word has its own stress and this never changes. Similar words, however, may have different stresses. Look at these words for example:

'**pho**tograph   pho'**to**grapher   photo'**gra**phic

As you can see the stress is on a different syllable in each word although the words are related.

Sometimes the same word has two different stresses and this can change the meaning, for example:

'**re**cord (the noun)   re'**cord** (the verb)

Unfortunately there are no rules to help you with word stress. When you learn a new word, you must learn how it is stressed.

Word groups

When we talk, we do not talk in single words and stop after each one. We talk in *groups* of words and each group is about the length of a breath. When we make sentences we stop between them, but we also take short stops at the end of the word groups. Look at the word groups in this sentence:

On Monday / I went to catch the train, / but when I got to the station / the trains were on strike./

Sentence stress

In these groups of words, some of them are *stressed*; that is, they are pronounced harder and sound more important. They are the words that stand out when you listen to a sentence. To show the stresses we will use marks like this ' and put them in front of the stressed syllable. So the mark on the word 'Monday means that the syllable **Mon** is the one that is stressed and sounds most important.

The stresses in the sentence we looked at earlier are:

On '**Mon**day I '**went** to '**catch** the '**train**, but '**when** I '**got** to the '**sta**tion the '**trains** were on '**strike**.

There are nine stressed words in this sentence.

In each word group one of the words sounds the most important and this is called the *nucleus*. We can change the meaning of a sentence by moving the nucleus, that is, by putting more stress on a different word and so making it the nucleus. For example, if you say:

I like your 'new coat, with the stress on the word **new**, this means that you like the new coat but not the old one.

If you say:

I like your new 'coat, with the stress on the word **coat**, the sentence now means that you like the coat but perhaps not the new shoes or hat.

What would the sentence mean if the stress were on the word **I**? And on the word **your**?

Intonation

Now that we have learnt about stress we must also learn about tones. Tones are the way that your voice moves up and down; every word group has a tone. The way we use these tones is called intonation, and it is the English intonation which makes English sound really English. You must learn the shapes of the English tones and also their meanings. It is possible in English to say the same sentence in different ways and so change the whole meaning.

When we are thinking about tones we must listen out for the nucleus of the word group; that is, the most important word. This is the word in which the voice moves most.

If the nucleus is at the beginning of a sentence and it goes down, then the rest of the sentence continues to go down. If the nucleus is at the end of the sentence, then most of the sentence is level and then goes up or down at the end. Look at the diagrams:

Jane's gone to ˈ↘London.

Types of tones

There are two main types of tones; *falling tones* (down tones) and *rising tones* (up tones). Sometimes they go together and make rise-fall tones (up-down tones) or fall-rise tones (down-up). Often certain tones are used for certain types of sentences. Here are some notes to help you.

Falling (down) tones

1. When we make a statement this is the tone we usually use. For example:

   He's very ↘old.

   It's a nice ↘house.

   It's on the big ↘table over there.

2. Questions that begin with a question word e.g. *what, where, who* and so on, usually have a falling tone. For example:

   Why's he doing ↘that?

   Who was that ↘man?

   What's he ↘doing?

Rising (up) tones

These tones are usually used when you ask questions without a question word, for example:

Is he ↗coming?

Are they on the ↗table?

Does he come ↗every week?

The answers to these questions would probably have a falling tone.

Tag questions
These are a little bit different. Look at this sentence.

He's ↘very good, ↘isn't he?

The question tag in this sentence is not really a question because the speaker is just checking the first statement. Both parts of the sentence have a falling tone.
Now look at this sentence.

He's ↘very good, ↗isn't he?

In this sentence the speaker is not very sure of the first statement and so makes it into a question. The first part of the sentence has a falling tone and the second part has a rising tone.

Fall-rise tones
With this tone the voice goes down first and then it goes up. We use this tone to show surprise.

John's got a new ↘car.

↘↗Really. He had a new one last month.

This tone also sounds *questioning*, as if to say 'This is so surprising. Are you sure?'

Rise-fall tones
This tone is the opposite of the fall-rise tone. With this tone the voice goes up first and then down.

This tone is used also for suprise but in a more definite way, without any question.

Susan's going to ↘Paris.

^Really, she's very ↘lucky.

This tone shows that you are *impressed*; the second person thinks it's good that Susan is going to Paris.

This is only a very short guide to stress and intonation, but it should help you when you listen to the dialogues in each lesson. There will be questions at the end of every dialogue to help you look out for different stresses and intonation. Here are a few notes to help you.

1. Try to break the sentences up into word groups before you repeat them. Take a breath between word groups.
2. Listen for the sentence stress; that is, the rhythm of English.
3. Listen for the most important word in each word group. This is the word which has the most stress, and where the tone changes.
4. Listen for the tones. Does the voice go up or down? Does it go up then down, or down then up? Use the rules above to help you.

PART 1

THE CONSONANTS

Introduction to consonants

In these lessons, we are going to practise listening to and pronouncing the English consonants. In parts 2 and 3 we will look at the pure vowels and diphthongs, but for now let us try to understand some of the words you will meet in the lessons on consonants. It will also help you pronounce the sounds a bit better if you understand a little about the way they are made and what happens when we speak.

Look at diagram 1.

1. The lungs give out the air we breathe in; it passes up the wind pipe to the vocal cords.
2. The vocal cords are very important; they may be open to make *voiceless* sounds or almost closed to make *voiced* sounds. The air pushes through the vocal cords and this makes them move, giving us voice (see diagram 2).
3. The soft palate can move up and down. When it is down, the air can pass out through the nose and this makes the nasal consonants. When it is up, the air cannot go out through the nose and so it passes out through the mouth to make all the other sounds.
4. The tongue can move to touch the top of the mouth and the teeth, and so stops or slows down the air. The front of the tongue can move to touch the teeth or the alveolar ridge, and the back of the tongue can move to touch the soft palate. Diagram 1 shows the different parts of the tongue.
5. The lips can close together to stop the air, or the bottom lip can move to the top teeth to slow down the air. They can also make many different shapes, which are very important for vowel sounds.

What is a consonant?

A consonant is a sound in which the air from the lungs is not allowed to pass out through the mouth without something interrupting it. The ways this can be done we will call, *how the sound is made*.

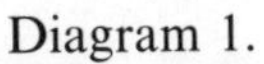

Diagram 1.

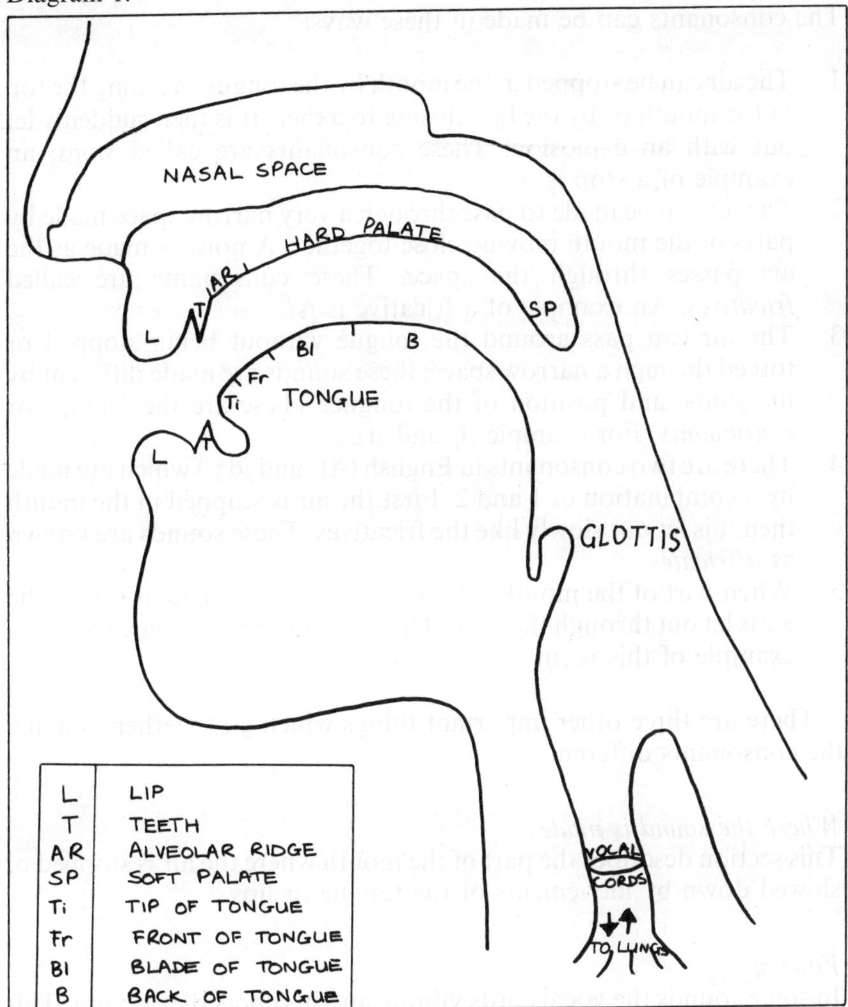

Diagram 2. The vocal cords

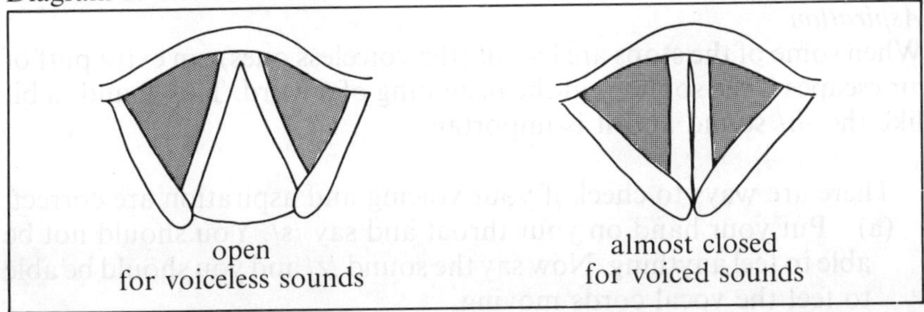

How the sound is made
The consonants can be made in these ways:

1. The air can be stopped in the mouth by the tongue touching the top of the mouth or by the lips closing together. It is then suddenly let out with an explosion. These consonants are called *stops*; an example of a stop is /t/.
2. The air can be made to pass through a very narrow space made by parts of the mouth moving close together. A noise is made as the air passes through the space. These consonants are called *fricatives*. An example of a fricative is /s/.
3. The air can pass around the tongue without being stopped or forced through a narrow space; these sounds are made different by the shape and position of the tongue. These are the *laterals* or *continuants*. For example /l/ and /r/.
4. There are two consonants in English (/tʃ/ and /dʒ/) which are made by a combination of 1 and 2. First the air is stopped in the mouth then it is let out slowly like the fricatives. These sounds are known as *affricates*.
5. When part of the mouth is closed and the soft palate is down, the air is let out through the nose. This makes the *nasal* consonants: an example of this is /m/.

There are three other important things which go together to make the consonants different:

Where the sound is made
This section describes the part of the mouth where the air is stopped or slowed down by movements of the tongue or lips.

Voicing
In some sounds the vocal cords vibrate and in others they do not. This makes the difference between voiced and voiceless sounds.

Aspiration
When some of the stops are let out (the voiceless ones), an extra puff of air escapes if the sound is at the beginning of a word. This sounds a bit like the /h/ sound and it is important.

There are ways to check if your voicing and aspiration are correct.

(a) Put your hand on your throat and say /s/. You should not be able to feel anything. Now say the sound /z/ and you should be able to feel the vocal cords moving.

(b) You can feel aspiration by putting your hand in front of your mouth. Firstly say the sound /p/. You should be able to feel the puff of air on your hand. Now say /b/ and you should not be able to feel this puff of air.

If you have any problems saying the sounds of English it often helps to look in a mirror. This will give you a better idea of where you are putting your tongue.

Listening pre-tests

Before you begin the lessons on consonants, do these two listening pre-tests. They will help you to find out which consonants you should practise most.

In each pre-test you will hear 60 pairs of words. Sometimes the words will be exactly the same, sometimes they will be slightly different. When you hear each pair, write down on a piece of paper S if the words sound the same, D if they sound different. For example, if you hear 'hat, hat' write S; if you hear 'hat, had' write D.

When you have listened to the 60 pairs of words in listening pre-test part 1, turn to the back of the book and . . .

1. Check your answers with the key on page 196.
2. Listen to the tape again, and this time, while you listen, read the words printed in the tapescript on page 196.
3. Look at the error identification chart on page 197. This will tell you which lesson you should concentrate on. For example, if you thought the two words in the first pair were the same you should study lessons 3 and 13.

Now do the same with listening pre-test part 2.
The key is on page 198.
The tapescript is on page 198.
The error identification chart is on page 199.

Lesson 1

The stops /p/ and /b/

How to pronounce these two consonants

How the sounds are made
These two consonants are both stops. The air coming from the lungs is stopped for a short time and let out explosively.

Where the sounds are made
Look at the diagrams. In 1 you can see that the air is stopped by the two lips being closed quite tightly. In 2 the lips are opened and the air passes out.

1

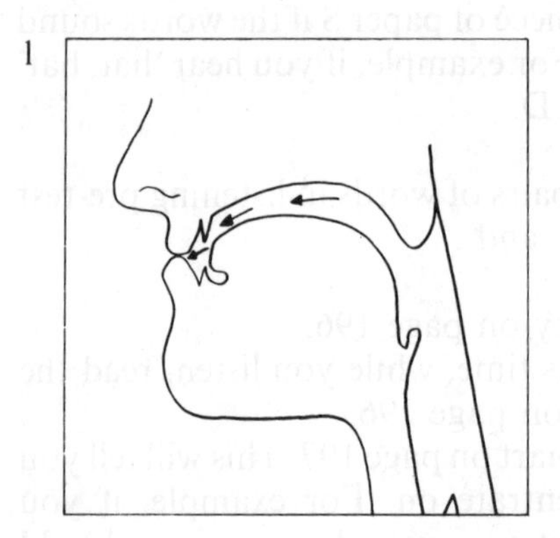

2

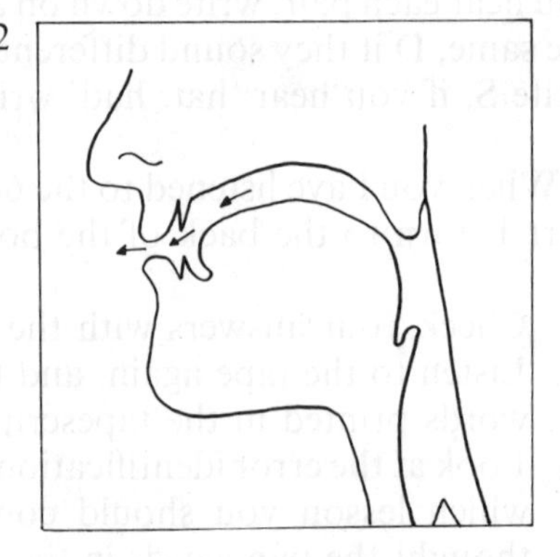

Voicing and length
/p/ is a voiceless sound; the vocal cords are not moving. It is a very short sound.
/b/ is a voiced sound; the vocal cords move to make this sound. It is a bit longer than /p/.

Aspiration
When /p/ is made at the beginning of a word there is an extra puff of air, a bit like the /h/ sound. /b/ is not aspirated.

Exercise 1a
Put your hand on your throat and say /p/ several times. You should not feel anything. Now say /b/ several times. You should be able to feel the vibration of the vocal cords moving. Now say /p/ /b/ /p/ and so on, and you should be able to feel this stopping and starting.

Exercise 1b
Put your hand in front of your mouth and say /p/. You should be able to feel the puff of air. Now say /b/. There should be no puff of air.

Spelling

/p/ is spelt with the letter 'p' or 'pp'.

/b/ is spelt with the letter 'b' or 'bb'.

There are a few words in English in which the 'p' and 'b' are *not* pronounced (e.g. pneumatic, receipt, thumb, comb).

Exercise 2
In this exercise you will hear ten words. You must decide whether, in each word, you hear the consonant /p/ or /b/. Show your answer by writing down p or b, and then correct your work. The correct answers are underlined in exercise 7 on page 8.

Exercise 3
Repeat these words, in which /p/ and /b/ come at the beginning.

pet, bet; pill, bill; pat, bat; park, bark; pay, bay.

Exercise 4
Repeat these words or groups of words, in which /p/ and /b/ come after a vowel.

apply, reply, repay, approach, appeal.
able, a brooch, a bead, abroad, a bend.

Exercise 5
Repeat these words in which /s/ comes before /p/. When these two sounds come together at the beginning of a word, the /p/ sound does not have any aspiration and it sounds a little more like the /b/ sound.

spy, speak, spend, spit, spell, spin.

Exercise 6

Repeat these words in which /p/ and /b/ come at the end of a word. In this position, the lips may stay closed after making the sound and there is not much explosion.

cheap, leap, top, shape, step.
rib, crib, cab, scrub, tube.

Exercise 7

Repeat the pairs of words. In each pair the one underlined is the one you heard in exercise 2. The other is almost the same, except that it has the other consonant.

pray, bray; posting, boasting; pox, box;
approach, a brooch; rope, robe; praise, braise.
pleading, bleeding; wrap it, rabbit;
pride, bride; paw, bore;

Exercise 8

Read through this dialogue and look at the questions at the end before you listen to the tape. Pat has never been to Beeston before and she can't find her friend's house. She asks a policeman.

Pat: Excuse me. I seem to be lost and I can't find my map.
Policeman: Yes, Beeston's a big place. People are always getting lost here.
Pat: I'm looking for Palmers the Bakers; my friend lives above the shop.
Policeman: Palmers the Bakers? I think it's past the library and just beside the butchers, opposite the book shop.
Pat: Past the library . . . beside the butchers . . . opposite the book shop . . . I hope I can find it now.
Policeman: I hope so too. There must be a party there because you're the ninth person to ask me today.

Now look at these questions.

1. Why does Pat repeat what the policeman says (line 8)? How does she say it?
2. Which is the most important word in the second part of line 2?
3. Which tone does Pat use for 'excuse me' (line 1)?

Exercise 9

Now read the part of Pat. She's a little worried because she's lost.

Exercise 10
Read the part of the policeman. He's very helpful.

Today's silly sentence

Barbara Baker baked beautiful bread while her brother Bob looked after the baby.

Group activities

1. Your teacher will say one word in each of these pairs of words. Listen carefully and decide which one it is.

1	2	1	2
pen	Ben	rope	robe
pig	big	nip	nib
pack	back	cap	cab
peach	beach	cup	cub

2. Now split into pairs and try the same thing with your partner.

3. Look at the list of words below. Each person in the group must think of a sentence using at least three of the words and then say it to the rest of the group. The rest of the group should listen carefully and decide which words he or she used.

please,	rub,	back,
potatoes,	put,	buy,
pass,	shop,	table,
big,	bag,	cup.

4. *Conversation practice*
Practise these conversations with a partner.

A.

Customer:

Could I have a bottle of [milk, / brandy, / Polish vodka, / grapefruit juice,] please?

Shop-keeper:

I'm sorry, we haven't got any [milk. / brandy. / Polish vodka. / grapefruit juice.]

B.

Customer:

Could I have a kilo of [peas, / beans, / ripe apples, / bananas, / parsnips,] please?

Shop-keeper:
I'm sorry, we . . .

Lesson 2

The stops /t/ and /d/

How to pronounce these two consonants

How the sounds are made
These two consonants are stops. The air coming from the lungs is stopped for a short time and let out explosively.

Where the sounds are made
Look at the two diagrams. In 1 you can see that the air is stopped by the front of the tongue touching the alveolar ridge. This ridge is behind your top teeth and it is important that you touch the ridge and not the teeth. In 2 you can see that the air is let out when the tongue is taken away from the alveolar ridge.

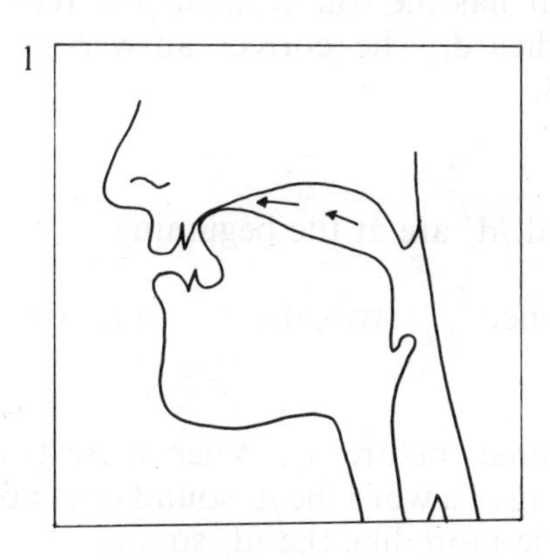

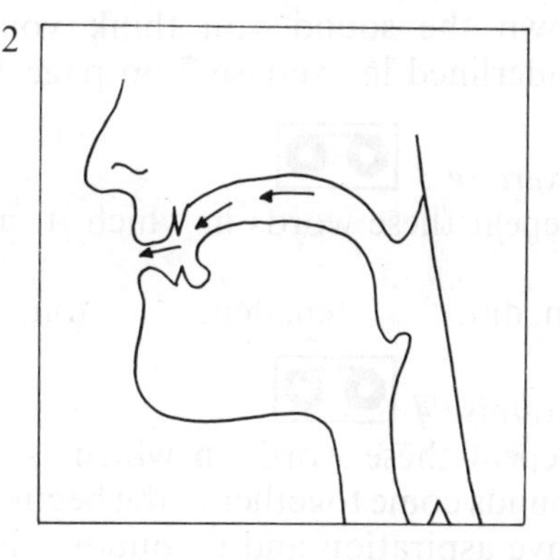

Voicing and length
/t/ is a voiceless sound; the vocal cords are not moving. It is a short sound.
/d/ is a voiced sound; the vocal cords move to make this sound. It is a longer sound.

Aspiration
When /t/ is made at the beginning of a word there is an extra puff of air

as it is let out. This extra puff sounds a bit like the /h/ sound. The /d/ sound is not aspirated.

Exercise 1a
Put your hand on your throat and say /t/ several times. You should not feel anything. Now say /d/ several times. You should be able to feel the vibration of the vocal cords moving. Now try /t/ /d/ /t/ and so on and you should feel the vibration stopping and starting.

Exercise 1b
Put your hand in front of your mouth and say /t/. You should be able to feel the puff of air. Now say /d/. There should be no puff of air.

Spelling

/t/ is spelt with the letters 't' or 'tt'. There are a few words, however, in which 'th' is pronounced as /t/ (e.g. Thomas, Thames). There are also a very few words in which 't' is not pronounced (e.g. castle).

/d/ is spelt with the letters 'd' or 'dd'.

Exercise 2
Decide whether each word you hear has the sound /t/ or /d/. Write down the sound you think you heard. The correct answers are underlined in exercise 7 on page 13.

Exercise 3
Repeat these words in which /t/ and /d/ are at the beginning.

tin, din; ten, den; ton, done; two, do; teal, deal.

Exercise 4
Repeat these words in which /s/ comes before /t/. When these two sounds come together at the beginning of a word the /t/ sound does not have aspiration and it sounds a little more like the /d/ sound.

stain, stairs, story, star, stamp, steer.

Exercise 5
Repeat these words with /t/ or /d/ in the middle. These sounds only have a weak explosion.

beating, beading; water, warder; latter, ladder;
writer, rider; sighting, siding.

Exercise 6

Repeat these words with /t/ or /d/ at the end. In a lot of these words the end is hardly pronounced at all and so there is not much explosion. The words ending in /d/ have a vowel which is a bit longer than those ending with /t/.

mat, mad; wrote, rode; late, laid; heat, heed; bit, bid.

Exercise 7

Repeat the pairs of words. In each pair the one underlined is the one you heard in exercise 2. The other is almost the same except that it uses the other consonant.

train, <u>drain</u>; tin, <u>din</u>; <u>ton</u>, done; <u>heat</u>, heed; <u>bright</u>, bride; fate, <u>fade</u>; <u>tearing</u>, daring; fright, <u>fried</u>; sight, <u>side</u>; <u>biting</u>, biding.

The pronunciation of the past tense '-ed'

The simple past tense in English is often made by adding '-ed' in the written form; for example the present *I walk* becomes *I walked* in the past. Although this ending is always written the same, we can say it in three different ways.

1. If 'ed' is added to a word ending with a voiceless consonant it is pronounced /t/. For example *washed* /wɒʃt/.
2. If 'ed' is added to a word ending with a vowel or voiced consonant, it is pronounced /d/. For example *played* /pleɪd/ and *robbed* /rɒbd/.
3. If 'ed' is added to a word that already ends in /t/ or /d/ we pronounce it as /ɪd/ and this adds an extra syllable to the word. For example *wait* in the past tense becomes *waited.* (/weɪt/ becomes /weɪtɪd/).

Now try the different endings in these exercises.

Exercise 8

Listen to the *last* sound in each of the words you hear and decide whether it is a /t/ or a /d/. All these words are past tense words spelt '-ed'. The correct answers are given in exercise 12 on page 14.

Exercise 9

Repeat these words. In all of them, the final '-ed' is pronounced as /t/.

rushed, wrapped, sipped, kicked, missed.

Exercise 10

Repeat these words. In all of them, the final '-ed' is pronounced as /d/.

loved, named, darned, lived, robbed.

Exercise 11

Repeat these words in which '-ed' is pronounced /ɪd/. Remember this happens because '-ed' comes after /t/ or /d/.

hated, floated, loaded, coated, sided.

Exercise 12

Repeat these words, which are the ones you heard in exercise 8. To help you pronounce the sound correctly, we have shown which ending it should be.

climbed	(/d/)	rained	(/d/)
fated	(/ɪd/)	slipped	(/t/)
splashed	(/t/)	wrapped	(/t/)
floated	(/ɪd/)	stacked	(/t/)
bashed	(/t/)	flamed	(/d/)

Exercise 13

Read through this dialogue. Look at the questions at the end before you listen to the tape.

Mrs Dent is at the station ticket office and is in a hurry to get to Dover.

Mrs Dent: A day return to Dover please.
Ticket Man: That'll be two twenty please.
Mrs Dent: Two twenty. Oh, could you tell me what time the train leaves?
Ticket Man: It goes in two minutes. You'd better hurry.
Mrs Dent: Oh! (rushes off) and how long does it take?
Ticket Man: Just under two hours—but you'll need your ticket . . .

Now look at these questions.

1. How does Mrs Dent speak to the ticket man? Is she polite?
2. Which tone does the ticket man use in line 5 (*You'd* . . .)?
3. Where is the stress on *minutes*? (line 5)

Exercise 14

Read the part of Mrs Dent. She's in a hurry.

Exercise 15
Read the part of the ticket man. He is very calm.

Today's silly sentence

Tiny Tim tried to tie the tail of his tiger Tiddles to a tall tree.

Group activities

1. Look at the pictures below. Take it in turns around the class to describe what Tony did yesterday. Think carefully about the ends of your verbs.

2. Make a sentence each describing one thing that you did yesterday. Tell the rest of the class.

3. Your teacher will say one word in each of these pairs of words. Listen carefully and decide which one it is.

1	2	1	2
ten	den	mat	mad
tip	dip	pat	pad
tin	din	bit	bid
tent	dent	seat	seed

4. *Conversation practice*
Practise these two short conversations with a partner.

A. At the station.

Passenger: What time does the train leave for [Dover / Devonport / Teddington / Southampton / Tunbridge / Tottenham] ?

Porter: At [ten past / twenty past / twenty-five past / ten to / twenty to / twenty-five to] ten.

B. In the street.

A: Excuse me. What's the best way to get to [Southport / the station / the delicatessen / Dover St. / The Strand] ?

B: I think you ought to catch [a bus. / a tram. / a train. / the underground. / the tube.]

C. Asking about trains.
Now put in the missing words when you ask these questions. The list of names should help you. Your partner should think of a suitable answer to your questions.

At what time . . . the train . . . ?
At which station . . . the train . . . ?
From which platform . . . the train . . . ?
Is there a train for . . . this morning?
How long . . . the train take to . . . ?

London	Dale	Diss	Derby
Dumbarton	Durham	Tenby	Tetbury
Tiverton	Tottington	Tilbury	Truro

Lesson 3

The stops /k/ and /g/

How to pronounce these two consonants

How the sounds are made
These two consonants are stops. The air coming from the lungs is stopped for a short time and then let out explosively.

Where the sounds are made
Look at the two diagrams. In 1 you can see that the air is stopped by the *back of the tongue* touching the soft palate. In 2 you can see that the air is let out when the tongue is taken away from the soft palate.

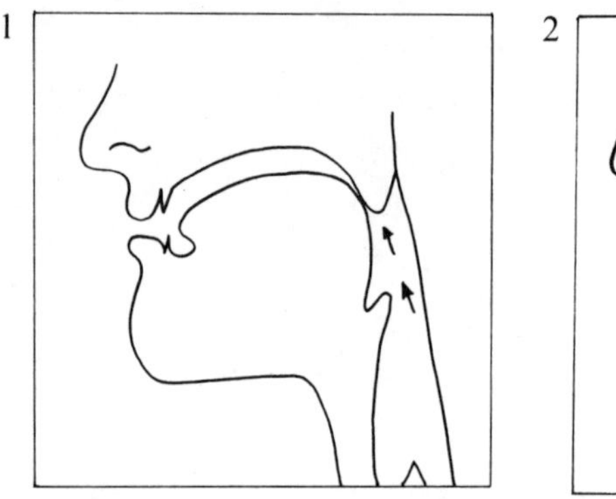

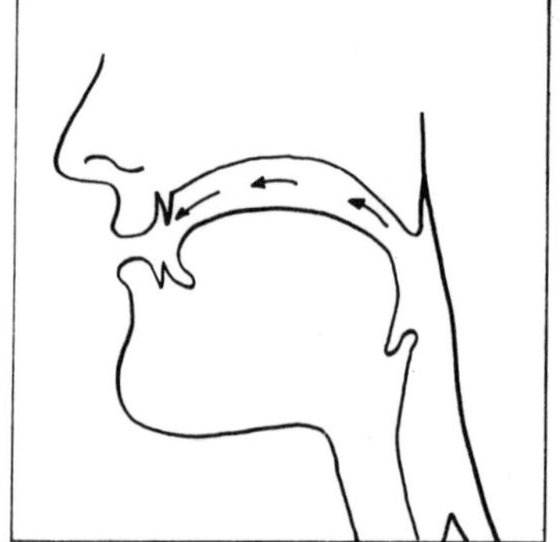

Voicing and length
/k/ is a voiceless sound; the vocal cords do not move to make this sound. It is a short sound.
/g/ is a voiced sound; the vocal cords move to make this sound. /g/ is slightly longer than /k/.

Aspiration
When /k/ is made at the beginning of a word there is an extra puff of air as it is let out. This extra puff of air (aspiration) sounds like the /h/ sound. /g/ is not aspirated.

Exercise 1a
Put your hand on your throat and say /k/ several times. You should not feel anything. Now say /g/ several times. You should be able to feel the vibration of the vocal cords moving. Now try /k/ /g/ /k/ and so on, and you should feel the vibration stopping and starting.

Exercise 1b
Put your hand in front of your mouth and say /k/. You should be able to feel the puff of air (aspiration). Now say /g/. There should be no puff of air.

Spelling
There are several ways in which /k/ can be spelt:
'k' as in: king, bake
'c' or 'cc' when followed by 'a', 'o' or 'u' as in:
came, cow, cure, accumulate, according
'ck' as in: black, stick
'ch' as in: ache, stomach
'qu' as in: bouquet, conquer.
/g/ is usually spelt with the letters 'g' or 'gg'. However, in a few words it is spelt as 'gh' (e.g. ghost), or 'gu' (e.g. guest). There are also a few words in which the letter 'g' is silent (e.g. sign, reign).

Exercise 2
Decide whether the words you hear have the /k/ or the /g/ sound. The correct answers are underlined in exercise 7 on page 20.

Exercise 3
Repeat these words with /k/ or /g/ at the beginning.

cut, gut; cash, gash; coat, goat; came, game; could, good.

Exercise 4
Repeat these words with /k/ or /g/ followed by /r/.

crate, grate; crime, grime;
crow, grow; crumble, grumble.

Exercise 5
Repeat these words with three consonants at the beginning: /s/ + /k/ + /r/. In these words /k/ loses its aspiration and sounds a little more like /g/.

scream, scrape, scratch, screw, script.

Exercise 6

Repeat these words in which /k/ or /g/ come after a vowel and do not have much explosion. The words ending in the /g/ sound have a vowel which is a bit longer than those ending in /k/.

lack, lag;
rick, rig;
flock, flog;
crack, crag;
frock, frog.

Exercise 7

Repeat the pairs of words. In each pair the one underlined is the one you heard in exercise 2. The other is almost the same, except that it has the other consonant.

crime, grime;
crumble, grumble;
cutting, gutting;
kilt, guilt;
slack, slag;
could, good;
curl, girl;
crew, grew;
clue, glue;
flocking, flogging.

Exercise 8

Read through this dialogue and look at the questions at the end before you listen to the tape.

Ken is ringing from Canada and wants to speak to his girlfriend Kate. It is a bad line and Gloria can't hear very well.

Ken: Hello, can I speak to Kate please?
Gloria: To Kate? I'm sorry Ken, she's gone to Greentown to get some Christmas cards.
Ken: Oh, can you give her a message?
Gloria: Yes, carry on, but speak clearly. I can't hear very well.
Ken: Tell her I'm coming tomorrow; I arrive at Gatwick at six o'clock.
Gloria: Tomorrow! Kate'll be so pleased. I'll give her the message. Have a good trip. Good-bye.

Now look at these questions.

1. Which tone did Gloria use when she said *tomorrow* (line 8)? Why did she say it like that?
2. Where is the stress in the word *tomorrow* (line 6)?
3. Where are all the stresses in line 4?

Exercise 9
Read the part of Ken. He's excited and anxious to speak to Kate. He has to speak quite slowly and clearly.

Exercise 10
Read the part of Gloria. She's finding it difficult to hear what Ken is saying.

Today's silly sentence

Gregory gave gorgeous gladioli to his girlfriend Gladys.

Group activities

1. Look at the dialogue between Ken and Gloria (exercise 8). Find two words beginning with /k/ or /g/ and make a sentence of your own with them. Read your sentence to the rest of the class.
2. Can you think of the words that go with the sentences below? Of course they begin with /k/ or /g/.

    1. Something that you drive.
    2. Somewhere that you grow flowers.
    3. Something to put on the floor.
    4. A visitor to your house.
    5. The opposite of dirty.

6. Something you shoot with.
7. Something to put on the fire.
8. A valuable metal.
9. A small tape.
10. Football, tennis and chess are all . . .

3. *Conversation practice*

Talking on the telephone. Find a partner to practise this with.

<table>
<tr><td>A: Could I speak to</td><td>Colin
Gregory
Karl
Gloria
Gladys
Ken</td><td>Campbell,
Gordon,
Clyde,
Goodman,
Gore,
Crudge,</td><td>please?</td></tr>
</table>

<table>
<tr><td>B: I'm sorry, . . .'s gone to</td><td>Keel.
Gatwick.
Kenya.
Greece.
Canada.
Cardiff.</td></tr>
</table>

A: Well, can I speak to . . . . . . (another name), then?

<table>
<tr><td>B: Hang on, I'll go and get</td><td>him.
her.</td></tr>
</table>

Lesson 4

The fricatives /f/ and /v/

How to pronounce these two consonants

How the sounds are made
All the sounds in Lessons 4 to 8 are known as fricatives. The air is not stopped from leaving the mouth as in the stop consonants, but is forced through a very narrow space made by parts of the mouth coming together. As the air moves through the space it makes a noise.

Where the sounds are made
To make the sounds /f/ and /v/ move the bottom lip up to the tips of the top teeth. The lip only needs to touch the teeth lightly so the air can pass between the teeth and the lip.

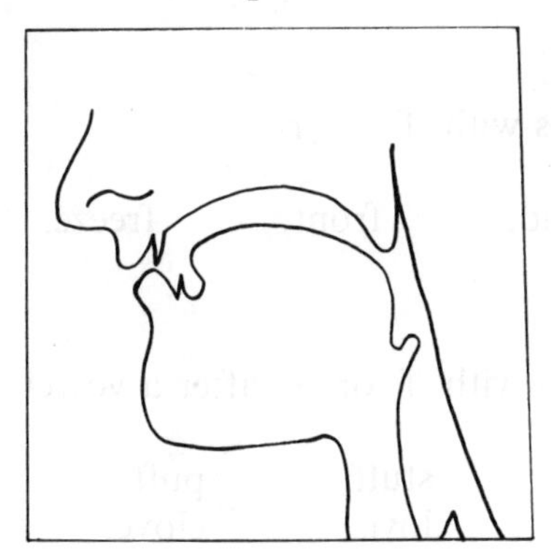

Voicing and length
/f/ is a voiceless sound; the vocal cords do not vibrate when you make this sound. It is a short sound.
/v/ is a voiced sound; the vocal cords vibrate when you make this sound. It is a slightly longer sound than /f/.

Exercise 1a
Put your hand on your throat and say /f/. You should not be able to feel anything. Now say /v/. You should be able to feel the vibration of the vocal cords. Try /f/ /v/ /f/ and so on, and you should be able to feel this stopping and starting.

Exercise 1b

These are easy sounds to check by looking in the mirror. You should be able to see your top teeth touching your bottom lip very lightly.

Spelling

/f/ is usually spelt as 'f' or 'ff'. However, there are some words in which it can be spelt as 'ph' (e.g. physical, photo), or as 'gh' (e.g. rough, cough).
/v/ is usually spelt as 'v'. However, in *of* the 'f' is pronounced /v/.

Exercise 2

Decide whether each word you hear has the /f/ or the /v/ sound. Write down the sound you think is correct. The answers are underlined in exercise 6 below.

Exercise 3

Repeat these words with /f/ or /v/ at the beginning.

fine, vine; fan, van; fat, vat; foul, vowel; few, view.

Exercise 4

Repeat these words with /f/ + /r/.

French, friend, front, freeze, fry.

Exercise 5

Repeat these words with /f/ or /v/ after a vowel.

wife, life, stuff, puff, lift.
live, wives, love, clove, glove.

Exercise 6

Repeat these words. The ones underlined are the ones you heard in exercise 2. The others are almost the same except that they use the other consonant.

rifle, rival; fine, vine;
file, vile; few, view;
feel, veal; fast, vast;
fail, veil; a life, alive;
fault, vault; leaf, leave.

Exercise 7

Read through this dialogue and look at the questions at the end before you listen to the tape.

Philip and his girlfriend, Vicky, are in a vegetarian restaurant looking at the menu.

Vicky: It makes a nice change coming to a vegetarian restaurant, doesn't it?
Philip: Mm, yes it does; what would you like from the menu?
Vicky: Have they got any fish?
Philip: No they haven't, only lots of vegetables and fresh fruit.
Vicky: In that case I'll have some French fried potatoes, fresh figs, trifle and coffee.
Philip: I hope you can finish all that, we have to leave by four o'clock!

Now look at these questions.

1. Listen to the stresses in *vegetarian* (line 1) and *vegetables* (line 5). Are they the same? How many syllables are there in *vegetables*?
2. Which is the most important word in line 4?
3. Which tone does Philip use in the second part of line 3?

Exercise 8

Read the part of Philip.

Exercise 9

Read the part of Vicky. She's enjoying her first visit to a vegetarian restaurant.

Today's silly sentence

Victor's friend Vincent rinsed his vests in vinegar.

Group activities

1. Your teacher will say one word in each of these pairs of words. Listen carefully and decide which one it is.

1	2	1	2
feel	veal	leaf	leave
fat	vat	thief	thieve
fail	vale	half	halve
few	view	off	of

2. Now split into pairs and try the same thing with your partner.

3. Here are eight pictures. The four on the top row are all things which begin with /f/; those on the bottom row begin with /v/. Write what you think the things are. Check your answers with your teacher. Now make a sentence using one of the words and read it to the rest of the class.

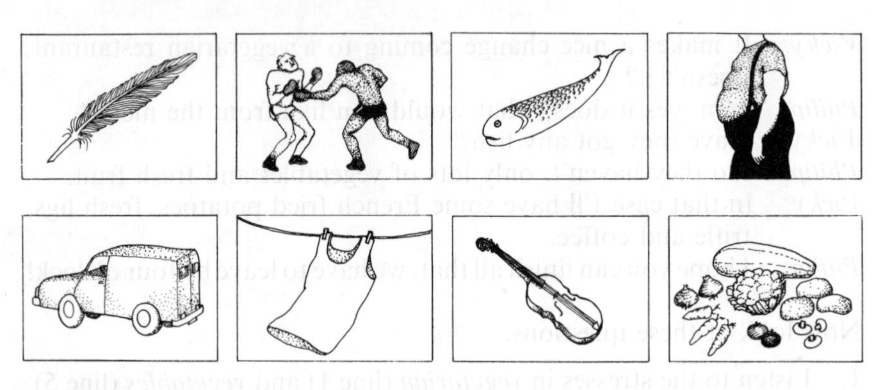

4. *Conversation practice*

You are ordering a meal in a restaurant. Practise this conversation with a partner.

Customer: First, I'd like	a fillet of sole a fillet steak some veal fricasse some pheasant a vol au vent some meat loaf	with	French fries. fried potatoes. French beans. cauliflower.

Waiter: (Writing down, repeats the order slowly.)

Customer: After, I'll have some	fresh fruit, figs, waffles, vanilla ice cream, coffee,	please.

Waiter: I'm sorry, I'm afraid we're out of . . .

Lesson 5

The fricatives /θ/ and /ð/

How to pronounce these two consonants

How the sounds are made
These two consonants are fricatives. Noise is made as air passes through a narrow space made by parts of the mouth coming together. These two sounds are the most difficult sounds to make in English so you may need a lot of practice with them.

Where the sounds are made
To make these consonants, move the tip of the tongue up behind the top teeth so that it lightly touches the bottom edge. Make sure that the tongue is *on* the teeth and not behind them on the alveolar ridge or you will make a /s/ sound. Be careful also not to press too hard because the air must move *between* the top teeth and the tongue.

If you find this sound very difficult to make, try putting your tongue tip between the top and bottom teeth to practise the sound (see diagram). When you can do it that way, try moving your tongue back behind the teeth to make the sound.

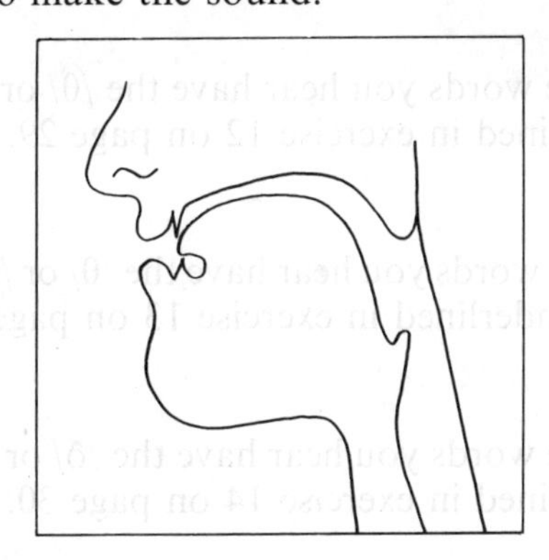

Voicing and length
/θ/ is a voiceless sound; that is the vocal cords do not vibrate when you make this sound. It is a short sound.
/ð/ is a voiced sound. The vocal cords vibrate when you make this sound. It is a slightly longer sound than /θ/.

Exercise 1a
Put your hand on your throat and say /θ/. You should not be able to feel anything. Now say /ð/. You should be able to feel the vocal cords vibrate when you say this sound. Now try /ð/ /θ/ /ð/ and so on, and you should be able to feel the vibration stopping and starting.

Exercise 1b
This is a mirror test. When you are making this sound properly the tongue should not be seen much between the teeth. Look in the mirror when you are trying the sounds in the practice position. Now move your tongue back to the normal position.

Spelling
Both /θ/ and /ð/ are always spelt with 'th'. To help you decide which sound to use at the *beginning* of a word it may be useful to remember that /ð/ usually comes in grammatical words such as *the, this, that* and so on. /θ/ comes at the beginning of all types of words, but not the grammatical ones.

Exercise 2
Decide whether the words you hear have the /θ/ or the /ð/ sound. The answers are in exercise 10 on page 29.

Exercise 3
Decide whether the words you hear have the /θ/ or the /s/ sound. The answers are underlined in exercise 11 on page 29.

Exercise 4
Decide whether the words you hear have the /θ/ or the /t/ sound. The answers are underlined in exercise 12 on page 29.

Exercise 5
Decide whether the words you hear have the /θ/ or /ð/ or the /z/ sound. The answers are underlined in exercise 13 on page 29.

Exercise 6
Decide whether the words you hear have the /ð/ or the /d/ sound. The answers are underlined in exercise 14 on page 30.

Exercise 7
Repeat these words which have /θ/ or /ð/ at the beginning.

thick,	thin,	thing,	think,	third.
this,	that,	they,	than,	then.

Exercise 8

Repeat these words which have /θ/ + /r/ at the beginning.

through, threat, thread, three, throne.

Exercise 9

Repeat these words which have /θ/ or /ð/ after a vowel.

bath, path, tooth, teeth, fourth.
bathe, rather, father, mother, further.

Exercise 10

Repeat these words. They are the ones you heard in exercise 2.

/ð/ therefore	/θ/ thick
/θ/ theory	/ð/ though
/θ/ through	/θ/ thirst
/ð/ thence	/ð/ those
/ð/ then	/θ/ thong

Exercise 11

Repeat the pairs of words. In this, and the next three exercises, the words underlined are the ones you heard in exercises 3 to 6. The other word in each pair is almost the same except that it has a different consonant.

thick, sick;
thigh, sigh;
mouth, mouse;
path, pass;
think, sink.

Exercise 12

thank, tank;
teeth, teat;
three, tree;
both, boat;
thug, tug.

Exercise 13

think, zinc;
breathe, breeze;
seethe, seas;
bath, bars;
teeth, tease.

Exercise 14

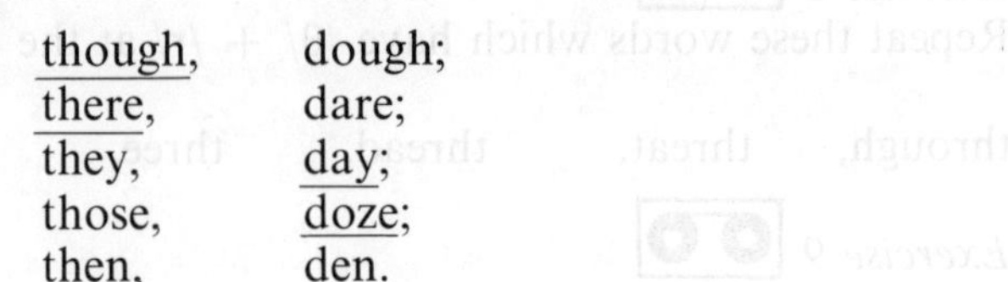

though, dough;
there, dare;
they, day;
those, doze;
then, den.

Exercise 16

Read through this dialogue and look at the questions at the end before you listen to the tape.

Timothy and Ruth are visitors to England.

Timothy:	A penny for your thoughts.
Ruth:	What? Oh, I was just thinking about next Thursday.
Timothy:	Why, what's happening then?
Ruth:	I'm going to Bidthorpe.
Timothy:	Bidthorpe? Where's that?
Ruth:	I'm not sure but I think it's about sixty miles east of London.
Timothy:	You'd better take your swimming costume then, that's in the middle of the North Sea!

Now look at these questions.

1. Where is the stress in the word *happening* (line 3)?
2. Which tone does Ruth use for *what* (line 2)?
3. Where are all the stresses in lines 6 and 7?

Exercise 17

Read the part of Timothy. He interrupts Ruth's thoughts.

Exercise 18

Read the part of Ruth. She's a bit worried about her trip on Thursday.

Today's silly sentence

Bertha poured three frothy beers for the three thirsty thieves.

Group activities

1. Divide into pairs. The first person says the number 3. The next one adds another 3 to make 33. Take turns adding another 3 and see how far you can go.

2. Practise this conversation with a partner.

A: Would you rather

have a Rolls Royce or a Mini? be the President of the United States or the Queen of England? travel by plane or by train? live in the country or in a big city? meet a famous footballer or a Nobel Prize winner? visit Canada or South Africa?

B: I'd rather . . .
or: Neither. I'd rather . . .

3. Thora is in hospital and she can't have a lot of the food she likes. She's lying in bed thinking about it. Look at the picture. Take turns around the class and make a sentence about one of the things. Begin: 'Thora's thinking about . . .'

4. *Conversation practice*
Practise this conversation with a partner.

A: Excuse me. Which bus goes to [Thorne / Thurley / Thornton / Thorpe / Thursby / Thornley] ?

B: The [3. / 33. / 333.] *

A: Thanks. What time's the next one?
B: At three. I think.

***Note**. We would say: The three.
The thirty-three.
The three, three, three.

Lesson 6

The fricatives /s/ and /z/

How to pronounce these two consonants

How the sounds are made
These two consonants are fricatives. Noise is made as air passes through a narrow space made by parts of the mouth coming together.

Where the sounds are made
Look at the diagram. To make these sounds, move the tip *and* the front of the tongue up so they lightly touch the alveolar ridge just behind the teeth. Be careful that the tongue is not on the teeth but just *behind* them.

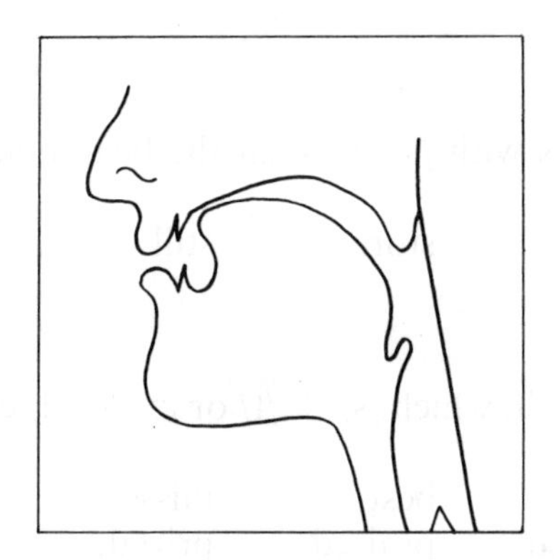

Voicing and length
/s/ is a voiceless sound; the vocal cords do not move when you make this sound. It is a short sound.
/z/ is a voiced sound; the vocal cords move to make this sound. It is a little bit longer than /s/.

Exercise 1
Put your hand on your throat and say /s/. You should not be able to feel anything. Now say /z/. You should be able to feel the vibration of the vocal cords. Now say /s/ /z/ /s/ and so on, and you should be able to feel the vibration stopping and starting.

Spelling

/s/ The most usual spelling is 's' or 'ss'. However, there are many words in which /s/ is spelt with 'c' (e.g. cease, peace). In a few words it can be spelt with 'sc' (e.g. science).

/z/ /z/ is often spelt with 'z' or 'zz' (e.g. zoo, dizzy). It can also often be spelt with 's' (e.g. rose, does, legs), but never at the beginning of a word.

Exercise 2

Decide whether each word you hear has the /s/ or the /z/ sound. The correct answers are underlined in exercise 8 on page 35.

Exercise 3

Repeat these words with /s/ or /z/ at the beginning.

soon,	soap,	seven,	soil,	sick.
cider,	cedar,	cinder,	Cynthia,	city.
zoo,	zinc,	zero,	zone,	zip.

Exercise 4

Repeat these words with /s/ + /t/ at the beginning.

stone,	stew,	store,	still,	stay.

Exercise 5

Repeat these words in which /s/ + /t/ or /z/ + /d/ come after a vowel.

mast,	fast,	best,	missed,	chest.
raised,	amazed,	praised,	prized,	closed.

Exercise 6

Repeat these words with /s/ + /t/ + /r/ at the beginning.

string,	strong,	strange,	stroke,	stripe.

Exercise 7

Repeat these words with /s/ or /z/ at the end.

mass,	toss,	pass,	kiss,	case.
jazz,	please,	craze,	toes,	rise.

Exercise 8

Repeat the pairs of words. The ones underlined are the ones you heard in exercise 2.

seal,	zeal;	Sue,	zoo;
loose,	lose;	peace,	peas;
ice,	eyes;	niece,	knees;
hiss,	his;	house (n.),	house (v.);
false,	falls;	fussy,	fuzzy.

The pronunciation of the plural endings 's' and 'es'

The plural form in English is usually made in two ways; by adding 's' or 'es' in the written form. 'es' is added if the singular of the word ends in 'ch' 's' or 'sh'. For example, 'watch' becomes 'watches'.

The 's' ending is pronounced in two different ways, and so there are three different plural endings altogether.

1. If you add 's' to a word ending in one of the voiceless sounds /t/, /k/ /f/ or /p/, it is pronounced /s/. For example, boat → boats, /bəʊt/→/bəʊts/.
2. If you add 's' to a word ending in a voiced sound (e.g. /d/, /g/) or a vowel, the 's' ending is pronounced /z/. For example, dog → dogs, /dɒg/→/dɒgz/, tree → trees, /triː/→/triːz/.
3. If you add 'es' to a word ending in /ʃ/, /tʃ/, /s/, /z/ it is pronounced /ɪz/ and adds an extra syllable to the word. For example, watch → watches, /wɒtʃ/→/wɒtʃɪz/.

Exercise 9

Repeat these words where 's' is added to a voiceless sound and is pronounced /s/.

cats, cakes, seats, cups, jokes.

Exercise 10

Repeat these words where 's' is added to a voiced sound or a vowel and is pronounced /z/.

plays, dogs, beds, lives, zoos.

Exercise 11

Repeat these words where 'es' is added to words ending in /tʃ/, /ʃ/, /s/ or /z/, is pronounced /ɪz/.

houses, matches, bushes, buses, crazes.

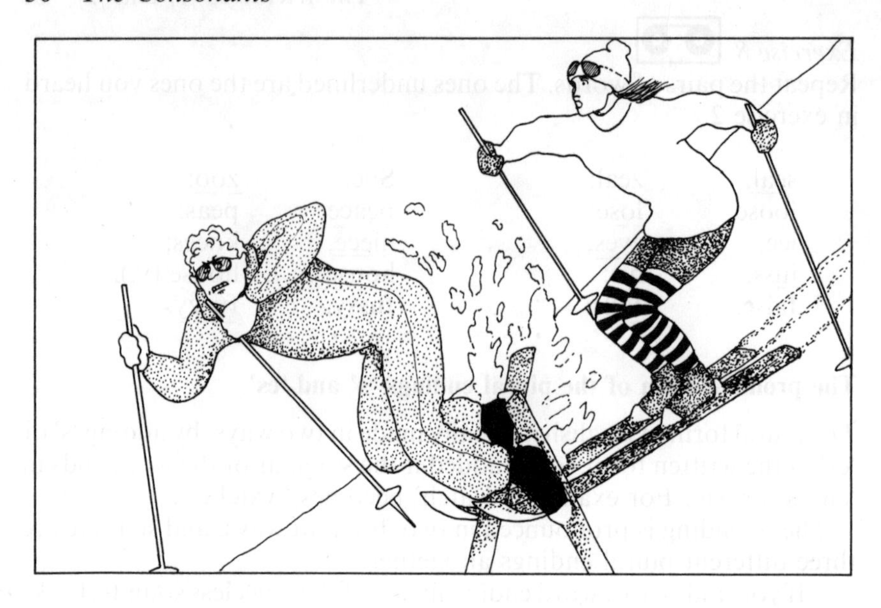

Exercise 12

Read through this dialogue and look at the questions at the end before you listen to the tape.

Sam, Sally and Sue are on a skiing holiday in Switzerland.

Sam: Did you see Sue on the slopes today?
Sally: Yes. She had some snazzy striped socks on, didn't she?
Sam: I meant, did you see what she did on her skis?
Sally: No, has she been causing trouble again?
Sam: Yes, she skied straight into Sven the instructor, covered him in snow and smashed his skis.
Sally: He won't be taking her to the disco tonight then.

Now look at these questions.

1. Which tone does Sally use to say *no* (line 4)?
2. Which is the most important word in line 7?
3. Which tone does Sally use for the tag, *didn't she* (line 2)?

Exercise 13

Read the part of Sam. He is amused by what happened to Sue.

Exercise 14

Read the part of Sally. She also thinks that Sue's accident is funny.

Today's silly sentence

'Cecil the serpent's lost his hiss,' said Zoe the zebra.

Group activities

1. Listen to the words your teacher says and decide which one of the pair it is.

1	2	1	2
sip	zip	niece	knees
Sue	zoo	trace	trays
sink	zinc	peace	peas
seal	zeal	cease	seas

2. Now try this with a partner.
3. *Plural game*
   Think of a noun and say it to the class. The person next to you must make it plural and then think of a word for the next person. See how long you can keep this going. Take care with the different endings and see if you can think of some to catch the group out.

Lesson 7

The fricatives /ʃ/ and /ʒ/

How to pronounce these two consonants

How the sounds are made
These two sounds are fricatives. Noise is made as air passes through a narrow space made by parts of the mouth coming together.

Where the sounds are made
Look at the diagram. The tongue is in almost the same position as it is for /s/ and /z/. The tip and front of the tongue lightly touch the alveolar ridge but /ʃ/ and /ʒ/ are different because the tongue also touches the front of the hard palate.

Another difference is the shape of the lips. Look at the photograph and you can see the lips should be rounded and compressed.

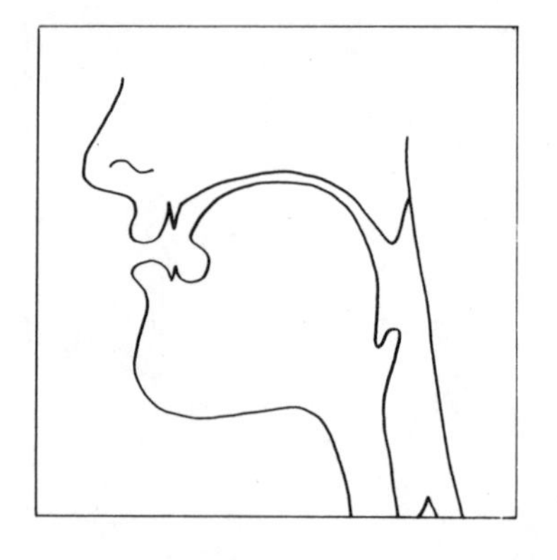

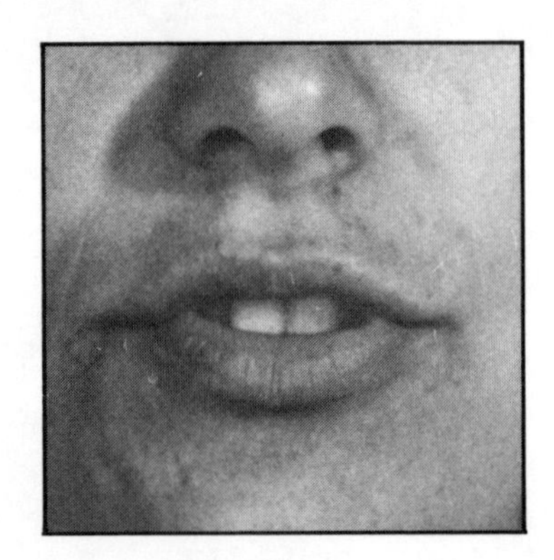

Voicing and length
/ʃ/ is a voiceless sound; the vocal cords do not vibrate when you make this sound. It is a short sound.
/ʒ/ is a voiced sound; the vocal cords vibrate when you make this sound. It is slightly longer than /ʃ/.

Exercise 1a
Put your hand on your throat and say /ʃ/. You should not be able to feel anything. Now say /ʒ/. You should be able to feel the vibration of

the vocal cords. Try /ʃ/ /ʒ/ /ʃ/ and so on, and you should be able to feel the vibration stopping and starting.

Exercise 1b
Look in the mirror for this one. Say /ʃ/ and check that the shape of your lips is the same as in the photograph. Now say /s/ /ʃ/ /s/ and so on, and you should see your lips move from spread to rounded.

Spelling

/ʃ/ The most usual spelling is 'sh' (e.g. should, shall, shell). However, there are many other spellings:
'ch' (e.g. machine),
's' or 'ss' when followed by 'u' (e.g. sure, assure), 'sch' (e.g. schedule). Note that many speakers of English, particularly in North America, pronounce this word /'skedʒəl/.
'ti', 'si', 'sci', 'ci', 'ce' in the middle of words (e.g. nation, mission, conscious, special, ocean).

/ʒ/ /ʒ/ can be spelt as 'si' in the middle of words (e.g. vision),
's' or 'z' when followed by 'u' (e.g. pleasure, azure),
'ge' at the end of some words (e.g. camouflage, garage).

Exercise 2
Decide whether the words you hear have the /s/ or the /ʃ/ sound. The correct answers are underlined in exercise 8 on page 40.

A special note on /ʒ/

The English words that use /ʒ/ are often borrowed from the French language. We have only a few words that begin /ʒ/ and these are all borrowed words e.g. gigolo. Many English speakers find /ʒ/ difficult to make at the end of words and so change it to /dʒ/ (the sound in lesson 10).

Listen to exercise 3 in which you will hear two different pronunciations of the same word. You can use either, but you may find the people around you use only one. Listen out for this.

Exercise 3
Listen only, do not repeat.

prestige, camouflage, barrage, gigolo, garage.

Did you notice that the first speaker pronounced /ʒ/, but the second pronounced /dʒ/?

Exercise 4 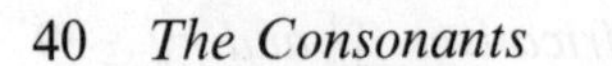

Repeat these words with /ʃ/ at the beginning.

shall, should, shoe, shop, sheet.

Exercise 5

Repeat these words with /ʃ/ + /r/ at the beginning.

shroud, shred, shrine, shrub, shrink.

Excerise 6

Repeat these words with /ʃ/ and /ʒ/ in the middle. Note that in the middle of words, /ʒ/ is the sound often used for the letter 's'.

bishop, cushion, ashore, machine, gashes.
pleasure, usual, leisure, division, casual.

Exercise 7

Repeat these words with /ʃ/ at the end.

rush, push, finish, cash, wash.

Exercise 8

Repeat the pairs of words. The ones underlined are the ones you heard in exercise 2.

sin,	shin;	Sue,	shoe;
solder,	shoulder;	sign,	shine;
sop,	shop;	sun,	shun;
ass,	ash;	puss,	push;
mass,	mash;	save,	shave.

Exercise 9

Read through this dialogue and look at the questions at the end before you listen to the tape.

Sheila has been trying on shoes for three hours. Mr Asher, the assistant, is trying to be patient.

Mr Asher: (sarcastically) Are you sure you wouldn't like to try this shade?

Sheila: Do you think I should? Beige won't match my shoulder bag . . .

Mr Asher: But it'll match your champagne-coloured shirt.

Sheila: No. Perhaps you could show me the first pair of shoes again—they were more fashionable.

Mr Asher: Why don't you try the shop next door—I'm sure they'll be able to help you.

Now look at the questions.

1. Where is the stress on the word *fashionable* (line 7)?
2. Which tone does Sheila use when she says *no* (line 6)?
3. Where are all the stresses on line 5?

Exercise 10
Read the part of Mr Asher. He's trying very hard to control his anger and not be rude to Sheila.

Exercise 11
Read the part of Sheila. She doesn't realize she's being very difficult.

Today's silly sentence

When ships come to shore, sailors usually rush to wash, shave, shine their shoes and go ashore.

Group activities

1. Look at these sentences that have been mixed up. See if you can sort them out.

   1. washing she her is hair?
   2. shampoo on put shelf the the.

3. washing dishes Shirley is the.
4. shiny the bush leaves has.
5. of cashier pay cake for portion the please the.
6. special drink for champagne is a occasions.
7. shave she him moustache told to his off.

2. Now you try it. Look through the exercises to find some words. Make a sentence and then mix it up before you read it to the class. See if they can sort it out.

3. You will need to use your memory! The first person starts the game by saying:

   'I rushed down to the shops to buy . . .' (adding something from the list).

   The next person repeats exactly the same sentence, but adds another item from the list, and so on.

   I rushed down to the shops to buy . . . some sheets
   some shoes
   some sugar
   a tape measure
   a sewing machine
   a washing machine

   (see if you can find any more with /ʃ/ or /ʒ/.)

Lesson 8

The fricative /h/

How to pronounce this consonant

How the sound is made
This sound is a fricative but it is a little different from the others. No parts of the mouth are moved to make this sound; the fricative noise is made by air being forced from the lungs.

Where the sound is made
The air from the lungs is pushed quite strongly through the glottis (look at Diagram 1 on page 3) and the noise is made in this part of the throat. Imagine you have been running and that you are out of breath. /h/ is very like the sound you would make. Be careful not to close the glottis too much; just leave your throat wide open and breathe strongly.

Voicing
/h/ is a voiceless sound. The vocal cords must be open to let the air pass through.

Exercise 1
Put your hand on your throat and say /h/. You should not feel any vibration.

Spelling
The most usual spelling of /h/ is with the letter 'h'. It can also sometimes be spelt with 'wh' (e.g. who).

N.B.—In many other languages, the letter 'h' is seen in writing but is not pronounced. Remember that in English it is nearly always pronounced as /h/ (except of course, in 'ch', 'gh', 'ph', 'rh', 'sh', 'th', 'wh'). There are, however, a few words in which the 'h' is not pronounced (e.g. hour, honest, heir), but these are rare.

Exercise 2
Decide whether each of the words you hear has the /h/ sound or not. The correct answers are underlined in exercise 6 on page 44.

Exercise 3

Repeat the pairs of words. One has /h/, the other does not.

I, high; eat, heat; ear, hear; ill, hill; old, hold.

Exercise 4

Repeat these words with /h/ at the beginning.

hell, heat, horse, hair, heart.

Exercise 5

Repeat these words with /h/ in the middle.

perhaps, behind, reheat, behave, ahead.

Note that the /h/ sound never comes at the end of words.

Exercise 6

Repeat the pairs of words. The ones underlined are the ones you heard in exercise 2.

edge,	hedge;	eight,	hate;
am,	ham;	ill,	hill;
old,	hold;	L (the letter),	hell;
arbor,	harbour;	all,	haul;
air,	hair;	I,	high.

Exercise 7

Read through this dialogue and look at the questions at the end before you listen to the tape.

Harry and June are at a party and June wants to know who everybody is.

June: Who's she?
Harry: Who?
June: Her.
Harry: Who do you mean, her?
June: Oh Harry! Her.
Harry: Who? With fair hair piled high on her head?
June: Yes, her.
Harry: Oh, that's Harriet. Henry's sister.
June: Henry? Who's he?
Harry: That's him, standing near the hall. Want to meet him, or her?
June: No. Just interested.

Now look at these questions.

1. Which tone does Harry use in line 2?
2. Which tone does June use in line 3?
3. Where is the stress in the word *interested* (line 11)? Is it the same as in the word *interest*?

Exercise 8

Read the part of June. June is not explaining things very well and she can't understand why Harry can't understand.

Exercise 9

Read the part of Harry. He's getting annoyed with Jane because she's being so vague.

Today's silly sentence

Henry and Harriet heaved in the heat to haul the heavy horse up the hill.

Group activities

1. Your teacher will say one word in each of these pairs of words. Listen carefully and decide which one it is. Then try it with a partner.

1	2	1	2
arm	harm	is	his
eat	heat	add	had
art	heart	eye	high
ill	hill	eight	hate

2. *Conversation practice*

Practise this conversation with your partner.

A: Excuse me, have you got a [hairbrush / handmirror / holiday brochure / hammer] ?

B: No, I'm sorry I haven't. Ask [him / her] over there, [he / she] might have one.

3. Here are ten pictures. The five on the left all begin with /h/, the ones on the right do not. Find the words, and match the pictures on the left with those on the right, so as to have pairs which sound almost the same. When you have done that, make up a sentence for each word, and say it to the class.

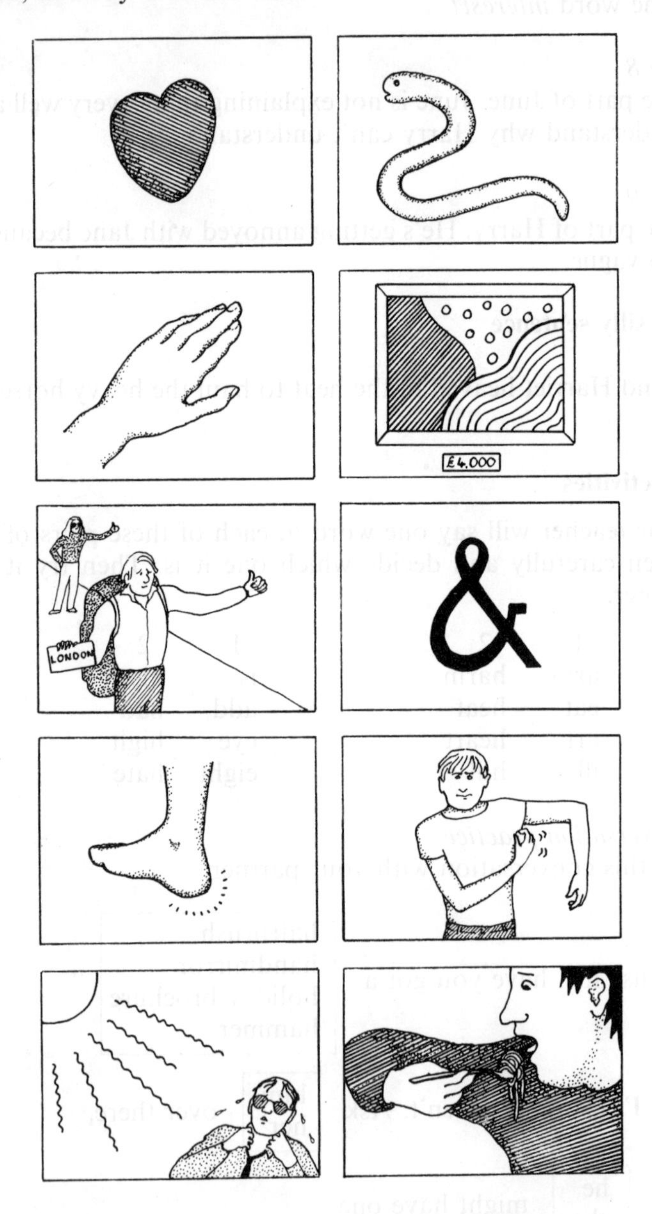

Lesson 9

The affricate /tʃ/

How to pronounce this consonant

How the sound is made

The sound /tʃ/ is an affricate. The affricates are made up of two sounds; a stop and a fricative. First the air is stopped in the mouth and, instead of being let out explosively, it is let out slowly through a narrow space. /tʃ/ is made up of the sounds /t/ and /ʃ/ but these are said very closely together. There is no vowel between them.

Where the sound is made

Look at the two diagrams. In 1 you can see where the tongue is when you say /t/. In 2 you can see where the tongue is for /tʃ/. The tip of the tongue stops the air at the alveolar ridge (as for /t/) but the front of the tongue is touching the hard palate and is preparing for the fricative part of the sound.

1

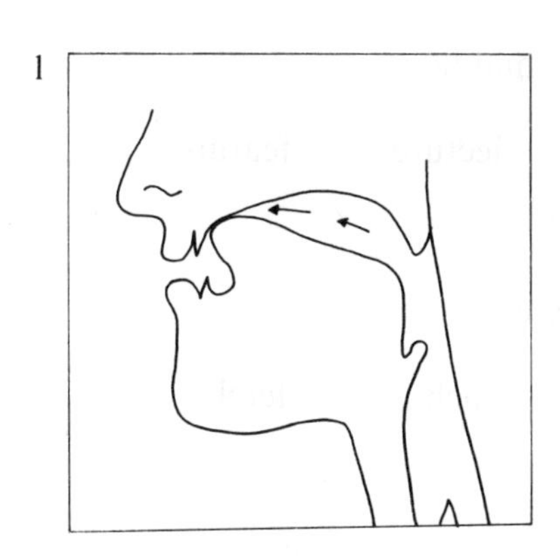

2

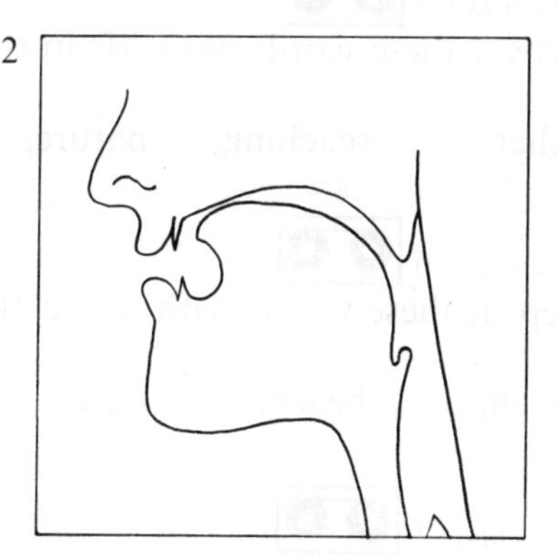

Voicing and length

/tʃ/ is voiceless; the vocal cords do not vibrate for the sound. It is a short sound.

Exercise 1

Put your hand on your throat and say /tʃ/. You should not feel any vibration.

Spelling
The most usual spelling for /tʃ/ is 'ch' (e.g. chin, chain). However, it can also be spelt as:
'tch' (e.g. match, watch),
't' when followed by 'ure' or 'eous' or 'ion' (e.g. nature, righteous, question).

Exercise 2
Decide whether each word you hear has the /t/ or the /tʃ/ sound. The correct answers are underlined in exercise 7 below.

Exercise 3
Decide whether each word has the /ʃ/ or the /tʃ/ sound. The correct answers are underlined in exercise 8 on page 49.

Exercise 4
Repeat these words with /tʃ/ at the beginning.

chin, cheap, cheer, charge, cheese.

Exercise 5
Repeat these words with /tʃ/ in the middle.

richer, reaching, nature, lecture, feature.

Exercise 6
Repeat these words with /tʃ/ at the end.

coach, beach, catch, such, fetch.

Exercise 7
Repeat these pairs of words. The ones underlined are the ones you heard in exercise 2.

time,	chime;	beat,	beach;
tin,	chin;	it,	itch;
test,	chest;	beating,	beaching;
cat,	catch;	wrote,	roach;
mat,	match;	tear (n.),	cheer.

Exercise 8

Repeat these pairs of words. The ones underlined are the ones you heard in exercise 3.

shin,	chin;	Shane,	chain;
sheet,	cheat;	sheep,	cheap;
mash,	match;	she's,	cheese;
cash,	catch;	mush,	much;
sheer,	cheer;	share,	chair.

Exercise 9

Read through this dialogue and look at the questions at the end before you listen to the tape.

Charlie's out shopping but he's not very good at it . . .

Charlie:	Have you got any cheddar cheese?
Shop Assistant:	No. I'm sorry . . .
Charlie:	Oh well, how about some cheshire cheese?
Shop Assistant:	No, this is not . . .
Charlie:	Well what cheese have you got?
Shop Assistant:	I'm sorry, the cheeseshop's next door. This is the butchers.

Now look at the questions.

1. How does the tone in line 2 tell you the shop assistant had not finished what she was saying?
2. Which is the most important word in line 5?
3. Which tone does Charlie use in line 1?

Exercise 10

Read the part of Charlie. He's very impatient and doesn't wait for the shop assistant to finish what she's saying.

Exercise 11

Now read the part of the shop assistant. She's trying very hard to explain.

Today's silly sentence

Charles tried to eat chicken and chips with Chinese chopsticks.

Group activities

1. Look at this picture. See how many sentences you can make up about it using the sound /tʃ/.

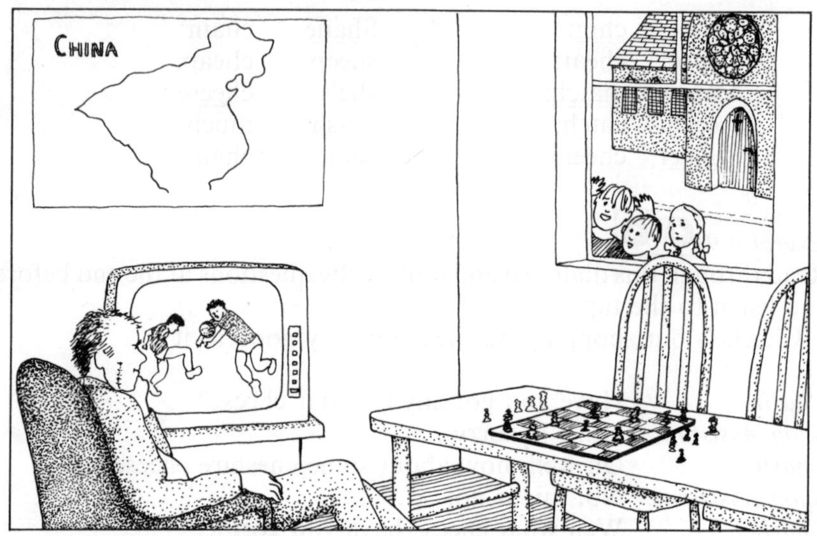

2. Your teacher will say one word in each of these pairs. Listen carefully and decide which one it is. Then try it with a partner.

1	2	1	2
chair	share	chick	tick
chin	shin	chap	tap
chop	shop	child	tiled
chew	shoe	chess	Tess
cheap	sheep	chart	tart

Conversation practice
Practise this conversation with a partner.

A: Excuse me, have you got any cheaper [chairs / chess sets / cheese / chutney / handkerchiefs / watches / Scotch] ?

B: Yes, [this is / these are] much cheaper.

Lesson 10

The affricate /dʒ/

How to pronounce this consonant

How the sound is made
This is the second of the affricate consonants. It is made up of the stop /d/ and the fricative /ʒ/. The air is stopped in the mouth for a short time and then let out slowly like a fricative.

Where the sound is made
Look at the two diagrams. In 1 you can see where the tongue is when you say /d/. In 2 you can see the position of the tongue for /ʒ/.

1

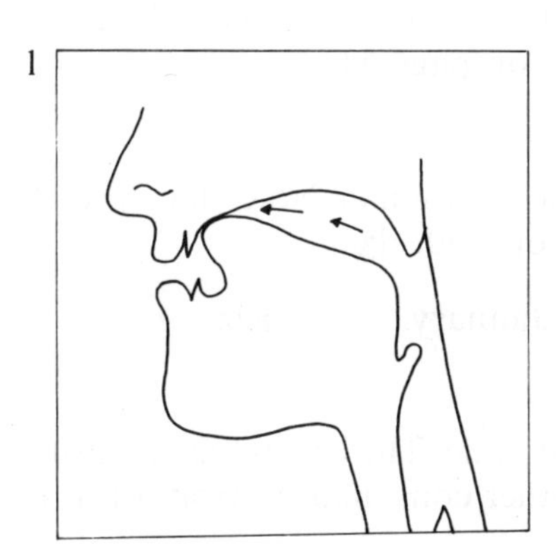

2

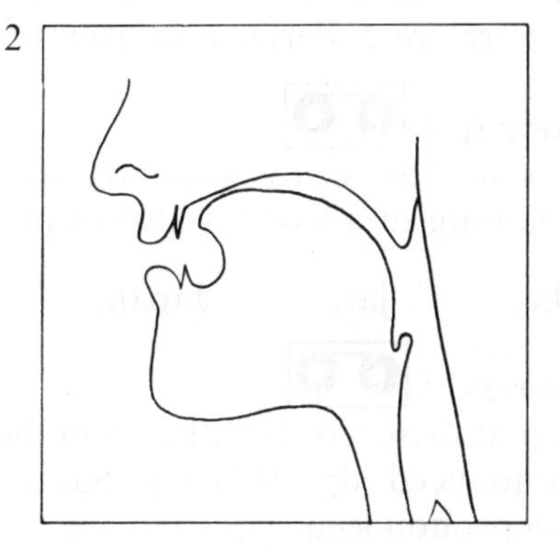

Voicing and length
/dʒ/ is a voiced sound. The vocal cords vibrate when you make this one. It is slightly longer than /tʃ/.

Exercise 1
Put your hand on your throat and say /dʒ/. You should feel the vibration of the vocal cords. Try saying /dʒ/ /tʃ/ /dʒ/ and so on, and you should feel the vibration stopping and starting.

Spelling
The most usual spelling is 'j' (e.g. jam, John). However, it can often be spelt as:

'g' before 'e' or 'i' (e.g. Belgium, gem),
'dg' (e.g. edge, judge),
'dj' (e.g. adjacent),
'gg' (e.g. suggest),
'di' (e.g. soldier).

A special note on /dʒ/

Remember that in lesson 7 (the fricative /ʒ/), we spoke about words spelt with 'g' which have been borrowed from French. Look again at the Special note on /ʒ/ on page 39, before you go on with this lesson.

Exercise 2
Decide whether each word has the /d/ or the /dʒ/ sound. The correct answers are underlined in exercise 8 on page 53.

Exercise 3
Decide whether each word has the /tʃ/ or the /dʒ/ sound. The correct answers are underlined in exercise 9 on page 53.

Exercise 4
Repeat these words with /dʒ/ at the beginning. Note that 'j' at the beginning of a word is always pronounced /dʒ/.

joke, jar, Japan, January, jazz.

Exercise 5
Repeat these words with /dʒ/ in the middle. The letters 'dg' are usually pronounced /dʒ/. When 'g' has another consonant in front of it, it is also pronounced /dʒ/.

badger, danger, urgent, engine, larger.

Exercise 6
Repeat these words in which 'g' is pronounced /dʒ/

age, rage, fragile, agenda, gouge.

Exercise 7
Repeat these words with /dʒ/ at the end.

edge, siege, large, purge, bulge.

Exercise 8

Repeat these pairs of words. The ones underlined are the ones you heard in exercise 2.

dale,	jail;	din,	gin;
aid,	age;	dam,	jam;
lard,	large;	deer,	jeer;
rid,	ridge;	Ed,	edge;
seed,	siege;	daunt,	jaunt.

Exercise 9

Repeat these pairs of words. The ones underlined are the ones you heard in exercise 3.

chest,	jest,	lunch,	lunge;
choke,	joke;	chin,	gin;
cheer,	jeer;	catches,	cadges;
rich,	ridge;	char,	jar;
perch,	purge;	larch,	large.

Exercise 10

Read through this dialogue and look at the questions at the end before you listen to the tape.

Jenny is coming through customs at the airport. She's looking a bit guilty.

Customs Officer: Could I just have a look at your luggage, please?
Jenny: Yes, but there are only a few jumpers in there.
Customs Officer: That's for me to judge.
Jenny: (Trying to distract him) I've been to Nigeria and the village markets . . .
Customs Officer: (Looking in bag, not distracted) And what about this jewellery here?
Jenny: (Smiling sweetly) Ah. I was just coming to that.

Now look at these questions.

1. What is the most important word in lines 6 and 7? Which tone is used in this sentence?
2. Where is the stress in the word *Nigeria* (line 4)?
3. Where are all the stresses in line 3?

Exercise 11

Read the part of the customs officer. He is speaking very formally and is not bothered by Jenny's attempts to distract him.

Exercise 12
Read the part of Jenny. She knows she's guilty and is trying all ways to avoid being caught.

Today's silly sentence

The judge sent Jim to jail for stealing gin and jam.

Group activities

1. Look at these descriptions and see if you can guess what the word is. All the words have /dʒ/ in them, but it may not be at the beginning.

    1. Something you put on bread.
    2. The Scots eat it for breakfast.
    3. A canal boat.
    4. You get this when you squeeze an orange.
    5. It pulls a train.
    6. He's in charge of a court.
    7. The tenth letter of the alphabet.
    8. The noise that money makes in your pocket.
    9. The first month of the year.
    10. Something that breaks easily is . . .

2. Choose one of these words and make your own sentence about it. Read it to the rest of the class.

Lesson 11

The nasal /m/

How to pronounce this consonant

How the sound is made
The three sounds in lessons 11, 12 and 13 are all nasals. The important thing making these sounds different from those we have already looked at is that the soft palate is down (see page 3). Part of the mouth is closed (like for the stops) but because the soft palate is down the air can pass out through the nose.

Where the sound is made
Look at the diagram. The lips are closed quite tightly and the air passes out through the nose because the soft palate is down. The lips do not open explosively (as in /b/ and /p/) but stay closed until the next sound is made.

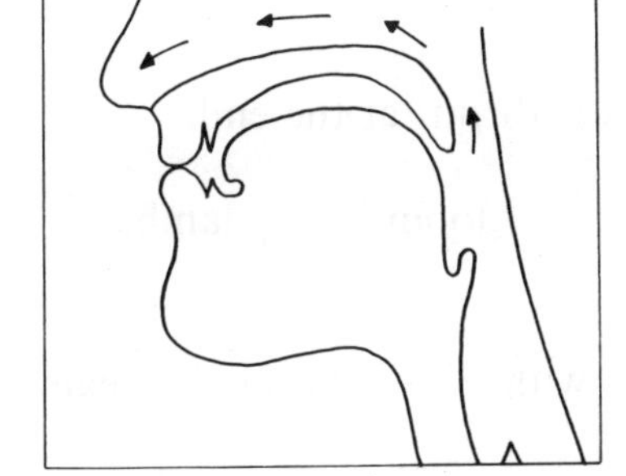

Voicing and length
/m/ is a voiced consonant. The vocal cords vibrate when you make this sound. It is quite a long sound.

Exercise 1
Put your hand on your throat and say /m/. You should feel the vibration of the vocal cords.

Exercise 2
Hold the tip of your nose and say /m/. You should feel a vibration in your nose as the air passes out.

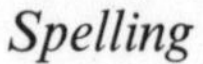

Spelling

/m/ is nearly always spelt as 'm' or 'mm'.
However, there are a few words in which 'mb' mn' are pronounced as /m/ (e.g. plumbing, damn).

Exercise 3

Decide whether each of the words you hear has the /m/ or the /b/ sound. The correct answers are underlined in exercise 9 below.

Exercise 4

Repeat these words with /m/ at the beginning.

man, March, mouse, move, miss.

Exercise 5

Repeat these words with /m/ in the middle.

remind, lemon, summer, among, demon.

Exercise 6

Repeat these words with /m/ followed by another consonant.

comfort, simple, number, dimple, symbol.

Exercise 7

Repeat these words with /m/ at the end.

steam, ham, loom, lamb, warm.

Exercise 8

Repeat these words with /s/ + /m/ at the beginning.

smart, Smith, smoke, smile, smaller.

Exercise 9

Repeat the pairs of words. The ones underlined are the ones you heard in exercise 3.

mind,	<u>bind</u>;	<u>my</u>,	by;
<u>mend</u>,	bend;	minder,	<u>binder</u>;
<u>rim</u>,	rib;	<u>gramme</u>,	grab;
<u>lamb</u>,	lab;	sum,	<u>sub</u>;
timer,	<u>Tiber</u>;	rum,	<u>rub</u>.

Exercise 10

Read through this dialogue and look at the questions at the end before you listen to the tape.

Margaret is Mr Mason's secretary. He wants her to work late tonight.

Mr Mason: Would you mind staying for a few more hours to finish this manuscript?
Margaret: No, I don't mind. I'm not doing much this evening.
Mr Mason: Oh good. I'll make sure you get something for staying behind.
Margaret: Mmm, a bit of extra money will be marvellous.
Mr Mason: Oh, I was thinking of a meat pie and a mug of coffee!

Now look at these questions.

1. Where is the stress in the word *marvellous* (line 6)?
2. Which tone does Mr Mason use when he says *Oh* in line 7?
3. Where are all the stresses in lines 1 and 2?

Exercise 11

Read the part of Mr Mason. He's being kind to Margaret as he realises there's a lot of work to do.

Exercise 12

Read the part of Margaret. She doesn't mind working late.

Today's silly sentence

Mary Smith and James McManus made marvellous muffins on Mondays.

Group activities

1. Look at the dialogue between Mr Mason and Margaret (exercise 10). See how many words you can find with the /m/ sound in them, and make one sentence each using at least one of them.

2. Use your dictionary and make a list of ten new words which begin with /m/. Read your list out to the others. See how long a list the whole class can make.

3. *Conversation practice*
   Practise this conversation with a partner.

A: Hey, where's [Malawi / Malaysia / Mali / Malta / Mexico / Monaco / Morocco] ?

B: Isn't it near . . .?

A: I don't think so [Mike. / Martin. / Raymond.]

B: Well, check it on the map.

A: Yes, but where is my map?

B: I think [Mary's / Muriel's / Maisie's] got it.

Lesson 12

The nasal /n/

How to pronounce this consonant

How the sound is made
/n/ is a nasal sound. Part of the mouth is closed and so the air is stopped from leaving the mouth in this way. The soft palate is down, however, and so the air can pass out through the nose.

Where the sound is made
Look at the diagram. The tip of the tongue is pressing against the alveolar ridge and so stops the air at that point. The soft palate is down and the air passes out through the nose.

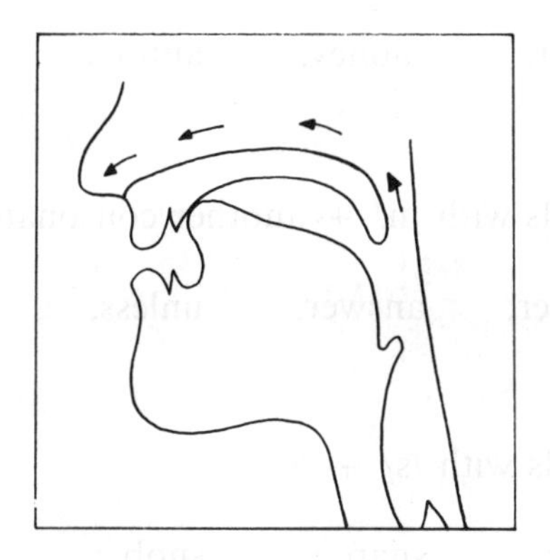

Voicing and length
/n/ is a voiced sound, the vocal cords vibrate when you make this sound. It is quite long.

Exercise 1a
Put your hand on your throat and say /n/. You should feel the vocal cords vibrating.

Exercise 1b
Hold your nose—you should feel some vibration in your nose when you are saying /n/. This is the air moving through the nose.

Spelling

/n/ is usually spelt with ‘n’ or ‘nn’.
Note that there are a few words in which ‘n’ has another consonant before it, but in which this first consonant is not pronounced (e.g. gnat, knit, know, pneumonia, sign—all the underlined are pronounced /n/).

Exercise 2

Decide whether each word you hear has the /n/ or the /d/ sound. The correct answers are underlined in exercise 9 on page 61.

Exercise 3

Repeat these words with /n/ at the beginning.

never, nurse, name, nut, note.

Exercise 4

Repeat these words with /n/ in the middle.

miner, dinner, money, annoy, funny.

Exercise 5

Repeat these words with /n/ + another consonant in the middle.

until, wonder, answer, unless, unhappy.

Exercise 6

Repeat these words with /s/ + /n/.

snow, snake, snap, snob, snail.

Exercise 7

Repeat these words with /n/ at the end.

pen, ton, mean, melon, done.

Exercise 8

Repeat these words with /n/ + /t/ at the end.

pint, tent, meant, punt, sent.

Exercise 9

Repeat these pairs of words. The ones underlined are the ones you heard in exercise 2.

nine,	dine;	know,	dough;
nip,	dip;	ban,	bad;
money,	muddy;	can,	cad.

Exercise 10

Read through this dialogue and look at the questions at the end before you listen to the tape.

John is trying to find an old friend, Nancy.

Ann: Hello, Newtown 694917.
John: Hello, is that Nancy?
Ann: Nancy? Nancy Noble? No, she doesn't live here anymore.
John: Oh dear. Do you know her new number?
Ann: Yes, I've got her number here. Have you got a pen, then you can take it down?
John: Yes, I've got one, carry on.
Ann: Her number's 979714. Oh but you won't find her there, she's gone to Canada for a month!

Now look at these questions.

1. Which tone does Ann use when she repeats Nancy's name (line 3)?
2. Which is the most important word in line 4? (*Do you know . . .*)
3. Where is the stress in *Canada* (line 9)?

Exercise 11

Read the part of Ann. She's trying to be helpful.

Exercise 12

Read the part of John. He's very keen to get in touch with Nancy.

Today's silly sentence

Nellie danced with her nephew Norman as the sun went down.

Group activities

1. *Number Game*
   Find a partner for this game. The first person starts with 9. The next person adds another 9 to make 99. Carry on adding another 9 and see how far you can go. Then try the same with 7.

2. Look at the picture and see how many sentences you can make using words with the /n/ sound in them.

3. *Conversation practice*
Practise this conversation with a partner.

<table>
<tr><td>A:</td><td>Hey. Do you know</td><td>Ian's
Norman's
Nigel's
Henry's
John's</td><td>telephone number?</td></tr>
</table>

B: Hmm. It's 99 1959.

A: No, that's not . . . 's, that's June's isn't it?

<table>
<tr><td>B:</td><td>Sorry, you're right. . . . 's is</td><td>29 3949.
97 9697.
69 9949.
19 2997.
79 4949.</td></tr>
</table>

A: Thanks.

Lesson 13

The nasal /ŋ/

How to pronounce this consonant

How the sound is made
This sound is nasal. Part of the mouth is closed and so the air is stopped from leaving this way. The soft palate is down and so the air passes out through the nose.

Where the sound is made
Look at the diagram. The back of the tongue is touching the soft palate and this stops the air passing out through the mouth. The soft palate is down and so the air goes out through the nose.

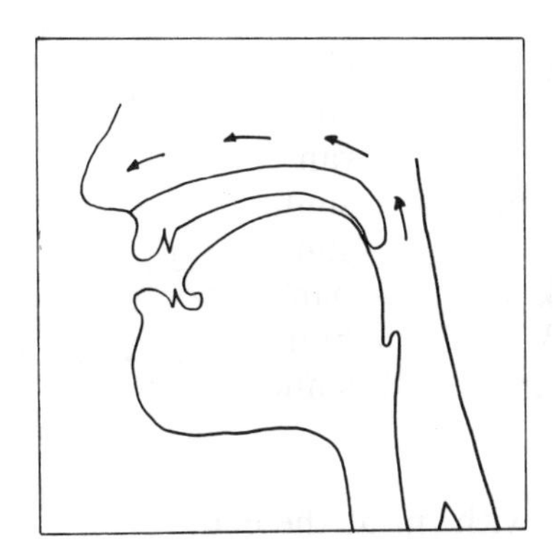

Voicing and length
/ŋ/ is a voiced sound and so the vocal cords vibrate. It is quite a long sound.

Exercise 1a
Put your hand on your throat and say /ŋ/. You should feel the vocal cords vibrating.

Exercise 1b
Hold the tip of your nose and say /ŋ/. You should feel the vibration in your nose as the air passes out.

Spelling

The most usual spelling of /ŋ/ is 'ng'.

'ng' is also sometimes pronounced /ŋ/ + /g/ (e.g. finger, anger). See exercise 6.

'nk' is pronounced /ŋ/ + /k/ (e.g. think, monkey). See exercise 7.

Note that /ŋ/ *never* comes at the beginning of words.

Exercise 2

Decide whether each of the words you hear has the /ŋ/ or the /n/ sound. The correct answers are underlined in exercise 9 on page 65.

Exercise 3

Decide whether each word you hear has the /ŋ/ or the /ŋk/ sound. The correct answers are underlined in exercise 10 on page 65.

Exercise 4

You will hear seven sentences. In each sentence, there is *one* of the three words on each line. Decide which of the three words you think you heard and write down A, B, or C. The answers are in exercise 11 on page 65.

	A /ŋ/	B /ŋk/	C /n/
1.	sing	sink	sin
2.	rang	rank	ran
3.	singing	sinking	sinning
4.	sung	sunk	sun
5.	bang	bank	ban
6.	bung	bunk	bun
7.	singer	sinker	sinner

Exercise 5

Repeat these words with /ŋ/ at the end.

sing, strong, hang, long, thing.

Exercise 6

Repeat these words with /ŋg/ in the middle.

finger, stronger, hunger, angry, language.

Exercise 7

Repeat these words with /ŋk/ in the middle or at the end.

monkey, ankle, think, sank, thank.

Exercise 8

Repeat these words with /ŋ/ in the middle.

singing, longing, hanging, singer, wronging.

Exercise 9

Repeat the pairs of words. The ones underlined are the ones you heard in exercise 2.

sing,	sin;	pang,	pan;
rang,	ran;	singing,	sinning;
gong,	gone;	king,	kin;
tongue,	ton;	clang,	clan;
robbing,	robin;	stung,	stun.

Exercise 10

Repeat the pairs of words. The ones underlined are the ones you heard in exercise 3.

king,	kink;	clung,	clunk;
sung,	sunk;	singer,	sinker;
ring,	rink;	flung,	flunk;
rang,	rank;	bring,	brink;
thing,	think;	bang,	bank.

Exercise 11

Repeat these sentences. They are the ones you heard in exercise 4.

1. Do you sing in the bath?
2. I ran but I missed the bus.
3. It was spring and the birds were singing.
4. The news was bad—the ship had sunk.
5. The bank opens at 9.30 in the morning.
6. A hamburger is minced meat in a bun.
7. My grandmother was a professional singer.

Exercise 12

Read through this dialogue and look at the questions at the end before you listen to the tape.

Ingrid and Martin are out in a new shopping precinct. Martin sees a man trying to attract their attention.

Martin: Ingrid, that man's trying to attract your attention.
Ingrid: Me? I don't know him. He must have made a mistake.

Martin: Look, he's waving his arms now and shouting something.
Ingrid: Oh, stop being silly. It's nothing to do with me.
Martin: He's rushing over now. He looks very angry. He's pointing at something.
Ingrid: I know why he's shouting now. You're up to your ankles in wet concrete!

Now look at these questions.

1. Where is the stress in the word *attract* (line 1)?
2. Which tone does Ingrid use when she says *me* (line 2)?
3. Where are all the stresses in line 4?

Exercise 13
Read the part of Martin. He's trying very hard to persuade Ingrid that the man is trying to attract her attention.

Exercise 14
Read the part of Ingrid. She can't understand why Martin is making so much fuss.

Today's silly sentence

The king angrily rang the gong, as he was dying of hunger.

Group activities

1. *Conversation practice*
   Practise this very short conversation. Note that Student B must change the verb to 'was . . .ing'. Be careful, because some of these will be pronounced with /ŋ/, and some others with either /ŋg/ or /ŋk/.

A: What were you doing when
- he rang
- it sank
- she thanked you
- he banged on the door
- the gong rang

?

B: I was . . .
- play the piano.
- watch a film.
- read.
- tidy the house.
- think.

2. Look at these descriptions. Can you guess what the words are. Of course they all have the /ŋ/ sound in them.

   1. You have four on your hand.
   2. You wear it on 1.
   3. Birds have two of them.
   4. English is . . .
   5. The opposite of shorter.
   6. You use it to tie up a parcel.
   7. This is when the sun goes down.
   8. The opposite of weak.

3. Fred is a 'peeping Tom'. He spent Saturday evening looking through keyholes. Describe what he saw.

Lesson 14

The lateral /l/

How to pronounce this consonant

How the sound is made
/l/ is a lateral sound and it is not like any of the other English sounds. It is called a lateral because the air passes around the sides of the tongue and then out through the mouth. The air is not stopped at all but the shape and movement of the tongue are important to make this sound.

Where the sound is made
To make the /l/ sound the tongue tip should press on the alveolar ridge. This stops the air from moving down the middle of the tongue, so it moves down the sides.

If you find this sound very difficult to make, try biting the tip of your tongue between your front teeth. This will force the air down the sides of your tongue and you will feel the /l/ sound. When you can do this, move your tongue back to the correct position and try making the sound that way.

1

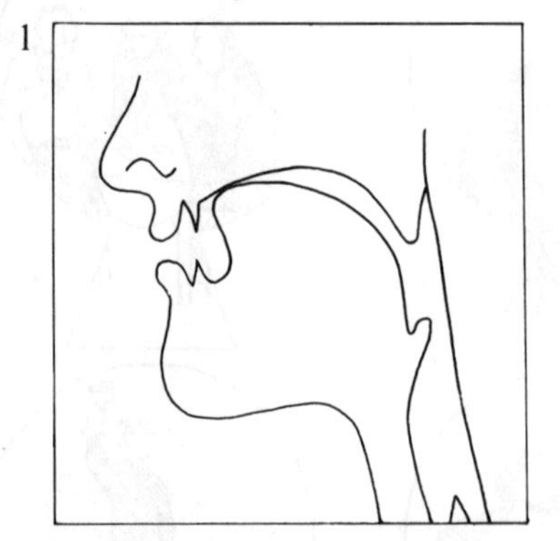

2

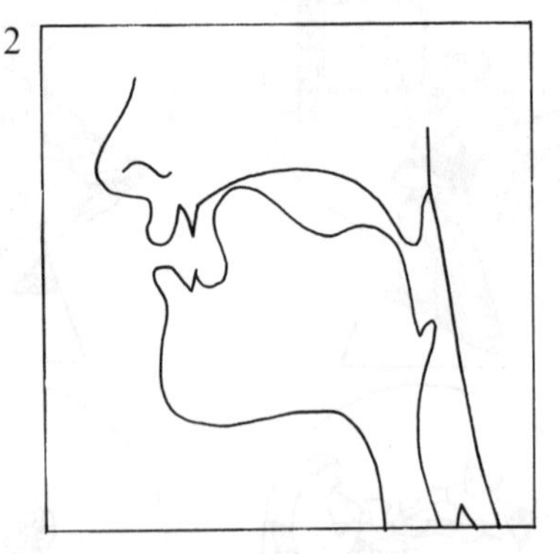

Look at the two diagrams. The first shows you how the /l/ sound is made when it comes before a vowel (e.g. land, slow, flat.) The second is slightly different and shows how /l/ is made when it comes before consonants and after vowels (e.g. help, feel, salt). The front of the tongue is the same but the back of the tongue is up a bit; this is almost the position it would be for the vowel /u/.

Voicing and length
/l/ is a voiced sound so the vocal cords vibrate when you make this sound. It is quite a long sound.

Spelling
/l/ is always spelt as 'l' or 'll'.
However there are many words with 'lm' or lk', in which the 'l' is not pronounced (e.g. calm, balm, folk, chalk).

Exercise 1
Put your hands on your throat and say /l/ with a vowel. You should be able to feel the vocal cords vibrating as you make the sound /l/.

The 'clear' and 'dark' /l/

Look at the diagrams on page 68. Remember there are two different /l/ sounds. The clear /l/ comes before vowels and the dark /l/ comes before consonants and after vowels, especially at the end of words. Listen to exercise 2 and you will hear the different /l/ sounds. The words with 'l' at the beginning will have a clear /l/, those with 'l' or 'll' after a vowel will have a dark /l/.

Exercise 2
Listen only; do not repeat.

lift, fill, let, fell, look, full.

Exercise 3
Repeat these words with a clear /l/ at the beginning.

lap, leap, lot, look, lane.

Exercise 4
Repeat these words with a dark /l/ at the end.

pull, pill, tell, pal, pool.

Exercise 5
Repeat these words with a clear /l/ in the middle.

filling, pulling, telling, tiling, peeling.

Exercise 6
Repeat these words with a dark /l/ and another consonant at the end.

kilt, pulled, pills, pearls, tails.

Exercise 7

Read through this dialogue and look at the questions at the end before you listen to the tape.

Lesley has just arrived at the Lane Gallery but it's full.

Attendant: Sorry miss, you can't go in there. The gallery's full.
Lesley: Oh no, I've got to see the Leonard Fullers before the gallery closes. I've come all the way from Lawton.
Attendant: I'm sorry, rules are rules. I can't let you in.
Lesley: But I'm leaving for Lebworth tonight. *Please* let me in.
Attendant: The people in that line in the hall are all waiting to have a look as well.
Lesley: But they're not leaving for Lebworth tonight. Please, can I go in?
Attendant: Oh alright love. Slip in quietly while I look the other way. But don't tell anyone else, will you!

Now look at these questions

1. How is Lesley speaking to the attendant. Does it matter if she doesn't get into the gallery?
2. Where is the stress on the word *tonight* (line 5)?
3. Where are all the stresses on lines 6 and 7.

Exercise 8

Read the part of the attendant. He is being friendly but firm.

Exercise 9

Read the part of Lesley. She's desperate to see the paintings and is pleading with the attendant.

Today's silly sentence

Lovely Lilly Livingstone used to live in Lincoln, but now she lives in London.

Group activities

1. Look at these sentences and see if you can sort them out.
    1. full is the gallery new?
    2. telling he's lies always.
    3. last night train was the late.
    4. long legs got hasn't very she.
    5. rail hold and onto you fall won't then the over.

2. Now you try the same thing with a partner. Look through the exercises and find some words with the /l/ sound in them. Make a sentence, mix it up and then see if your partner can sort it out.
3. Look at this picture. How many things can you find in it with the /l/ sound in them.

4. *Conversation practice*
   Practise this conversation with a partner.

Visitor:
Excuse me. Could you tell me where

Len Miller Lesley Hall Harold Black Miss Laughton

lives?

Local: . . .? Oh, I know! First on the left into

Fuller Rd. Milne St. Lane St. Fall Ave.

Visitor: First left. . . . (repeats the street).
Local: You'll find a large block of flats on the left.
Visitor: Do you know which floor?
Local: No, but the names are listed in the hall.
Visitor: Thanks very much.

Lesson 15

The continuant /r/

How to pronounce this sound

How the sound is made
The consonant /r/ is a *continuant* and it is almost like a vowel. It is the shape of the tongue in the mouth, and its movements, which are important in this sound. It is not like most of the other consonants as the tongue touches only the back teeth.

Where the sound is made
Look at the diagram, and you can see the shape of the tongue. The front of the tongue is *near* the alveolar ridge but does not touch it. The sides and the back of the tongue are also raised, and so the whole tongue is shaped like a saucer (see diagram). The air passes over the saucer and out through the mouth.

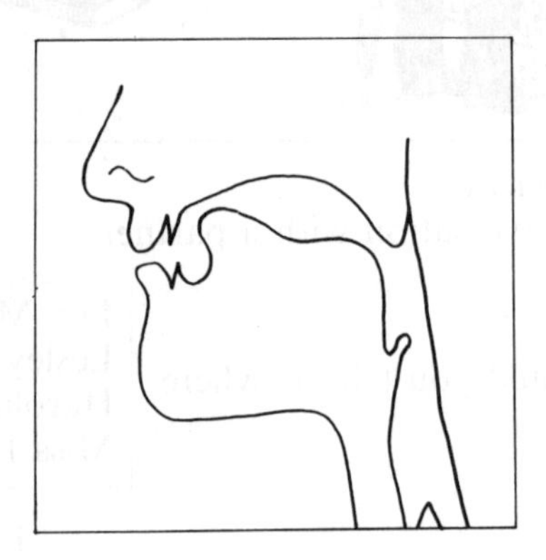

There are many different ways of making the /r/ sound. You may find the people around you making it in a different way, so listen for this. The way described here is that of Southern England and is acceptable everywhere.

Voicing and length
/r/ is a voiced sound. It is quite a long sound.

Exercise 1
Put your hand on your throat and say /r/. You should feel the vibration of the vocal cords moving.

Spelling
/r/ is usually spelt as 'r' or 'rr'.
Sometimes it can be spelt as
'wr' (e.g. write, wretch),
'rh' (e.g. rhythm, rhetoric).

Exercise 2
Decide whether each word you hear has the /l/ or the /r/ consonant. The correct answers are underlined in exercise 9 on page 74.

Exercise 3
Repeat these words with /r/ at the beginning.

red, raft, rot, root, raid.

Exercise 4
Repeat these words with /r/ in the middle.

caring, turret, carrot, sharing, peering.

Exercise 5
Repeat these words with /tr/ or /dr/ at the beginning.

trip, drip; train, drain; try, dry; troops, droops; trunk, drunk.

Exercise 6
Repeat these words. Note that 'r' at the end of a word, or if it has another consonant after it, is usually *not pronounced.* But, there are many English speakers (especially in North America) who do pronounce it.

car,	fewer,	far,	tier,	cheer.
starting,	feared,	parked,	skirt,	cheered.

The linking /r/

Although 'r' at the end of a word is not usually pronounced, it *is* pronounced if the next word starts with a vowel. We will practise this in exercise 7.

Exercise 7

Repeat these short sentences with a linking /r/. 'r' at the end of a word is pronounced because the next word begins with a vowel.

The car and the bike.
It's for Anne.
Put the beer on the table.
There's more over there on the table.

The intrusive /r/

It is difficult to say two vowels one after the other, so English speakers sometimes put an /r/ sound between the vowel sounds to link them. We will practise this in exercise 8.

Exercise 8

Repeat these short sentences, and listen for the intrusive /r/.

1. India and Africa.
2. Anna and Bill.
3. Stella asks the way.

Exercise 9

Repeat the pairs of words. The ones underlined are the ones you heard in exercise 2.

leer,	rear;	play,	pray;
lot,	rot;	blue,	brew;
lice,	rice;	laid,	raid;
lower,	rower;	lift,	rift;
flute,	fruit;	stalling,	storing.

Exercise 10

Read through this dialogue and look at the questions at the end before you listen to the tape.

Fred and Rosemary are talking about their friend Ronald.

Fred: Ronald's got a new car. It's a red one I think.
Rosemary: Really! What happened to that old car of his?
Fred: Didn't you hear the story? It's been going round for ages.
Rosemary: Oh, was he responsible for that crash on the ring road?
Fred: Yes, that was him. Straight over the railway line, just missed the river and then right into a new Rolls Royce!
Rosemary: Perhaps the new car'll be luckier for him.

Now look at these questions.

1. Which tone did Rosemary use for *really* (line 2)?
2. There are some examples of linking 'r's in the dialogue. Can you find them?
3. Which is the most important word in line 7?

Exercise 11
Read the part of Fred.

Exercise 12
Read the part of Rosemary.

Today's silly sentence

Ronald the rabbit raced after the red rooster.

Group activities

1. Your teacher will say one word in each of these pairs of words. Listen carefully and decide which one it is.

1	2	1	2
read	lead	red	led
write	light	rain	lane
root	loot	Rhine	line
rice	lice	wrong	long

2. Now try the same thing with a partner.

3. The prefix *re-* means 'to do again'. For example: 'I read my favourite book again' becomes 'I re-read my favourite book'. Change the verbs in these sentences by adding the prefix *re-*.

   You've failed the exam—you must *take* it *again.*
   This soup is cold—would you *heat* it *again*?
   She kept disappearing and *appearing again.*
   The shop is open from 9 to 12; it *opens again* at 2.30 in the afternoon.
   There are 33 mistakes in this letter—would you *type* it *again*?
   The football match was a draw—the teams will *play* it *again* next week.
   I hope you can read my letter—I don't want to *write* it *again.*
   When he lost his job as a driver, he had to *train again* as a mechanic.

4. *Conversation practice*
   Very often you have to re-do something differently because it was wrong the first time. With a partner, read and complete this dialogue.

A: You look fed up. What's wrong?

B: I've got to

re-write this letter.
re-take the exam.
re-organise my holiday.
re-arrange my . . .
re-think my . . .
re-make . . .

A: Really—why?
B: Oh, because . . .

Lesson 16

The semi-vowel /j/

How to pronounce this sound

How the sound is made

The sound /j/ is a semi-vowel. It is pronounced more like a vowel than a consonant because the air is not stopped or forced through a narrow space. The shape and movements of the tongue are important when you make this sound.

Where the sound is made

Look at the diagram. The front of the tongue is near the alveolar ridge but does not touch it. It is pulled away from this position very quickly. Be careful that the tongue does not touch the alveolar ridge or you may make a /d/ or /dʒ/ sound.

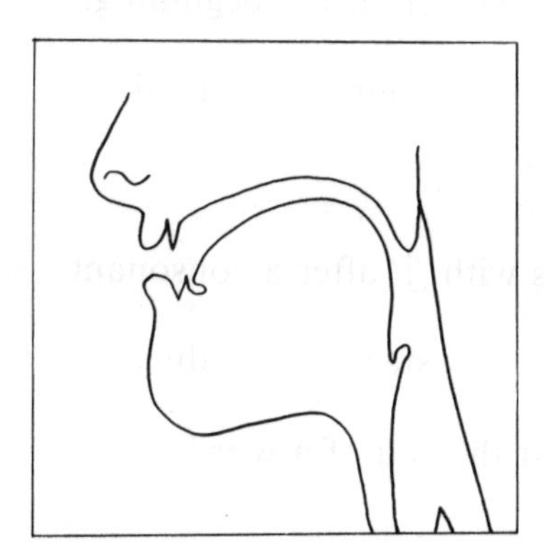

Voicing and length

/j/ is voiced so the vocal cords vibrate when you make this sound. It is quite a short sound.

Exercise 1

Put your hand on your throat and say /j/. You should feel the vibration of the vocal cords when you make this sound.

Spelling

/j/ is *usually* spelt as:

'y' (e.g. young, yes),
'i' when followed by another vowel (e.g. onion).

It often comes before the following vowels:

'u' (e.g. pure, cure),
'ew' (e.g. few, new),
'eau' (e.g. beauty),
'eu' (e.g. feud).

Exercise 2

Decide whether the words you hear have the /j/ sound or not. The correct answers are underlined in exercise 6 below.

Exercise 3

Decide whether the words you hear have the /j/ or the /dʒ/ sound. The correct answers are underlined in exercise 7 on page 79.

Exercise 4

Repeat these words with /j/ at the beginning.

yes, yard, your, used, unit.

Exercise 5

Repeat these words with /j/ after a consonant.

tune, hue, stew, duty, beauty.

/j/ never comes at the end of a word.

Exercise 6

Repeat these pairs of words. The ones underlined are the ones you heard in exercise 2.

yet,	ate;	used,	oozed;
due,	do;	beauty,	booty;
yearn,	earn;	yam,	am;
yon,	on;	yawning,	awning;
hue,	who;	your,	or.

Exercise 7

Repeat these pairs of words. The ones underlined are the ones you heard in exercise 3.

yet,	jet;	yolk,	joke;
you,	Jew;	yard,	jarred;
yon,	John;	year,	jeer;
yam,	jam;	yule,	jewel;
your,	jaw;	yacht,	jot.

Exercise 8

Read through this dialogue and look at the questions at the end before you listen to the tape.

John has just seen Judy at a party. He doesn't know her and he is too friendly. Judy's not very pleased.

John: Hello. Haven't I seen you somewhere before?
Judy: No, I'm sure you haven't. I've never seen you before.
John: Yes you have. You used to go down to the youth club in Yarmouth.
Judy: No I didn't, you've made a mistake.
John: I know. You used to go yachting . . . last year . . . in Yelton.
Judy: No really. I'm sure we've never met.
John: Oh well, you know me now . . . like a coffee?

Now look at these questions.

1. Which tone does Judy use in the second part of line 2 (*I've never . . .*)?
2. Where is the stress in *mistake* (line 5)?
3. Where are all the stresses in the second part of line 3?

Exercise 9

Read the part of John. He's trying very hard to get to know Judy.

Exercise 10

Read the part of Judy. She's getting very annoyed with John.

Today's silly sentence

The young and beautiful Yolanda yearned for Yorick's new yellow yacht.

Group activities

1. Charlie's in prison. He's not very happy because he's thinking about all the things he did before he was put in prison. Look at the pictures and describe what Charlie *used to* do.

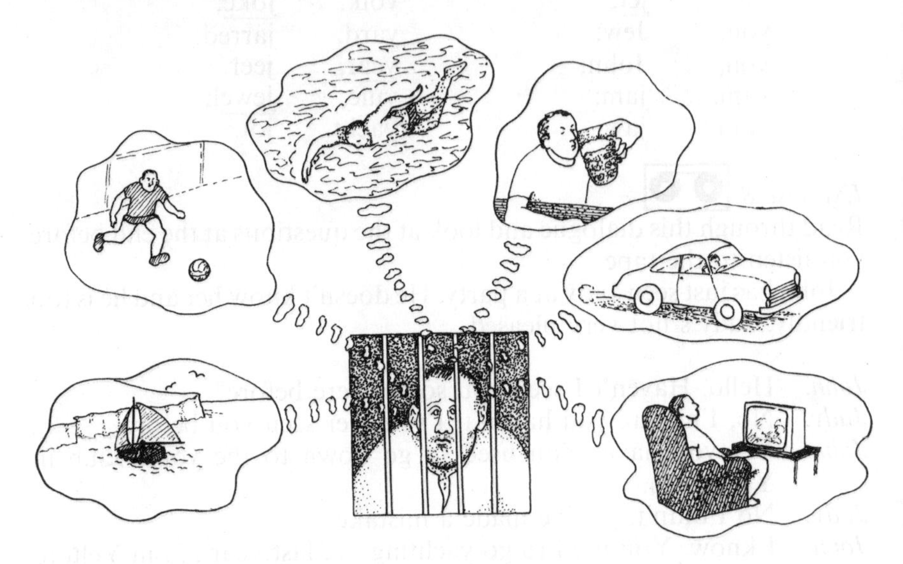

2. Your teacher will say one word in each set of three words. Listen carefully and decide which one it is.

1	2	3
debt	yet	jet
dot	yacht	jot
deer	year	jeer
dam	yam	jam

3. Now try the same thing with your partner.

4. *Conversation practice*
With a partner, read and complete this dialogue.

A: You used to [sail / skate / play the piano / ski / read] a lot, didn't you?

B: Yes, I used to, but . . .

Lesson 17
The semi-vowel /w/

How to pronounce this consonant

How the sound is made

/w/ is a semi-vowel. It is more like a vowel than a consonant as the air is not stopped or forced through a narrow space. It is the shape of the mouth and lips, and the position of the tongue which are important in this sound.

Where the sound is made

There are two things to think about when you make this sound. There is a diagram and a photograph to help you.

1. The back of the tongue moves up to be near the back of the palate, almost like the sound /u/. It then moves away very quickly. When you make this sound be careful that the back of your tongue does not touch your palate. If you find this sound difficult, try making the vowel sound /u/ first (see page 135) and then move your lips as described below.

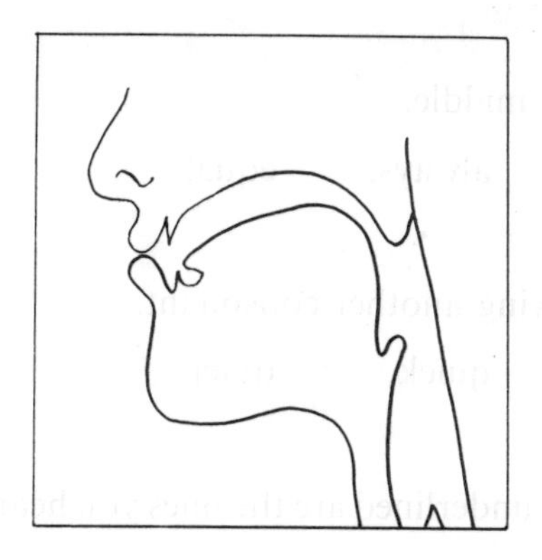

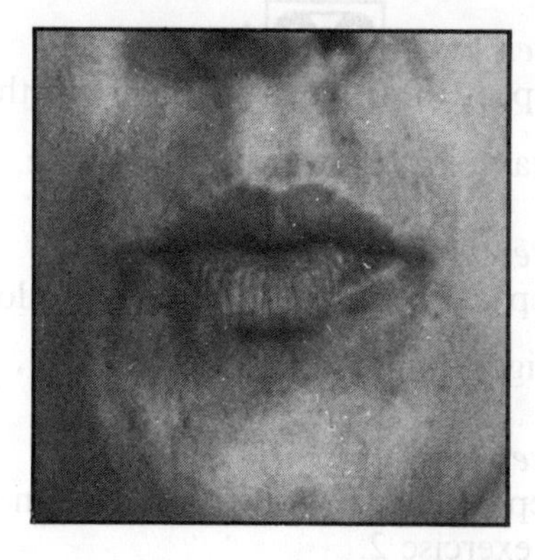

2. In the photograph you can see the shape of the lips. They are tightly rounded and they protrude to make this sound. They come apart quickly at the same time as the tongue moves away from the palate.

Voicing and length
/w/ is voiced so the vocal cords vibrate to make this sound. It is a short sound.

Exercise 1a
Put your hand on your throat and say /w/. You should be able to feel the vibration of the vocal cords.

Exercise 1b
Look in the mirror and say /w/. Check that your lips are the same shape as those in the photograph. Your lips should be closed tightly together and you should not be able to see your teeth.

Spelling
The most usual spelling is 'w' (e.g. wet, window).
It can also be spelt 'wh' (e.g. which, why).
In a few other words, /w/ is pronounced before a vowel (e.g. one, suite), but does not appear in the spelling.

Exercise 2
Decide whether each word you hear has the /w/ or the /v/ sound. The correct answers are underlined in exercise 6 below.

Exercise 3
Repeat these words with /w/ at the beginning.

we, what, war, wood, why.

Exercise 4
Repeat these words with /w/ in the middle.

away, reward, beware, always, equal.

Exercise 5
Repeat these words with /w/ following another consonant.

twig, twin, dwarf, quick, quiet.

Exercise 6
Repeat the pairs of words. The ones underlined are the ones you heard in exercise 2.

wheel, veal; weir, veer;
wail, veil; wiser, visor;
worse, verse; wend, vend;
why, vie; wane, vein;
wet, vet; west, vest.

Exercise 7

Read through this dialogue and look at the questions at the end before you listen to the tape.

Wendy is visiting the Doctor. She's very slow and the Doctor's in a hurry to see all his patients.

Doctor Wilson:	What exactly is wrong with you?
Wendy:	Well, you see it's . . .
Doctor Wilson:	And when did this start?
Wendy:	Um . . . Wednesday it was I think, but . . .
Doctor Wilson:	And where exactly is the pain?
Wendy:	Well it was here, but then it went over there . . .
Doctor Wilson:	I see, well one of these tablets after meals will do the trick. Next please!

Now look at these questions

1. Which is the most important word in line 1? Where is the stress in this word?
2. Which tone does Doctor Wilson use in line 3?
3. Where are all the stresses in lines 7 and 8?

Exercise 8

Read the part of Doctor Wilson. He is very impatient and has no time to listen to Wendy.

Exercise 9

Read the part of Wendy. She is very slow at explaining things and isn't very sure what to say.

Todays silly sentence

Here's why we should beware of wearing a wig in windy weather.

Group activities

1. Look at the picture. Imagine you are a reporter and you have just arrived on the scene. Ask your partner as many questions as you can using the question words which, why, where and so on.

2. Ask questions around the class now using the question words. One student asks a question e.g. Where do you come from? The next students replies and then thinks of another question.

3. *Conversation practice*
   Practise this conversation with a partner.

A: Which one of these jumpers would you like?

B: Oh, the [white / green / yellow / blue / woollen / orange / striped] one would be nice.

PART 2

THE VOWELS

Introduction to vowels

What is a vowel?

A vowel is a sound made by the vocal cords. Vowels are made different by changing the shape of the mouth and the position of the tongue.

There is nothing to stop the air moving out of the mouth or to slow it down, as there is in consonants.

The soft palate is always up to make the English vowels, so no air passes through the nose. There are no nasalised vowels in English.

Vowels are always voiced sounds. When we make vowels, the vocal cords are always vibrating; if they weren't vibrating, we wouldn't hear anything because no noise is made in the mouth. Remember to put your hand on your throat; you should always be able to feel the vibration when you make a vowel.

How do we make the different vowel sounds?

We do not stop the air as it leaves the mouth and so do not change the sound in this way; vowels sounds are made different by different *shapes* of the mouth. This is done in three ways:

1. *Moving the jaw*
   The jaw can be moved to make the mouth wide open, nearly closed, or any position in between.

   To help you feel this movement of the jaw, try saying the words 'car' and 'key'. In the first word the jaw should be open and in the second word it should be almost closed.

2. *Moving the tongue*
   The tongue can change its shape very easily; and it is the movements of the tongue which are the most important for making vowels sounds. It can move up at the front, in the middle, or at the back. Of course there are also a lot of other positions in between these.

   To help you feel the movements of your tongue, try saying the words 'tea' and 'two'. In the first word your tongue should move up at the front, and in the second word it should move up at the back.

3. *Moving the lips*
   The lips can make a lot of different shapes which will change the sound of a vowel. The lips can move from being round to spread, with a lot of different shapes in between.
   To test your lip movements you will need to look in a mirror. Say the words 'mean' and 'moon'. In the first word your lips should be spread, and in the second word they should be round.
   For each vowel sound you must think about each of these things carefully; to help you, each section will give careful descriptions of the movements.

Types of vowels

There are two types of vowels that we will be talking about in this book.

1. *Pure vowels*
   These vowels have only one sound in them and they can be short or long. The long vowels will have ː written after them. Try saying, for example, the words 'bid' and 'bead' (/bɪd/ and /biːd/). The difference between these two words is that the first has a short vowel and the second has a long vowel.

2. *Diphthongs*
   These sounds are made up of two vowels and they are always long. For example, the vowel in the word 'play', /pleɪ/, is a diphthong. In section 2 we will be looking only at the pure vowels; in section 3 we will be looking at the diphthongs.

How the pure vowels are described

To help you with each of the different movements that you must put together to make the vowel sounds, each vowel will be described under the following three headings: *The tongue, The mouth and lips,* and *Length.*

1. *The tongue*
   Because the tongue is so important in making vowel sounds, we will be using a vowel chart to help show you where the tongue should go to make each vowel.

This is a vowel chart:

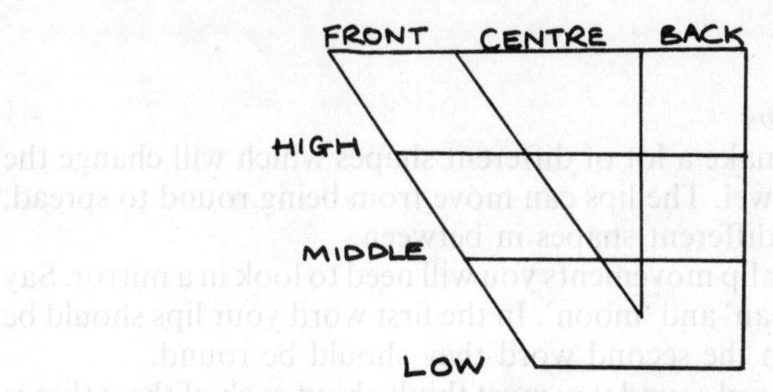

You can see that it is a diagram that divides the mouth into sections. We can say whether the tongue should be in a high, middle or low position, and whether we are talking about the front, centre or back of the tongue.

Here is one example (the /i:/ sound) to show how the chart works. Here is a drawing of the position of the tongue for this vowel:

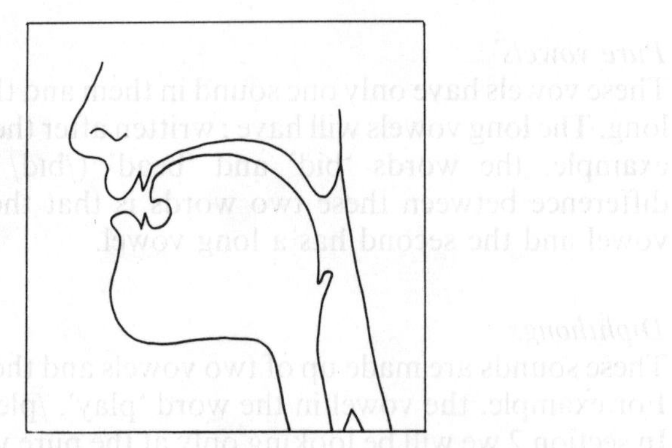

Now let us put it in the vowel chart and put a dot on it to show that the tongue is high and to the front:

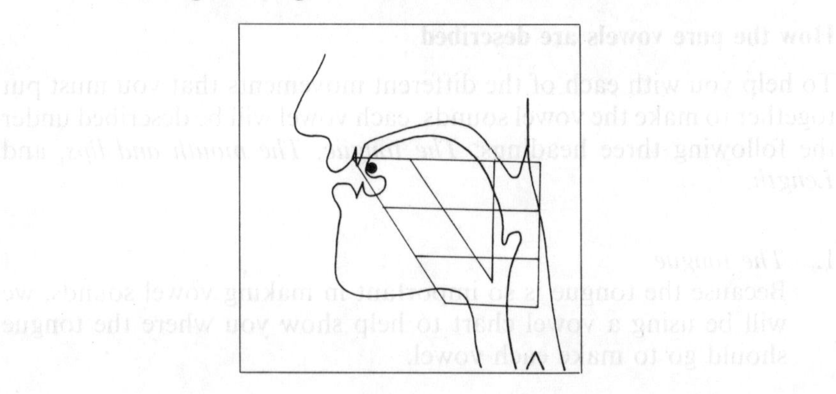

Now we will take away the drawing of the mouth and we are left with the vowel chart showing the position of the tongue:

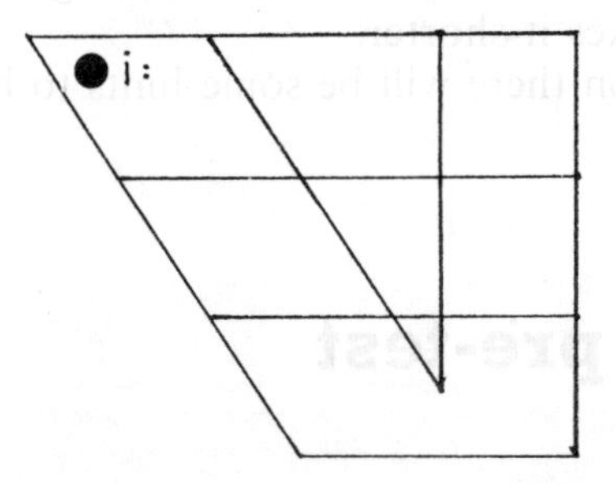

2. *The mouth and lips*
To help you with the lip shapes and the position of your jaw, we will be using photographs like this:

/iː/

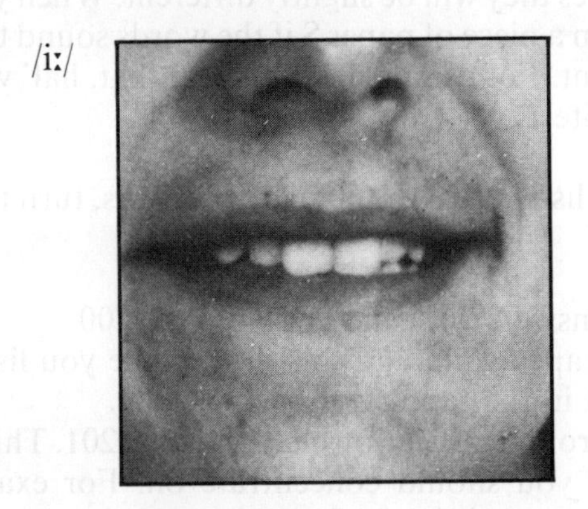

If you are worried about the way you are using your lips to make a vowel sound, look in a mirror and check the shape you are making with the one in the photograph.

3. *Length*
As we said before, some pure vowels are short and some are long. However the length of the vowels may be changed by the sound that comes after them in a word. If a vowel is followed by a voiceless consonant (for example /t/, /s/, /f/) then it may be made shorter. If a vowel is followed by a voiced consonant (for example /d/, /z/, /v/) it may be made longer. To test this, say the words 'beat' /biːt/ and 'bead' /biːd/. The two words have the same long vowel /iː/ but it is made longer in the second word because it is followed by a voiced consonant.

In this way it is even possible that a short vowel e.g. /ɪ/ in 'bid', can be longer than a long vowel e.g. /iː/ in 'beat'. This is because the voiced consonant makes the vowel longer and the voiceless consonant makes it shorter.

In each lesson there will be some hints to help you with this.

Listening pre-test

Before you begin the lessons on vowels, do the listening pre-test. It will help you to find out which vowels you should practise most.

You will hear 60 pairs of words. Sometimes the words will be exactly the same, sometimes they will be slightly different. When you hear each pair, write down on a piece of paper S if the words sound the same, D if they sound different. For example, if you hear 'hat, hat' write S; if you hear 'hat, hot' write D.

When you have listened to the 60 pairs of words, turn to the back of the book and . . .

1. Check your answers with the key on page 200.
2. Listen to the tape again, and this time, while you listen, read the words printed in the tapescript on page 200.
3. Look at the error identification chart on page 201. This will tell you which lessons you should concentrate on. For example, if you thought the two words in the first pair were the same, you should study lessons 23 and 25.

Lesson 18

The pure vowel /iː/

How to pronounce this vowel

The tongue
Look at the vowel chart and the diagram. You can see that the front of the tongue should be very high and to the front of the mouth.

If you move your tongue too far forward you will stop the air—but try to put it as far forward as you can without doing this.

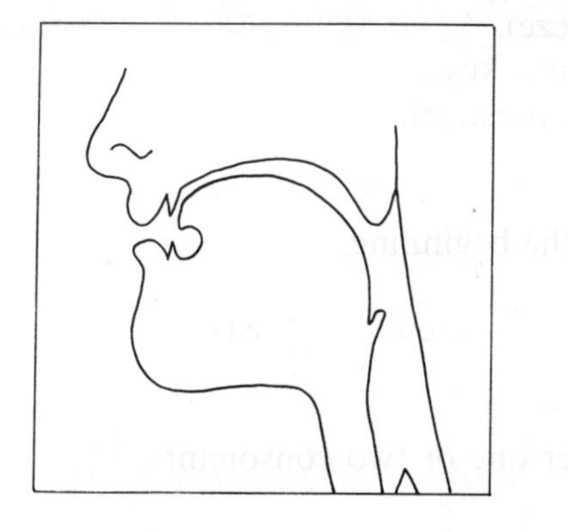

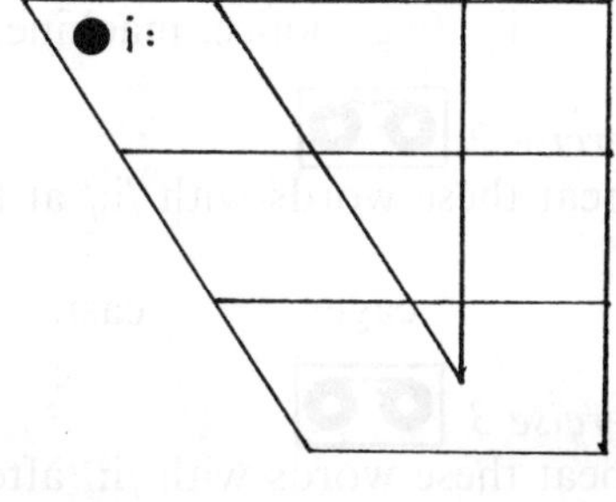

The lips and the mouth
The lips should be spread and the mouth should be slightly open.

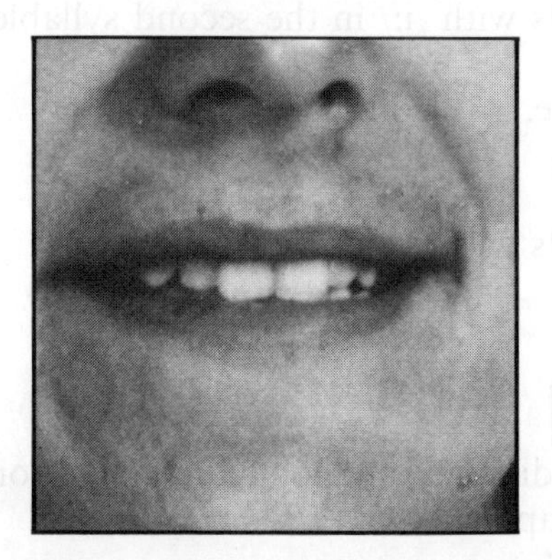

Length
/iː/ is a *long* vowel, but remember it may be changed by the sound that comes after it in the word. It may be longer if it is followed by a voiced consonant and shorter if it is followed by a voiceless consonant.

Exercise 1
Listen only, do not repeat. Note how, in the words with *voiced* consonants, the /iː/ is longer than in the words where the vowel is followed by a *voiceless* consonant.

need, eat; peas, peace; cheese, chief.

Spelling
/iː/ can be spelt in these ways:
'ee' (e.g. three, cheese, leek),
'ea' (e.g. season, leap, seat),
'e' (e.g. be, these, complete),
'ie' (e.g. piece, siege, frieze),
'ei', 'ey' (e.g. seize, receive, key),
'i' (e.g. police, machine, prestige).

Exercise 2
Repeat these words with /iː/ at the beginning.

eat, eager, east, even, easy.

Exercise 3
Repeat these words with /iː/ after one or two consonants.

piece, cream, leaf, sheep, bean.

Exercise 4
Repeat these words with /iː/ in the second syllable.

asleep, believe, complete, machine, police.

Exercise 5
Repeat these words with /iː/ at the end.

sea, three, key, be, knee.

Exercise 6
Read through this dialogue and look at the questions at the end before you listen to the tape.

Pete is walking through the town where he lives and is stopped by a policewoman.

Policewoman: Excuse me, have you seen a green car go by?
Pete: A green car? No, I'm sorry I haven't.
Policewoman: You see there's been a robbery at the key factory.
Pete: Oh, what did they steal?
Policewoman: A lot of keys and fifteen thousand pounds.
Pete: Fifteen thousand! But why keys?
Policewoman: They're all copies of the prison keys. The thieves will probably set their friends free . . .
Pete: Your chief won't be very pleased, will he!

Now look at these questions.

1. Which tone does Pete use in line 4?
2. What is *won't* the short form of? (line 9).
3. Where are all the stresses in line 3?

Exercise 7
Read the part of the policewoman. She's very worried about the burglary.

Exercise 8
Read the part of Pete. He's not very worried about the burglary.

Today's silly sentence

Three sleepy sheep see a bee eat a piece of cheese.

Group activities

1. Look at the dialogue on page 93. How many words can you find with the /iː/ sound in them? Now each student must make a sentence of his or her own using at least two of the words and read it to the class.

2. Now try this game. One person starts off by saying the word 'seat'. The next person must change the word by putting a different sound at the beginning, for example 'beat'. The next person must change the end of the word, for example 'bean'. The vowel must stay the same and you cannot say the same word twice. Take turns to change the beginning and the end as you go round the class, and keep going until you can think of no more words.

3. *Conversation practice*
   The sentences in this dialogue have been mixed up. Work with another student and sort them out.

   How many sheep were in that field yesterday?
   Yes, Steve.
   Well there are fourteen there now.
   Hey, Jean.
   We'd better see if we can find them. Mr Green'll be furious.
   We counted them; there were eighteen.

Lesson 19

The pure vowel /ɪ/

How to pronounce this vowel

This vowel is very similar to /iː/, so you should be very careful to make a difference between the two. The next lesson (lesson 20) will help you with this.

The tongue
Look at the vowel chart and the diagram. The front of the tongue is high to make this sound, but you can see from the vowel chart that it is not as high or as far forward as it is for /iː/.

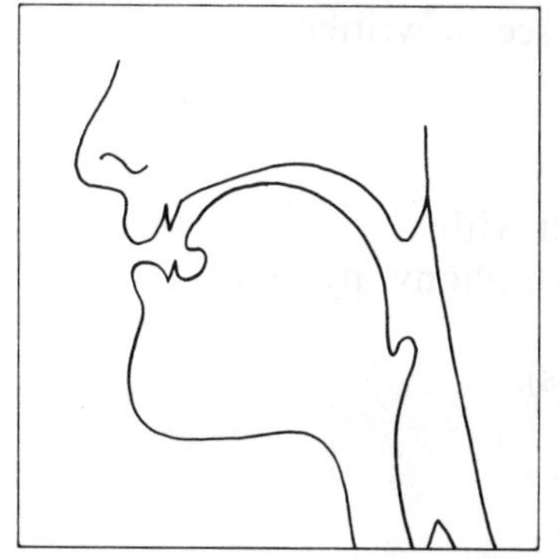

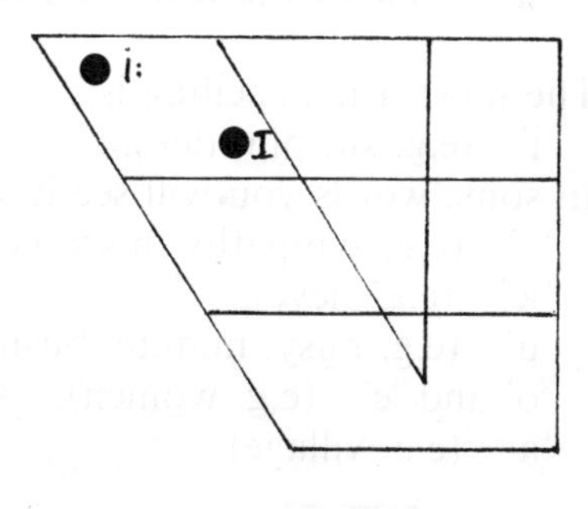

The lips and mouth
The lips are spread but not as widely spread as for /iː/. The mouth should be slightly open.

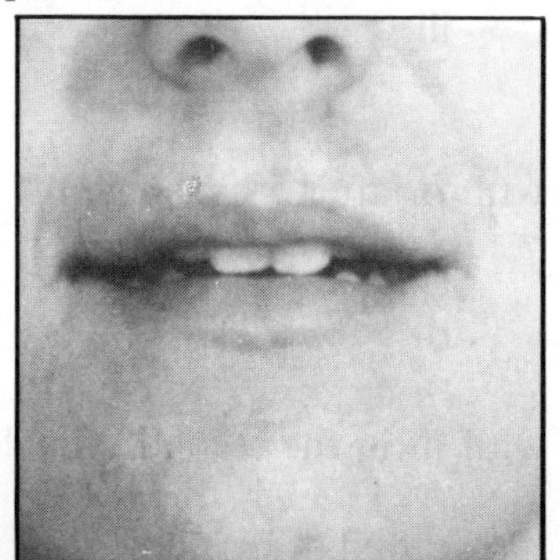

If you have a problem making the difference between /ɪ/ and /iː/, check the shape of your mouth in a mirror with the pictures. Say /ɪ/ and then /iː/. You should see the lips changing shape.

Length
/ɪ/ is a short sound. Remember, however, that it may be changed by the sound that comes after it in the word. It may be made longer if it comes before a voiced consonant and shorter if it comes before a voiceless consonant.

Exercise 1
Listen only. Note how, in the words with *voiced* consonants, the /ɪ/ is longer than in the words in which the vowel is followed by a *voiceless* consonant.

rib, rip; big, bit; sing, sick.

Spelling
Here are some of the ways you will see /ɪ/ written.

The most usual spelling is:
'i' (e.g. sit, pip, tick).
In some words you will see it spelt with:
'y' (e.g. sympathy, mystery, symphony, pyramid),
'ie' (e.g. sieve),
'u' (e.g. busy, minute, business),
'o' and 'e' (e.g. women),
'a' (e.g. village).

Exercise 2
Repeat these words with /ɪ/ at the beginning.

ink, it, ill, itch, is.

Exercise 3
Repeat these words with /ɪ/ after a consonant.

big, little, ship, thin, busy.

Exercise 4
Repeat these words with /ɪ/ in the second syllable.

landed, waited, rabbit, clinic, cooking.

Exercise 5

Read through this dialogue and look at the questions at the end before you listen to the tape.

Linda is in a flat agency, looking for somewhere to live.

Bill: Sit down and I'll look in my books and see what I've got for you.
Linda: Just a little flat will do . . . with a big kitchen, perhaps.
Bill: Little flat, big kitchen. Ah I've got just the thing.
Linda: Can I see it? Is it near?
Bill: Yes, it's this one upstairs. Nice and handy.
Linda: Handy? Handy for what?
Bill: Well, I'll give you a ring in the mornings and you can drop in with a cup of coffee!

Now look at these questions.

1. Which tone does Linda use when she says *handy?* in line 7?
2. Where is the stress in *upstairs* (line 6)?
3. Which is the most important word in the second part of line 4?

Exercise 6

Read the part of Bill. He's being helpful but has a bit of a joke with Linda.

Exercise 7

Read the part of Linda. She's a bit worried about finding a flat.

Today's silly sentence

Which big tin did Bill kick under the kitchen sink?

Group activities

1. *The number game*
   Find a partner for this game. The first person says the number 6 and then the other person adds another 6 to make 66. Carry on in this way adding another 6 each time and see how far you can go.

2. Look at these pictures. Describe the people you see in them.

Here are some words to help you:
big, pretty, silly, thin, little, filthy, feeling sick.

3. *Conversation practice*
Practise this conversation, using any of the items from this list (or any others you can think of).

a tin of figs	some milk
a packet of thin dry biscuits	six sausages
six big eggs	some spinach
a cake mix	some tinned fish

A: I'm going down the street. Do you need anything?
B: Yes. You could get me . . .
A: (Writing down) . . . Anything else?
B: Oh, and we also need . . .
A: OK. . . . Is that all?
B: I think so. Oh, no! Get . . . as well.
A: . . . That all?
B: Yes. Could you read the list back?
A: OK. You want . . .

Lesson 20

Comparing the vowels /ɪ/ and /iː/

This lesson will help you with the vowels /ɪ/ and /iː/ that we looked at in lessons 18 and 19. This is to make sure that you can *hear* the difference between them and pronounce them both well.

How to pronounce these vowels

These are important things to remember.

The tongue
Look at the vowel chart.

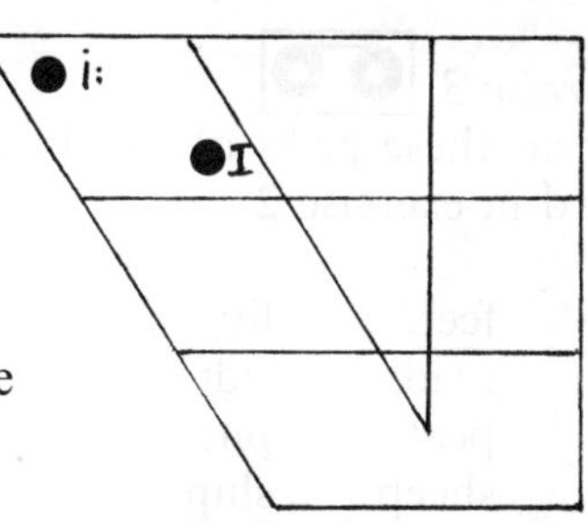

Remember that for /iː/ the tongue is high and to the front, for /ɪ/ the tongue is not so high and not so near the front, but it is still high and to the front of the mouth.

The mouth and lips
Look at the photographs.

The lips are spread.

/iː/

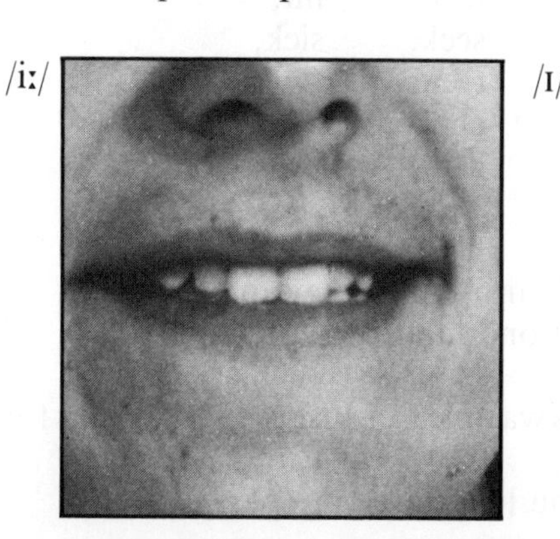

The lips are *loosely* spread and more relaxed.

/ɪ/

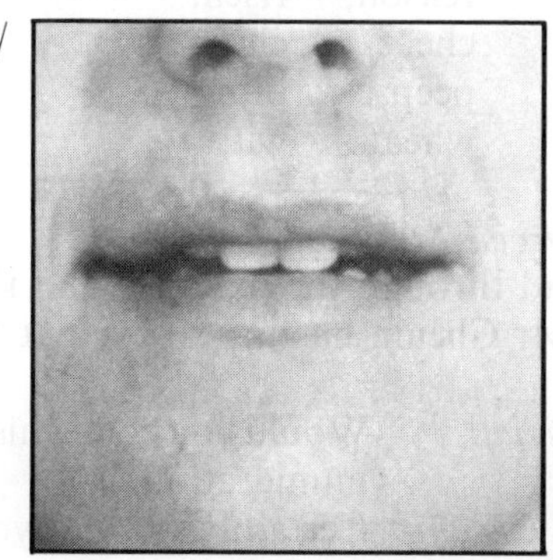

Length
/iː/ is a long sound. /ɪ/ is a short sound.
But remember that both sounds may be made longer if they are followed by a voiced consonant, for example, /b/ /z/ /v/ /d/. They may be made shorter if they are followed by a voiceless consonant, for example /p/ /s/ /t/ /f/.

Exercise 1
Listen only.

beat,	bit;	bean,	bin;
deep,	dip;	dean,	din;
keep,	kip;	keen,	kin.

Exercise 2
Decide whether each word you hear has the /iː/ or the /ɪ/ vowel. The correct answers are underlined in exercise 3.

Exercise 3
Repeat these pairs of words. The ones underlined are the ones you heard in exercise 2.

feet,	fit;	seen,	sin;
read,	rid;	heel,	hill;
peat,	pit;	sleek,	slick;
sheep,	ship;	seeks,	six;
reach,	rich;	least,	list.

Exercise 4
Repeat some more pairs of words which have /iː/ and /ɪ/.

bean,	bin;	heat,	hit;
reason,	risen;	seek,	sick;
cheat,	chit;	teens,	tins;
peep,	pip;	cheap,	chip;
wheat,	wit;	leak,	lick.

Exercise 5
Read through the dialogue and then listen to the tape.
Mr Cheam has just arrived at London airport.

Official: Would you come this way please? Just a few questions for immigration.
Mr Cheam: Certainly. Would you like to see my passport?

Official:	Yes please. Which plane did you come in on?
Mr Cheam:	British Airways from India, Delhi.
Official:	Do you live in India?
Mr Cheam:	No, I was there on business.
Official:	How long are you staying in England?
Mr Cheam:	About six weeks. I'm here on business too.
Official:	Where will you be staying?
Mr Cheam:	Tinton for three weeks, then Pinlow for three.
Official:	Good, no problems. Enjoy your visit to England.

Now look at these questions.

1. Which is the most important word in line 6?
2. Where are all the stresses in line 11?
3. What tone does Mr Cheam use for *certainly* in line 3?

Exercise 6
Read the part of the immigration official.

Exercise 7
Read the part of Mr Cheam. He's being polite and helpful.

Today's silly sentence

These six sleek sheep sleep on their feet.

Group activities

1. Look through the dialogue above. How many words can you find with the /iː/ and /ɪ/ sounds. Make your own sentence using one each of these words and then read your sentence to the class.

2. Your teacher will say one word in each of these pairs of words. Listen carefully and decide which one it is.

1	2	1	2
peek	pick	seat	sit
leek	lick	green	grin
peat	pit	lean	Lynne
reap	rip	sheep	ship

3. Now do the same thing with a partner.

Lesson 21

The pure vowel /e/

How to pronounce this vowel

1. *The tongue*

Look at the vowel chart and the diagram. You can see that the front of the tongue is raised to the middle of the front of the mouth. If you open your mouth slightly you should see your tongue just behind, and half-way between, your top and bottom teeth.

The vowel chart shows you that the tongue is lower in the mouth than it is for /iː/ and /ɪ/.

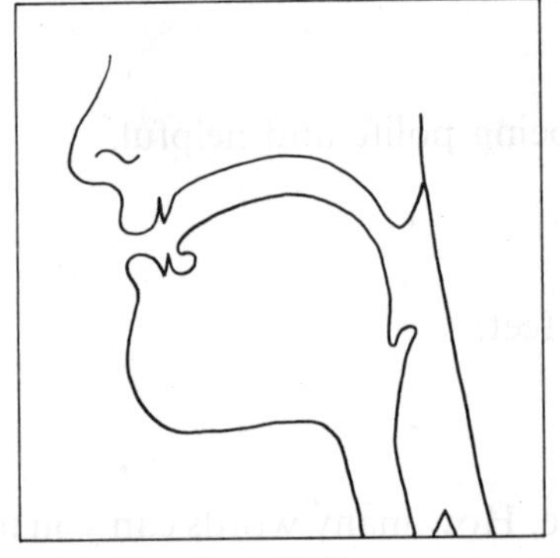

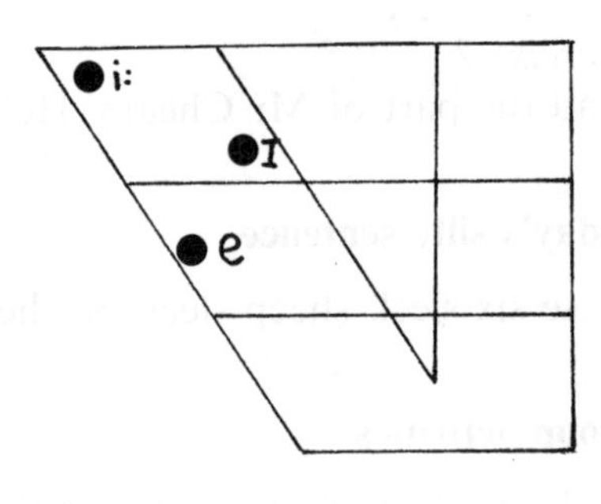

2. *The mouth and lips*

The lips are loosely spread and the mouth is slightly open to make this sound. Look at the photograph and check in the mirror that you are making the sound in the same way, and that your lips look the same.

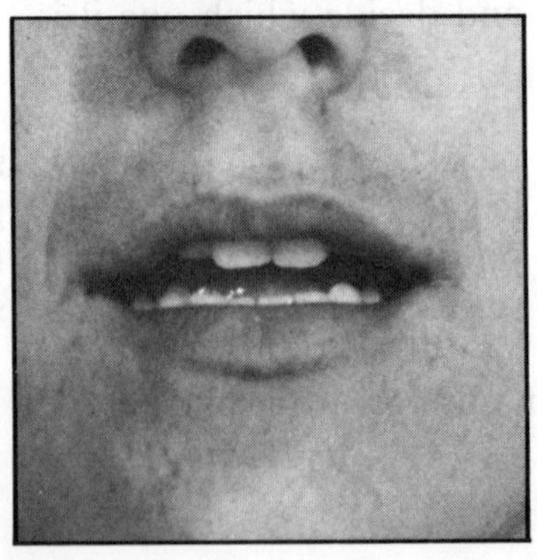

3. *Length*

/e/ is a short sound. Remember, however, that it will be shortened if it is before a voiceless consonant. It will be made longer if it is before a voiced consonant.

Exercise 1

Listen only.

wet, when; jet, gem; debt, dead.

Spelling

The most usual spelling of /e/ is with 'e' (e.g. bed, leg, nest, went, when).

But it can also be spelt as:

'ea' (e.g. head, dead, breath),

'a' (e,g, many, any).

Exercise 2

In this exercise we will compare *three* vowel sounds. Decide whether each word you hear has the /iː/, the /ɪ/ or the /e/ vowel. The correct answers are underlined in exercise 5.

Exercise 3

Repeat these words with /e/ at the beginning.

any, ever, essence, anything, end.

Exercise 4

Repeat these words with /e/ after a consonant.

said, set, never, better, fetch.

Exercise 5

Repeat the groups of words. The ones underlined are the ones you heard in exercise 2.

beat,	bit,	bet;	teens,	tins,	tens;
least,	list,	lest;	neat,	knit,	net;
lead,	lid,	led;	wean,	win,	when;
peat,	pit,	pet;	heed,	hid,	head;
seeks,	six,	sex;	each,	itch,	etch.

Exercise 6

Read through this dialogue and look at the questions at the end before you listen to the tape. Ben and Jenny are friends.

Ben: Can you lend me ten pounds?
Jenny: What do you want to borrow ten pounds for?
Ben: I promised I'd mend the tennis net . . .
Jenny: Tennis net? What have you done to it?
Ben: Well, Ken bet me I couldn't jump over it . . .
Jenny: I see, and he won the bet!

Now look at these questions.

1. Which is the most important word in line 1?
2. Which tone does Ben use in line 3?
3. Which tone does Jenny use for *tennis net* in line 4?

Exercise 7

Read the part of Ben. He's worried because he needs some money.

Exercise 8

Read the part of Jenny. She's curious to know why Ben needs the money.

Today's silly sentence

The jelly Ned made for Ted never set.

Group activities

1. Your teacher will say one of the words in each set of three. Listen carefully and decide which one it is.

1	2	3
seat	sit	set
reach	rich	wretch
dean	din	den
read	rid	red
bead	bid	bed

2. Now try the same thing with a partner.

3. Look at these 8 pictures. Decide what the words are. Of course, they all have the /e/ sound in them.

4. Now each student must make up his or her own sentence using one of these words. Read your sentence to the rest of the class.

5. *Conversation practice*
   Practise this conversation with a partner

A:	Hello,	Ben. Ted. Fred. Ken.	Have you seen	Nellie Jenny Betty Wendy	?

B:	. . .? She's	Ed's Len's Brett's	friend, isn't she?

A:	Yes. She said she'd meet me at	ten. ten past ten. seven. ten to seven. eleven.

B: Sorry, can't help you.

A: Oh, well never mind. . . . always forgets.

Lesson 22

The pure vowel /æ/

How to pronounce this vowel

The tongue
Look at the vowel chart and the diagram. You can see that the front of the tongue is at the bottom of the mouth and just behind the bottom teeth. The tongue is lower than it is for /e/, as you can see in the vowel chart.

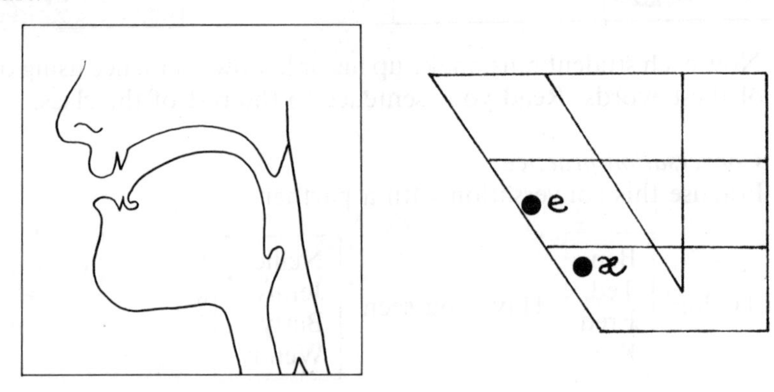

The lips and mouth
The mouth is open wider than it is for /e/. Check the shape of your lips when you are saying this sound by looking in the mirror. Are they the same as the picture?

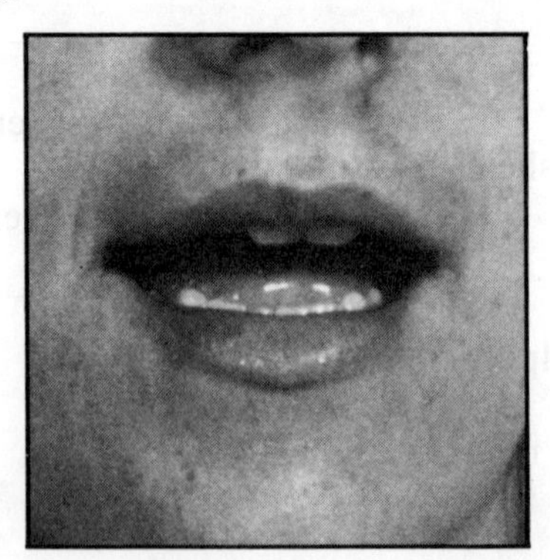

Length
/æ/ is a short vowel. Remember, however, that it can be made a little longer when it is followed by a voiced consonant, and shorter when it is followed by a voiceless consonant.

Exercise 1
Listen only. Remember /æ/ sounds shorter before a voiceless consonant and longer before a voiced consonant.

pat, pad; sack, sad; wrap, ram; tack, tan.

Spelling
/æ/ is nearly always spelt as ‘a’ (e.g. sat, pat, lack).

Exercise 2
Decide whether each word you hear has the /e/ or the /æ/ vowel. The correct answers are underlined in exercise 5 below.

Exercise 3
Repeat these words with /æ/ at the beginning.

at, apple, atom, as, am.

Exercise 4
Repeat these words with /æ/ after one or two consonants.

band, fat, stamp, cramp, black.

Exercise 5
Repeat the pairs of words. The ones underlined are the ones you heard in exercise 2.

met,	mat;	bend,	band;
pen,	pan;	ten,	tan;
set,	sat;	wreck,	rack;
ketch,	catch;	bet,	bat;
expend,	expand;	men,	man.

Exercise 6
Read through the dialogue and look at the questions at the end before you listen to the tape.

Ann is in the street trying to buy a newspaper. The newspaper seller is shouting to attract customers.

Newspaper Seller:	Get your Manchester News here. Smash and grab at the jewellers!
Ann:	Really, did they catch the man who did it?
Newspaper Seller:	Yes. Read all about it, accident at Hanley.
Ann:	Anyone killed?
Newspaper Seller:	Three . Manchester News, tonight's match on the back page.
Ann:	Who won the match?
Newspaper Seller:	Hanley Athletic. Do you want a copy?
Ann:	No, I know all the news now!

Now look at these questions.

1. Which tone does Ann use in line 5?
2. Where is the stress in the word *accident* (line 4)? Is it the same in the word *accidental*?
3. Where are all the stresses in line 3?

Exercise 7
Read the part of the newspaper seller. He is talking to Ann and trying to sell his newspapers.

Exercise 8
Read the part of Ann.

Today's silly sentence

Pat's so mad at the fat black cat.

Group activities

1. Look at these newspaper headlines. Write two or three sentences that you think would be underneath the headlines in the paper. Read your sentences to the class and see if they have the same.

    1. Bank robbery at Hanley.
    2. Hanley Athletic win cup.
    3. Serious accident, Black Hill. 3 killed.
    4. Manchester goes Conservative.
    5. Blackrock gets new pool.
    6. Valuable cat lost—reward offered.

2. The four pictures on the left all have the /e/ sound. The four on the right are almost the same, except that they have the /æ/ sound. Work out what the words are and match up the pictures. Now see if you can make up eight sentences which use the words. Read them out to the class.

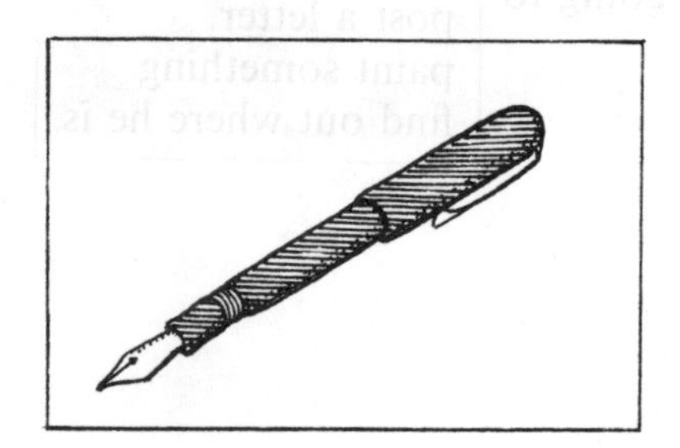

10

3. *Conversation practice*
Practise this conversation with a partner.

B must listen carefully to *A*'s question to give the right answer.

A: What's that man doing with that

stamp
apple
map
raquet
jacket
can of paint

?

B: I don't know. He's probably going to

put it on.
play tennis.
eat it.
post a letter.
paint something.
find out where he is.

Lesson 23

The pure vowel /ʌ/

How to pronounce this vowel

The tongue
This vowel is similar to /æ/ (lesson 22) and so you may have some difficulty making them sound different. Look at the vowel chart and the diagram. You can see that the front of the tongue is lower and a bit further back than it is for /æ/. The front of the tongue is not behind the bottom teeth now, but a little bit away from them and almost touching the bottom of the mouth. The middle of the tongue is raised to the middle of the mouth.

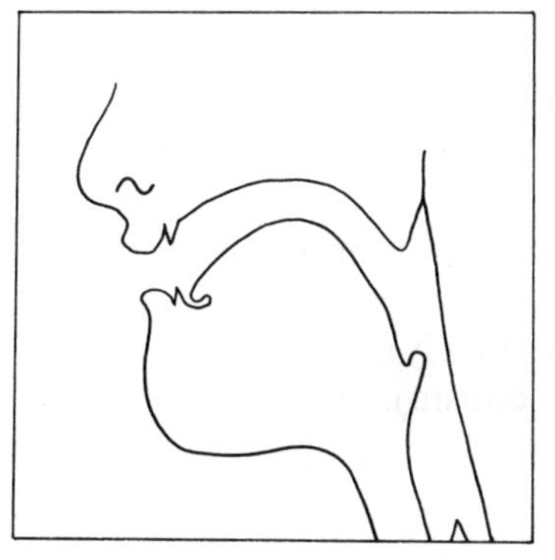

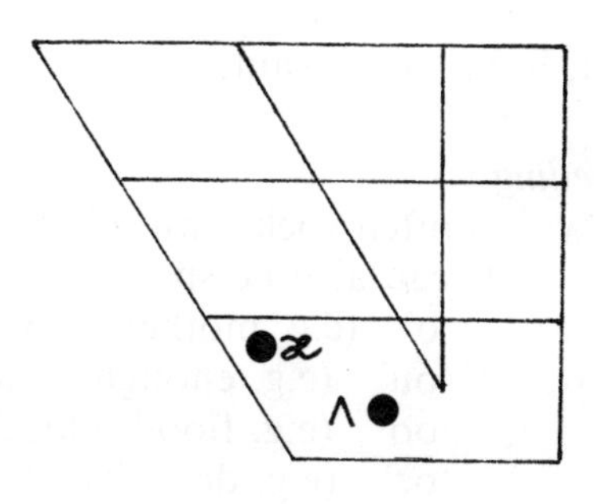

The mouth and lips
The mouth is open for this sound as you can see in the photograph.

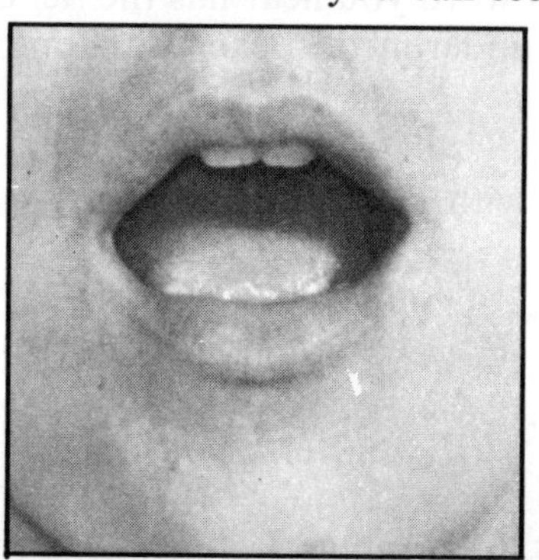

Length
/ʌ/ is a short vowel. However, it sounds very short if it is followed by a voiceless consonant. It sounds longer if it is followed by a voiced consonant.

Exercise 1
Listen carefully for the difference between /ʌ/ and /æ/. The first word of each pair has the vowel /æ/ and the second word of each pair has the vowel /ʌ/.

Listen and do not repeat.

match, much; lamp, lump; dam, dumb; bad, bud; hat, hut.

Listen to this exercise again if you are still having trouble in hearing the difference.

Exercise 2
Listen, do not repeat. Remember /ʌ/ sounds longer when it is followed by a voiced consonant.

hut, hub; shut, shun; rut, run.

Spelling
/ʌ/ is often spelt with 'u' (e.g. sun, gun, jump, cut).
It can also be spelt as:
'o' (e.g. mother, Monday, lovely),
'ou' (e.g. enough, young, cousin),
'oo' (e.g. flood, blood),
'oe' (e.g. doesn't).

Exercise 3
Decide whether each word you hear has the /æ/ or the /ʌ/ vowel. The correct answers are underlined in exercise 6 on page 113.

Exercise 4 
Repeat these words with /ʌ/ at the beginning.

ugly, under, other, up, utter.

Exercise 5
Repeat these words with /ʌ/ after a consonant.

butter, mother, young, shut, southern.

Exercise 6

Repeat these pairs of words. The ones underlined are the ones you heard in exercise 3.

lamp,	lump;	cap,	cup;
hat,	hut;	batter,	butter;
cat,	cut;	ban,	bun;
bang	bung;	mash,	mush;
stamp,	stump;	match,	much.

Exercise 7

Read through this dialogue and look at the questions at the end before you listen to the tape.

Ann is starting a new job at the bank and Mr Bunn, the manager, is telling her what to do.

Mr Bunn: Now don't forget you must shut up the drawers and put the cover on the typewriter.
Ann: But Mr Bunn . . .
Mr Bunn: You must lock up the money in the safe and you must shut the front door.
Ann: But Mr Bunn, the tea girl doesn't . . .
Mr Bunn: Tea girl? You're the tea girl! What are you worrying me for? I thought you were the new cashier.
Ann: Sorry Mr Bunn. Shall I run upstairs and make some tea?

Now look at these questions.

1. Which tone does Mr Bunn use when he says *tea girl* (line 7)?
2. Where are all the stresses in lines 1 and 2?
3. Which is the most important word in line 8 (I thought. . .)?

Exercise 8

Read the part of Mr Bunn. He's speaking very formally to his new employee and is very angry when he finds out who she is.

Exercise 9

Read the part of Ann. She's trying very hard to tell Mr Bunn she's not the cashier.

Today's silly sentence

My country cousin, Cuthbert, loves to jump in muddy puddles.

Group activities

1. Imagine you are going on holiday. Look at the pictures and talk about the things you mustn't forget to do.
   'I musn't forget to . . .'

2. Your teacher will say one word in each of these pairs of words. Listen carefully and decide which one it is.

1	2	1	2
track	truck	lack	luck
cat	cut	sack	suck
bat	but	cap	cup
sang	sung	match	much

3. Now try the same thing with a partner.

4. *Conversation practice*
   Practise this conversation with a partner.

A: Going to the match on | Sunday
Monday | ?

B: Can't. My cousin's coming up from | the country
Buxton
Muddlum
Lumsdum | for a couple of days.

A: Well, bring him too. We're going to see | Dumhead
Rumley
Umbridge | versus | Crumley.
Tonbridge.
Hutton.

B: I'll ask him. I'll give you a ring before lunch on ...

A: Fine! Hope you can come.

Note. All these place names have the sound /ʌ/.

Lesson 24

Revision of the pure front vowels

How to pronounce these vowels

Now let us look at all the vowels we have practised in lessons 18 to 23. These vowels are all front vowels because it is the front of the tongue which is moved to make these sounds.

The tongue
Look at the vowel chart. You can see that front vowels can be made at the top, in the middle, or at the bottom of the mouth.

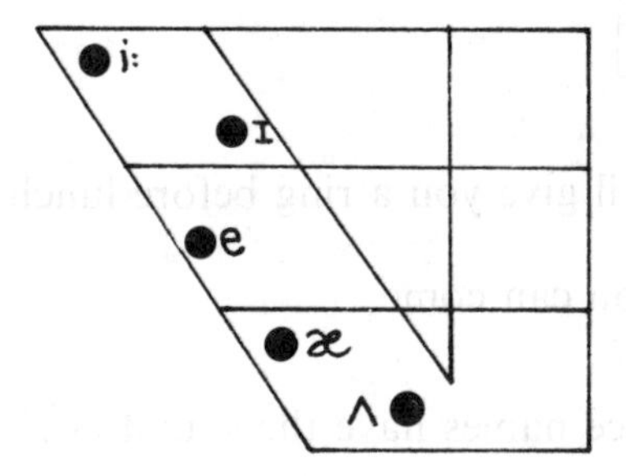

The mouth and lips
Look at the photographs. As the tongue is moving from the top of the mouth to the bottom of the mouth (that is moving from /iː/ to /ʌ/) the mouth becomes more and more open. In the same way the lips become less spread.

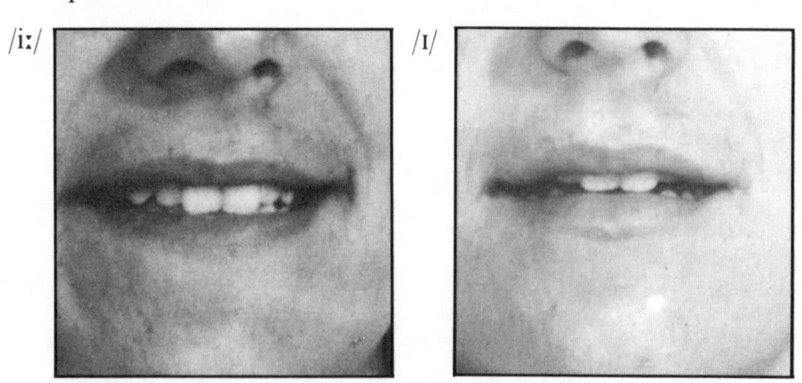

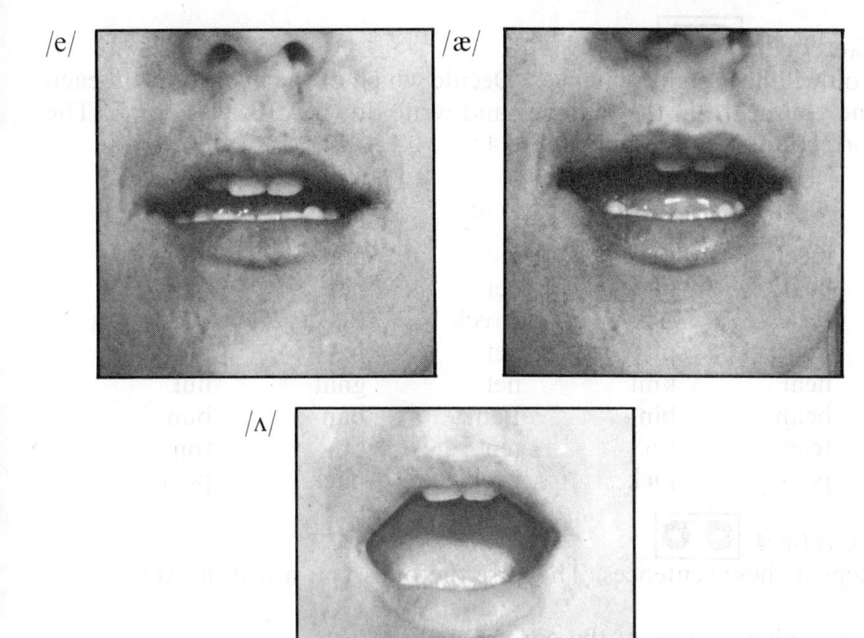

Look in the mirror and say these five vowels. You should see the mouth and lips changing. Check your lips with the lips in the photographs.

Exercise 1

Decide which of the five vowels you hear in each word. The correct answers are underlined in exercise 2.

Exercise 2

Repeat these groups of five words. The ones underlined are the ones you heard in exercise 1.

meet,	mit,	met,	mat,	mutt.
beat,	bit,	bet,	bat,	but.
reek,	rick,	wreck,	rack,	ruck.
Pete,	pit,	pet,	pat,	putt.
neat,	knit,	net,	gnat,	nut.
bean,	bin,	Ben,	ban,	bun.
teen,	tin,	ten,	tan,	ton.
peak,	pick,	peck,	pack,	puck.

Exercise 3

You will hear eight sentences. Decide which of the five words on each line you heard in the sentence and write down A, B, C, D or E. The correct answers are in exercise 4.

	A /iː/	B /ɪ/	C /e/	D /æ/	E /ʌ/
1.	meet	mit	met	mat	mutt
2.	beat	bit	bet	bat	but
3.	reek	rick	wreck	rack	ruck
4.	Pete	pit	pet	pat	putt
5.	neat	knit	net	gnat	nut
6.	bean	bin	Ben	ban	bun
7.	teen	tin	ten	tan	ton
8.	peak	pick	peck	pack	puck

Exercise 4

Repeat these sentences. They are the ones you heard in exercise 3.

1. They met us at the corner of the street.
2. I'll bet you ten dollars that you can't do it.
3. They stacked the bottles on the rack.
4. Don't pat that dog; it bites.
5. Her room was kept very neat and tidy.
6. Throw them in the bin, will you.
7. This bag weighs a ton.
8. I'll pick you up at three.

Lesson 25

The pure vowel /ɑː/

The vowels in lessons 25 to 30 are back vowels. That is because it is the back of the tongue which is important when you make these vowels.

How to pronounce this vowel

The tongue
Both the front of the tongue and the back of the tongue are low in the mouth when you make this sound, and so the air passes through a wide opening.

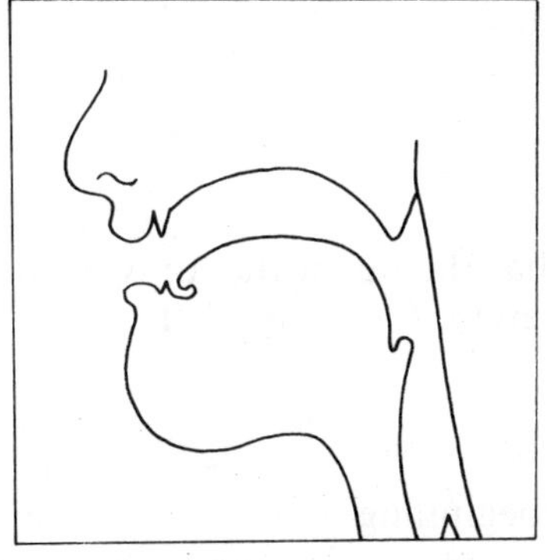

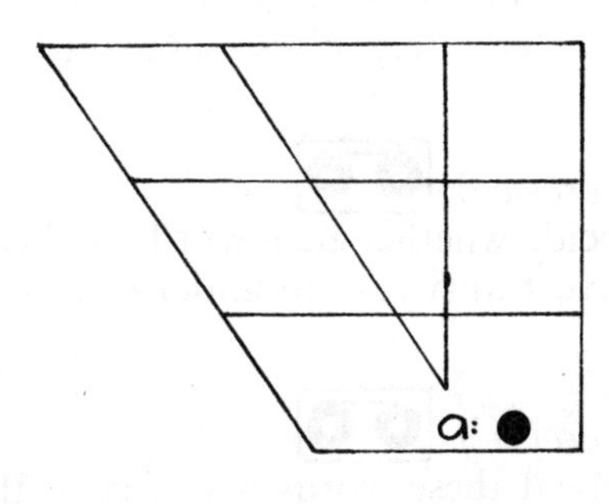

The mouth and lips
Look at the photograph. The mouth is wide open and the lips are rounded.

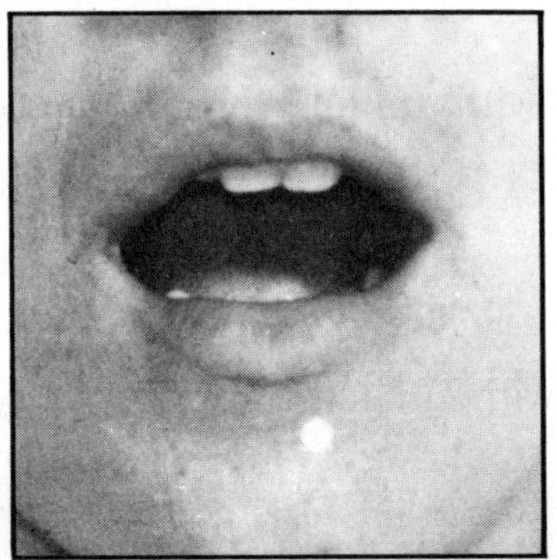

Length
/ɑː/ is a long vowel. Remember, however, that it is made shorter when it comes before a voiceless consonant. It is longer when it comes before a voiced consonant.

Exercise 1
Listen only; do not repeat.

cart, calm; dark, darn; lark, lard.

Spelling
/ɑː/ is usually spelt as:
'a' (e.g. father, tomato, after),
'ar' (e.g. farm, large, part, arm).
But it can also be spelt as:
'al' (e.g. calf, palm, half, calm),
'ear' (e.g. heart),
'au' (e.g. laugh),
'er' (e.g. clerk, sergeant).

Exercise 2
Decide whether each word you hear has the /æ/ or the /ɑː/ vowel. The correct answers are underlined in exercise 6 on page 121.

Exercise 3
Repeat these words with /ɑː/ at the beginning.

after, arms, argument, aunt, ask.

Exercise 4 
Repeat these words with /ɑː/ after one or two consonants.

half, hearty, bark, start, clerk.

Exercise 5
Repeat these words with /ɑː/ in the second syllable of a word or group of words.

tomato, a car, the park, a mast, an aunt.

Exercise 6

Repeat these pairs of words. The ones underlined are the ones you heard in exercise 2.

had, hard;
cap, carp;
Pam, palm;
pat, part;
am, arm;

bad, bard;
massed, mast;
pack, park;
lad, lard;
ant, aunt.

Exercise 7

Read through this dialogue and look at the questions at the end before you listen to the tape.

Mark and Martha are hurrying along the street to get to the cinema on time.

Martha: Hurry up, the film's starting—can't you run any faster?
Mark: Oh I'm trying. Who's starring?
Martha: Charles Carnforth—he's in all the disaster films.
Mark: Oh, is it 'Star Disaster'?
Martha: That's right, not hard to guess what it's about.
Mark: Martha, stay calm, but I saw it last week.

Now look at these questions.

1. Which tone did Mark use when he said *Martha* (line 6)?
2. Where is the stress in the word *disaster* (line 3)?
3. Where are all the stresses in line 3?

Exercise 8

Read the part of Martha. She's getting a bit angry with Mark because he's being so slow.

Exercise 9

Read the part of Mark. He's already seen the film and is worried that Martha will be angry.

Today's silly sentence

Charming Charley asks Martha Farnsbarns for a dance at the barn dance.

Group activities

1. Take turns around the class to say one of these words. The rest of the class must decide if it is in group 1 or 2.

1	2
chat	chart
Dan	darn
back	bark
hat	heart
lack	lark
ban	barn
match	march

2. Now each student must think of a sentence using one of the words. Read your sentence to the class.

3. Look at the map below. Working in pairs, ask each other how to get from:

   Farnton to Darnley
   Scarsley to Narmton
   Parsley to Larmsley

   In your reply, use expressions such as:

   Go to . . .
   Turn left at . . . to . . .
   Go straight through . . . to . . .
   Go straight on to . . .

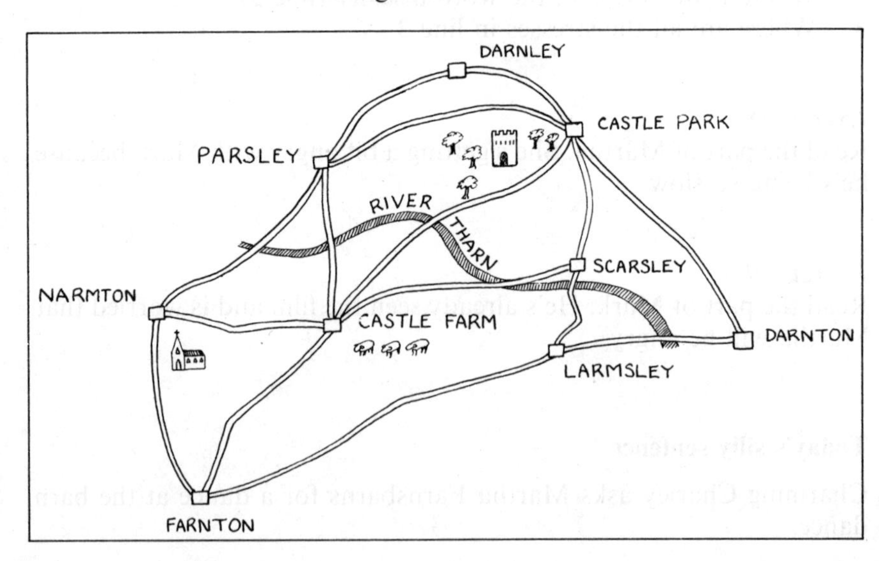

Lesson 26

The pure vowel /ɒ/

How to pronounce this vowel

The tongue
The back and the front of the tongue are low when you make this sound. The back, however, is a little bit higher than for /ɑː/. Look at the diagram and the vowel chart and you can see the position of the tongue.

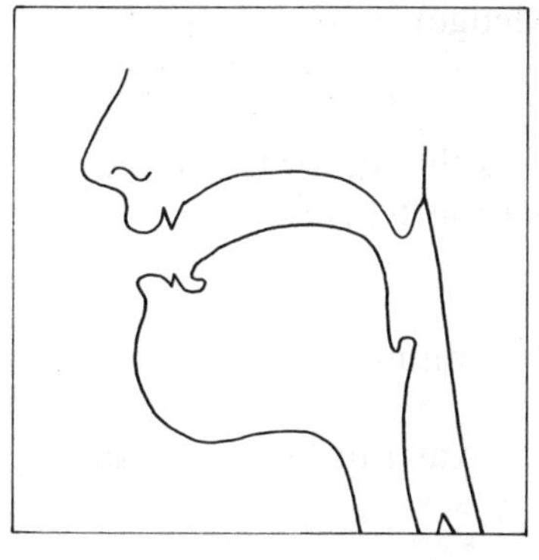

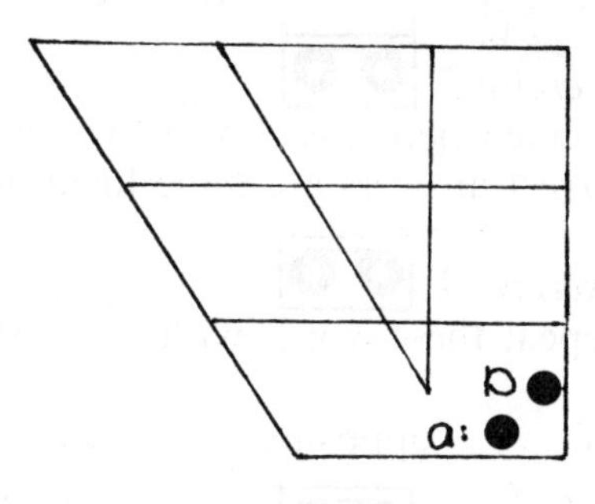

The mouth and lips
Look at the photograph. The mouth is open but not as wide as it is for /ɑː/. Look in a mirror when you are practising this sound and check the shape of your lips with the photograph. The lips are rounded when you make this sound.

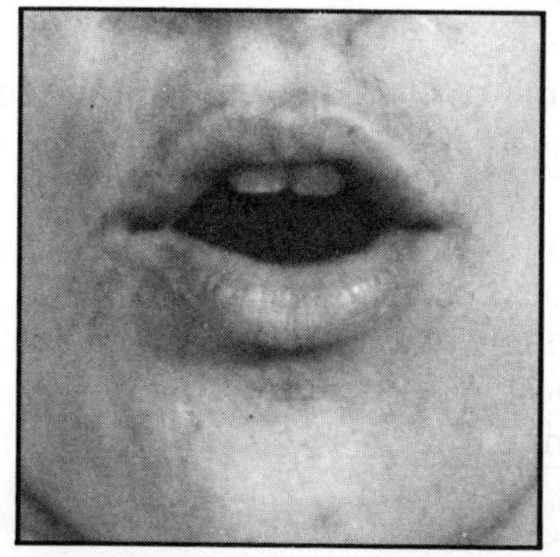

Length

/ɒ/ is a short sound. It sounds very short when it is followed by a voiceless consonant and sounds slightly longer when it is followed by a voiced consonant.

Exercise 1

Listen only; do not repeat.

cot, cod; lock, long; flock, flog.

Spelling

/ɒ/ is usually spelt as:

'o' (e.g. dog, lock, bother, fog),

'a' (e.g. was, swan, what, yacht),

But in some words it can be spelt as:

'au' (e.g. sausage, because, Australia),

'ou' or 'ow' (e.g. cough, knowledge).

Exercise 2

Decide whether each word you hear has the /ɑː/ or the /ɒ/ vowel. The correct answers are underlined in exercise 5 below.

Exercise 3

Repeat these words with /ɒ/ at the beginning.

off, opposite, olive, Australia, odd.

Exercise 4

Repeat these words with /ɒ/ after a consonant or a group of consonants.

John, body, strong, bottle, impossible.

Exercise 5

Repeat these pairs of words. The ones underlined are the ones you heard in exercise 2.

<u>cart</u>,	cot;	lark,	<u>lock</u>;
part,	<u>pot</u>;	<u>sharp</u>,	shop;
calf,	<u>cough</u>;	<u>barks</u>,	box;
<u>darn</u>,	Don;	<u>tart</u>,	tot;
impassable,	<u>impossible</u>;	mark,	<u>mock</u>.

Exercise 6

Read through this dialogue and look at the questions at the end before you listen to the tape.

Bob has just come back from holiday and is talking to his friend Dot.

Dot: Did you get lots of hot sun on your holiday?
Bob: Don't talk to me about holidays.
Dot: Why not? Did something go wrong?
Bob: Yes, I got lost and got on the wrong plane.
Dot: And where did you get off?
Bob: In Oslo, and there was a lot of snow about!

Now look at these questions.

1. Where is the stress in the word *about* (line 2)?
2. Which tone does Bob use in line 2?
3. Which is the most important word in the second part of line 6?

Exercise 7

Read the part of Dot. She's being very friendly.

Exercise 8

Read the part of Bob. He's feeling very miserable because he's had a bad holiday.

Today's silly sentence

Don and Dot Mogg have long blond hair.

Group activities

1. *The word game*
   Start this game with one person saying the word *sock*. The next person changes the first sound in the word, for example *lock*. Then change the last sound, for example *lot* and so on. The vowel always stays the same. Go round the class. If you can't think of a word drop out, and carry on until only one person is left.

2. Look at this picture. How many sentences can you make using the /ɒ/ sound?

3. *Conversation practice*
Practise this conversation with a partner.

A:	I've got to get	a some	lock for the door. dog collar. bottles of wine. cough mixture.

B:	Moggs Bloggs Goughs Dons	is a good shop. In	Long Strong Hogg Forest	Street.

A:	The one opposite the	bank? chemist? butcher? post office?

B: That's the one.

Lesson 27

The pure vowel /ɔː/

This sound is very similar to /ɒ/, so take care to make them sound different.

How to pronounce this vowel

The tongue
The back of the tongue is a little bit higher than it is for /ɒ/ Look at the diagram and you can see that the front of the tongue is low and the back is raised to about the middle of the mouth.

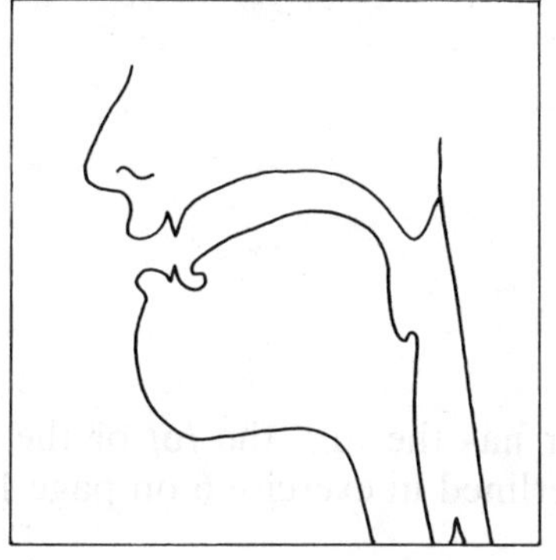

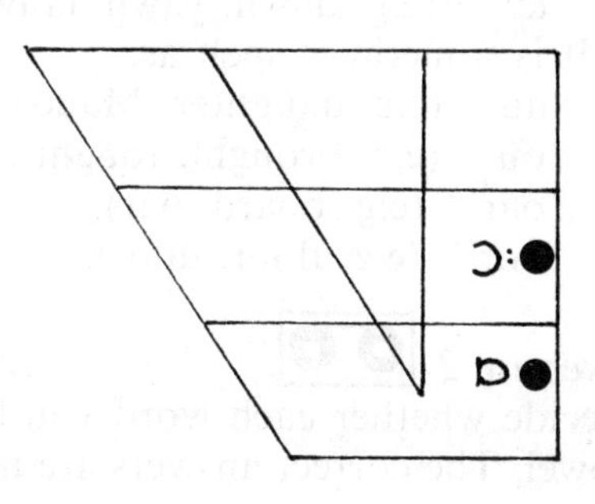

The mouth and lips
Look at the photograph. The mouth is a little more closed than it is for /ɒ/ and the lips are rounded.

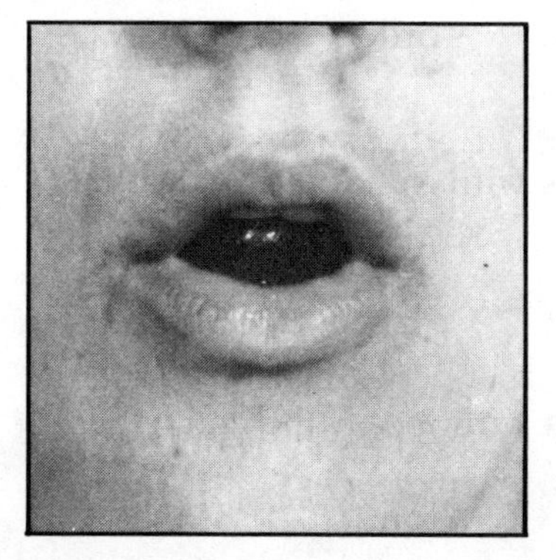

Look in a mirror when you are practising this sound and check that the shape of your lips is the same as in the photograph. Say the /ɒ/ sound first and then say /ɔː/. You should feel your jaw move and see your mouth close a little bit.

Length
/ɔː/ is a long vowel, but remember it may be shorter if it comes before a voiceless consonant or longer if it comes before a voiced consonant.

Exercise 1
Listen only; do not repeat.

caught, cord; bought, born; walk, worn.

Spelling
/ɔː/ is often spelt as:
'or' (e.g. lord, ford, short),
'a' (e.g. war, tall, walk),
'aw' (e.g. dawn, yawn, crawl).
It is sometimes spelt as:
'au' (e.g. daughter, Maud),
'ou' (e.g. brought, fought),
'oar' (e.g. board, oar).
'oor' (e.g. floor, door).

Exercise 2
Decide whether each word you hear has the /ɑː/, the /ɒ/ or the /ɔː/ vowel. The correct answers are underlined in exercise 6 on page 129.

Exercise 3
Repeat these words with /ɔː/ at the beginning.

ought, author, order, always, awkward.

Exercise 4
Repeat these words with /ɔː/ after a consonant.

lord, short, war, tall, walk.

Exercise 5
Repeat these words with /ɔː/ at the end.

door, oar, four, saw, more.

Exercise 6

Repeat the groups of words. The ones underlined are the ones you heard in exercise 2.

cart,	cot,	caught;	part,	pot,	port;
darn,	Don,	dawn;	barn,	Bonn,	born;
card,	cod,	cord;	hark,	hock,	hawk;
stark,	stock,	stalk;	tart,	tot,	taught.

Exercise 7

Read through this dialogue and look at the questions at the end before you listen to the tape.

Paul Broughton, a famous footballer, is being interviewed on television.

T.V. Interviewer: And when were you first taught the sport?
Paul Broughton: I played with a ball before I could walk, but I had my first game at four.
T.V. Interviewer: And you've always played since then?
Paul Broughton: Yes, and I've brought home forty-four different trophies.
T.V. Interviewer: Do you think your children ought to be footballers?
Paul Broughton: My daughters think the idea's awful.

Now look at these questions.

1. Which tone does the interviewer use in line 4?
2. Where is the stress in the word *footballers* (line 7)?
3. Where are all the stresses in line 8?

Exercise 8
Read the part of the interviewer. He does not know Paul Broughton and so is speaking quite formally.

Exercise 9
Read the part of Paul Broughton. He's been interviewed a lot of times before.

Today's silly sentence

The horse-stall Paul bought is far too short for his tall horse.

Group activities

1. *The number game*
   Split into pairs. The first person says the number 4. The next person adds another 4 to make it 44. Carry on in this way and see how far you can go.

2. Look at the lists of words. One person will say one of the words and the other students must decide whether the word has the /ɒ/ /ɔː/ or /ɑː/ sound in it. Take turns around the class so each person has a turn at saying a word.

1	2	3
pot	port	part
tot	taught	tart
cod	cord	card
stock	stork	stark

3. *Conversation practice*
   Practise this conversation with a partner.

A:	Is	Paul Claude Maud George	taller or shorter than	my daughter Paula	?

B:	Oh, I think	he's she's	about	4 inches 4 centimetres	taller. shorter.

Lesson 28

The pure vowel /ʊ/

How to pronounce this vowel

The tongue

Look at the vowel chart and the diagram. For the /ʊ/ sound, it is not the very back part of the tongue which is important, but the part towards the middle. This part of the tongue is raised quite high.

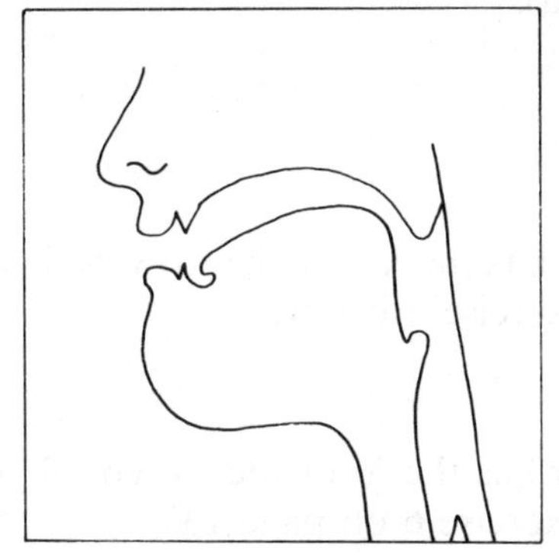

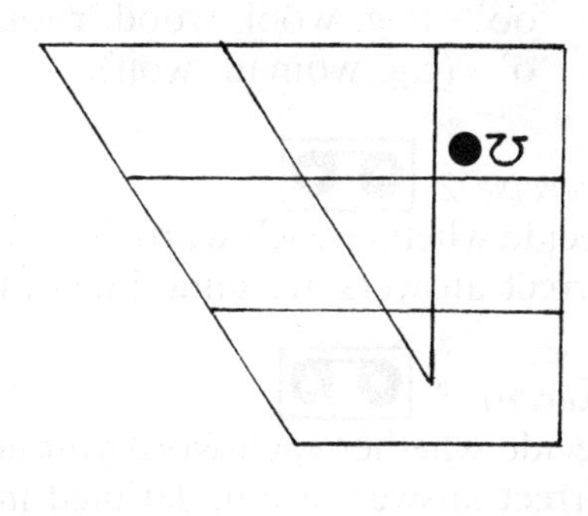

The mouth and lips

The lip shape is important for this sound. You can see in the photograph that the lips are rounded and quite close together.

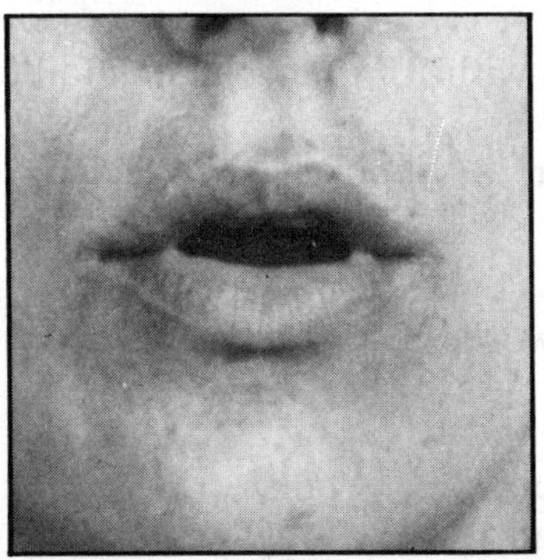

When you are practising this sound look in the mirror to make sure your lips are the right shape. Say the vowel /ɑː/ and then move to /ʊ/. You should see the lip shape changing.

Length

/ʊ/ is a short vowel. It is very short when it is followed by a voiceless consonant and a little bit longer when it is followed by a voiced consonant.

Exercise 1

Listen only; do not repeat,

shook, should; foot, full; put, puss.

Spelling

/ʊ/ is often spelt as:

'u' (e.g. pull, put).

It can also be spelt as:

'ou' (e.g. should, would, could),

'oo' (e.g. wool, wood, rook),

'o' (e.g. woman, wolf).

Exercise 2

Decide whether each word you hear has the /ɔː/ or the /ʊ/ vowel. The correct answers are underlined in exercise 5 below.

Exercise 3

Decide whether each word you hear has the /ɪ/ or the /ʊ/ vowel. The correct answers are underlined in exercise 6 on page 133.

N.B. /ʊ/ never appears at the beginning or at the end of a word.

Exercise 4

Repeat these words with /ʊ/ after one or more consonants.

crook, butcher, shook, wooden, cooking.

Exercise 5

Repeat the pairs of words. The ones underlined are the ones you heard in exercise 2.

port, put; talk, took;
bawl, bull; fought, foot;
Paul, pull; fall, full;
wall, wool; ward, wood;
cork, cook; gored, good.

Exercise 6

Repeat the pairs of words. The ones underlined are the ones you heard in exercise 3.

pit,	put;	kick,	cook;
bill,	bull;	lick,	look;
pill,	pull;	tick,	took;
rick,	rook;	fit,	foot;
will,	wool;	fill,	full.

Exercise 7

Read through this dialogue and look at the questions at the end before you listen to the tape.

Bill is in the local library.

Bill: I'm looking for a cookery book.
Assistant: What sort of cookery book?
Bill: I'd like a book of recipes.
Assistant: Have a look on the top shelf, that's full of books like that.
Bill: (looks in book and closes it) Good, I'll put it back now.
Assistant: That was quick.
Bill: Yes, I only wanted to see how to boil an egg.

Now look at these questions.

1. Which is the most important word in line 1?
2. Which tone does the assistant use in line 6?
3. Where are all the stresses in line 7?

Exercise 8

Read the part of Bill.

Exercise 9
Read the part of the assistant. She's being very helpful.

Today's silly sentence

The cook threw her cookery book at the cuckoo which was looking at her pudding.

Group activities

1. Look at the dialogue on page 133. How many words can you find using the /ʊ/ sound? Write a sentence each using one of these words.

2. Your teacher will say one word in each set of three. Listen carefully and decide which one it is.

1	2	3
pit	put	port
bill	bull	bawl
kick	cook	cork
fill	full	fall
fit	foot	fought

3. Now try the same thing with a partner.

4. *Conversation practice*
Practise this conversation with a partner.

A: Look! Would you put those [eggs / glasses / cups / bottles] on that wooden bench?

B: I don't know if I should. They might break there.

A: Well, put them on the table, then!

Lesson 29

The pure vowel /uː/

How to pronounce this vowel

The tongue
Look at the vowel chart and the diagram. The back of the tongue is very high at the back of the mouth. You can see on the vowel chart that /uː/ is made higher and further back than /ʊ/.

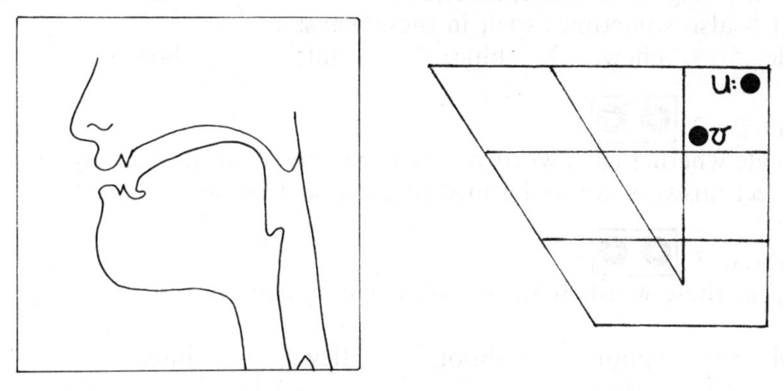

The mouth and lips
The mouth is almost closed and the lips are rounded.

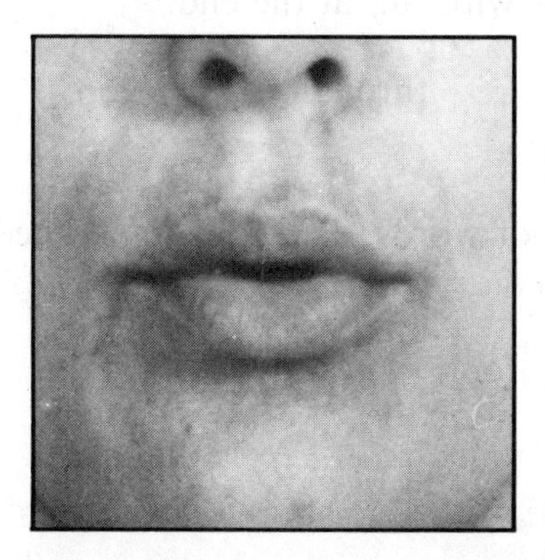

Look in the mirror when you practise this sound. Check that the shape of your lips is the same as in the photograph.

Length
/uː/ is a long vowel. Remember, however, that it sounds very long when it is followed by a voiced consonant and a bit shorter when it is followed by a voiceless consonant.

Exercise 1
Listen only; do not repeat.

groove, group; lose, loot; soon, suit.

Spelling
/uː/ is often spelt as:
'oo' (e.g. tooth, fool, spoon, food),
'ou' (e.g. youth, through, soup, group),
'o' (e.g. two, lose, move, do).
It is also sometimes spelt in these ways:
rude, chew, blue, suit, shoe.

Exercise 2
Decide whether each word you hear has the /ʊ/ or the /uː/ vowel. The correct answers are underlined in exercise 5 below.

Exercise 3
Repeat these words with /uː/ after one or two consonants.

fool, spool, shoot, flew, juice.

Exercise 4
Repeat these words with /uː/ at the end.

too, shoe, through, zoo, who.

Exercise 5
Repeat these pairs of words. The ones underlined are the ones you heard in exercise 2.

full, fool; wood, wooed;
pull, pool; should, shooed;
soot, suit; could, cooed.

Exercise 6
Read through this dialogue and look at the questions at the end before you listen to the tape.

Prue is at a party and a detective comes up to her and asks her some questions.

Detective: Have you seen Sue? She's the girl in the long boots.
Prue: Well she was standing near that group, having some food.
Detective: Was she with a youth in a blue suit?
Prue: A blue suit? Yes I think she was. Why? Who's he?
Detective: He's a murderer on the loose!
Prue: Oh, is that true! Poor Sue.

Now look at these questions.

1. Which is the most important word in the first part of line 2?
2. Which tone does the detective use in line 3?
3. Where is the stress in the word *murderer* (line 5)?

Exercise 7
Read the part of the detective. He's very worried about Sue.

Exercise 8
Read the part of Prue. She's trying to be helpful.

Today's silly sentence

Sue threw soup at the youth in blue.

Group activities

1. Your teacher will say one word in each of these pairs of words. Listen carefully and decide which one it is.

1	2
pull	pool
soot	suit
wood	wooed
could	cooed

2. Now work in pairs. Take turns to say one of these words and your partner must decide which sound the words have in them.

3. Now use one of the words to make a sentence. Read your sentence to the rest of the group and they must decide which sound is in the word you chose.

4. *Conversation practice*
Practise this conversation with a partner.

A: Where's [Prue / Sue / Lulu] ?

B: . . .? She went out at about [two. / twenty to two. / twenty-five to two. / ten past two. / two twenty.]

A: Who with?
B: Oh, a group from school.
A: Where did they go?

B: To [school, / the pool, / Tooting,] I think.

Lesson 30

Revision of the pure back vowels

How to pronounce these vowels

The tongue

Look at the vowel chart. You can see how the vowels change. /ɑː/ is made with the back of the tongue low in the mouth, and /uː/ is made with the tongue high in the mouth. The other sounds come between these two. When you try exercise 1, see if you can feel your tongue moving in this way.

Exercise 1

Repeat each vowel.

/ɑː/ /ɒ/ /ɔː/ /ʊ/ /uː/

The mouth and lips

As the back of the tongue moves higher in the mouth, the mouth closes more and more. Look at the photographs and you can see the difference in the shape of the lips for all the back vowels. They are all rounded.

Look in a mirror when you practise the vowel sounds. Check the shape of your lips with the photographs.

/ɑː/

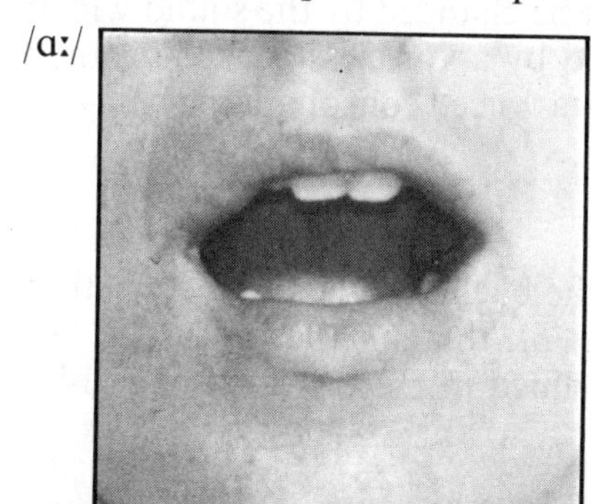

/ɒ/

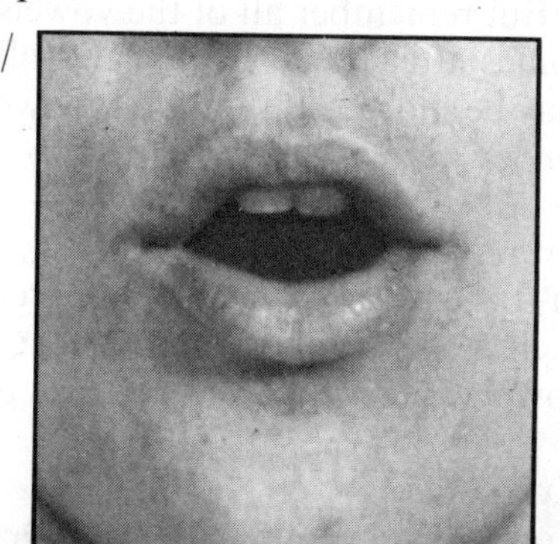

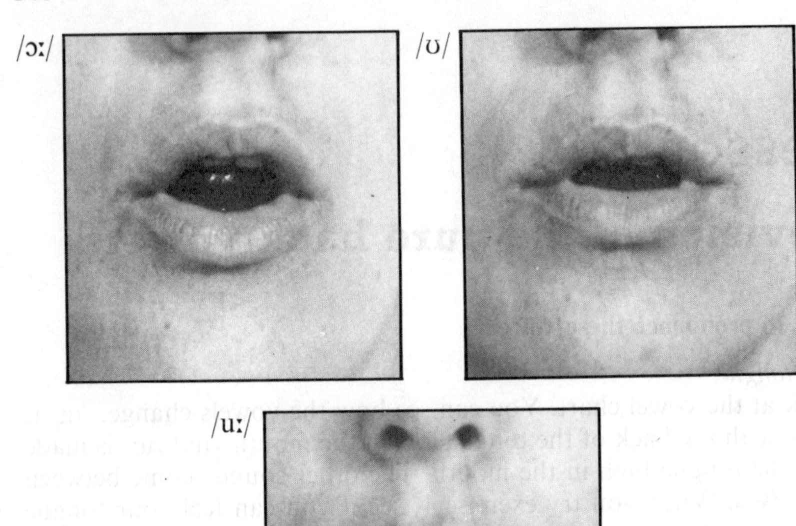

Exercise 2
Repeat each vowel.

/ɑː/ /ɒ/ /ɔː/ /ʊ/ /uː/

Length
/ɑː/, /ɔː/ and /uː/ are all long vowels.
/ʊ/ and /ɒ/ are short vowels.

But remember all of the vowels can be changed by the sound which comes after them. If they are followed by a voiceless consonant they may be shorter. If they are followed by a voiced consonant they may be longer.

Exercise 3
In this exercise, we will compare *all* the back vowels. Decide whether each word you hear has the /ɑː/, the /ɒ/, the /ɔː/, the /ʊ/ or the /uː/ vowel. The correct answers are underlined in exercise 5 on page 141.

Exercise 4
You will hear nine sentences. Decide which of the words on each line

you heard and write down A, B, C, D or E. Where there is a blank, this shows that no word exists in English. The correct answers are in exercise 6 below.

	A /ɑː/	B /ɒ/	C /ɔː/	D /ʊ/	E /uː/
1.	cart	cot	caught	—	coot
2.	—	wad	ward	wood	wooed
3.	card	cod	cord	could	cooed
4.	guard	god	gored	good	—
5.	marred	mod	Maud	—	mood
6.	—	Poll	Paul	pull	pool
7.	tart	tot	taught	—	toot
8.	part	pot	port	put	—
9.	—	sot	sought	soot	suit

Exercise 5

Repeat the groups of words. The ones underlined are the ones you heard in exercise 3. Where there is a blank, this shows that no word exists in English.

/ɑː/	/ɒ/	/ɔː/	/ʊ/	/uː/
cart	cot	caught	—	coot
—	wad	ward	wood	wooed
card	cod	cord	could	cooed
guard	god	gored	good	—
marred	mod	Maud	—	mood
—	Poll	Paul	pull	pool
tart	tot	taught	—	toot
part	pot	port	put	—
—	sot	sought	soot	suit

Exercise 6

Repeat these sentences. They are the sentences you heard in exercise 4.

1. Shove it in the cart!
2. Your wife's in Ward 2, Mr Brown.
3. Where's the cord of my dressing gown?
4. Mm! That was a good dinner, Chris!
5. Take no notice; he's in a bad mood again.
6. He landed flat on his face in a pool of muddy water.
7. What on earth were you taught when you went to school?
8. I do hope I get a part in that play!
9. I don't think that'll suit you very well.

Lesson 31

The pure vowel /ɜː/

This vowel and the vowel in lesson 32 are central vowels. For these vowels it is the middle of the tongue which is important, and the back and the front of the tongue are low in the mouth. The two central vowels are very similar, so take care when you are practising them.

How to pronounce this vowel

The tongue
Look at the vowel chart and the diagram. You can see that the front and the back of the tongue are low in the mouth, but the middle of the tongue is quite high.

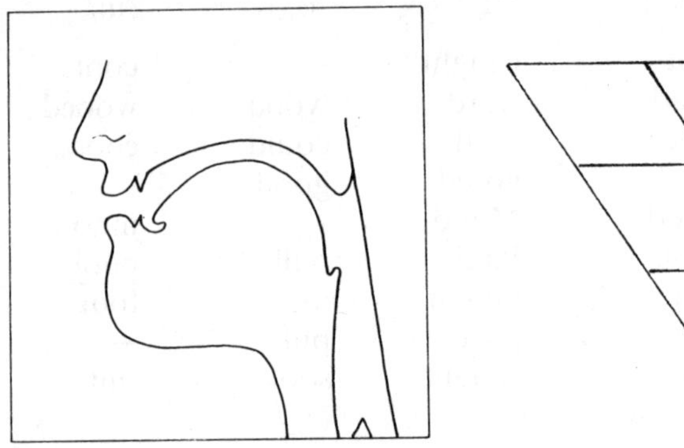

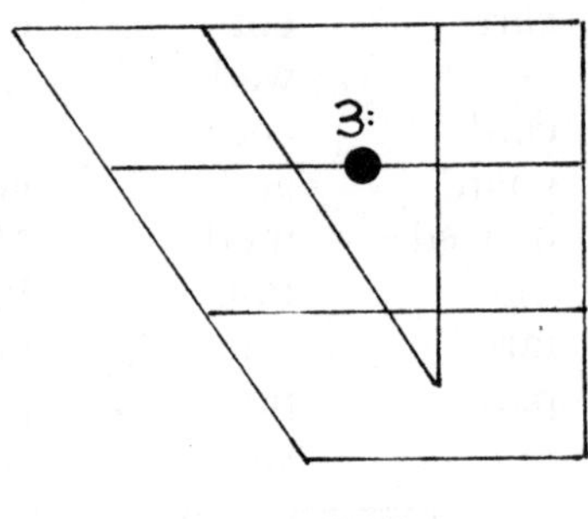

The mouth and lips
The mouth is nearly closed and the lips are loosely spread. Look at the photograph and you can see the shape of the lips. Look in a mirror when you practise this sound and check that the shape of your lips is the same as in the photograph.

Length
/ɜː/ is a long sound. It sounds very long in a stressed syllable. Remember, if /ɜː/ comes before a voiced consonant it sounds longer. If it comes before a voiceless consonant it sounds shorter. Listen to the words in exercise 1.

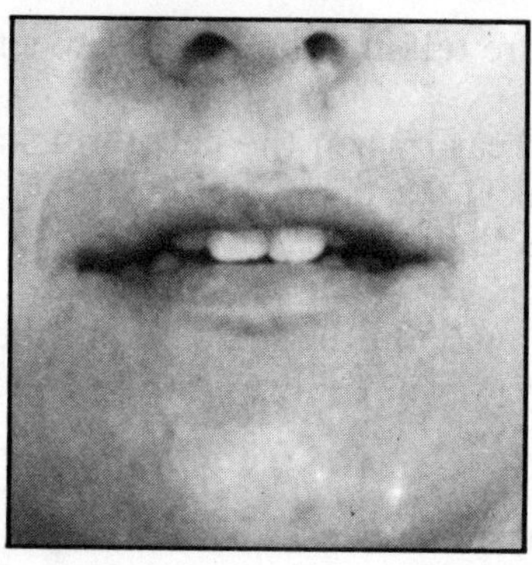

Exercise 1
Listen only; do not repeat.

earl, curse; fern, skirt; girl, surf.

Spelling
/ɜː/ is often spelt as:
'ur' (e.g. church, purse, curl),
'ir' (e.g. girl, skirt, first),
'er' (e.g. fern, her, serve),
'ear' (e.g. earth, early).
It can also be spelt as:
'our' (e.g. journey),
'w' + 'or' (e.g. world, word).

Exercise 2
Repeat these words with /ɜː/ at the beginning.

early, earth, earl, urge, urn.

Exercise 3
Repeat these words with /ɜː/ after a consonant.

serve, birth, worm, nurse, first.

Exercise 4
Repeat these words with /ɜː/ after a consonant and at the end.

stir, fur, her, purr, blur.

Exercise 5
Read through the dialogue and look at the questions at the end before you listen to the tape.

Bert and Shirley are talking about the new term at college.

Shirley: Have you heard when the new term starts?
Bert: Yes, I think it starts on the third.
Shirley: Thursday's the third, isn't it?
Bert: That's right.
Shirley: I'm going away on the first, I won't be back for the third.
Bert: Oh Shirley. You're always the same; you'll never learn anything.

Now look at the questions.

1. Which tone does Shirley use when she says *isn't it* (line 3)?
2. Is the tone in the first part of the sentence the same?
3. Where are all the stresses in line 2?

Exercise 6
Read the part of Shirley. She doesn't really mind missing the beginning of term.

Exercise 7
Read the part of Bert. He's telling Shirley off for missing the start of term.

Today's silly sentence

The thirty-third Earl of Splurge flirts with Bert's girlfriend Myrtle.

Group activities

1. Look at these descriptions and see if you can guess what the word is. Of course they all have the /ɜː/ sound in them.

    1. The opposite of late.
    2. Something that flies.
    3. A place where people go to pray.
    4. The day after Wednesday.
    5. Something that men wear.
    6. When you put something in the fire it . . .
    7. First, second, . . .

2. Look at the dialogue on page 144. Go round the class and make a list of all the words with the /ɜː/ sound in them.

3. Write one sentence each using one of these words. Read your sentence to the rest of the class.

4. *Conversation practice*
   Practise this conversation with a partner.

A: Bert and Shirley are	in China. going to church. working in the bookshop. living in a flat. playing tennis.

B: They *were* . . ., but now they're . . . (think of something suitable).

Lesson 32

The pure vowel /ə/

How to pronounce this vowel

The tongue
Look at the vowel chart and the diagram. The middle of the tongue is quite high, and the back and the front of the tongue are low in the mouth when you say this sound. The middle of the tongue is a bit lower than it is for the /ɜː/ sound.

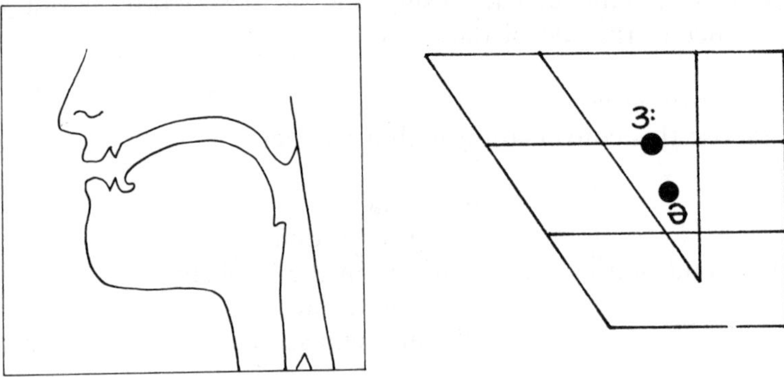

The mouth
Look at the photograph. The mouth is nearly closed and the lips are loosely spread.

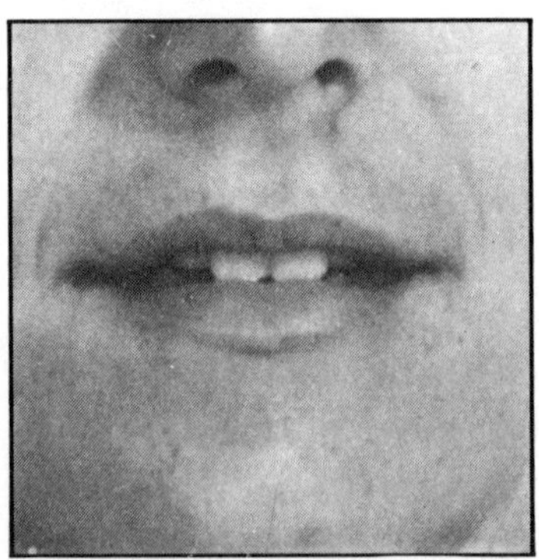

Length
/ə/ is always a short sound. Listen to the phrases in exercise 1. The words *a* and *the* both have the /ə/ in them when they are not stressed.

Exercise 1

a book, the book; a pin, the pin; a man, the man.

Spelling

This vowel sound can be spelt in a lot of different ways. It is different from other vowel sounds as it is only heard in unstressed syllables—these are the words or parts of words which do not stand out or sound important.

Some words always have the /ə/ in syllables which are never stressed. For example "Britain' /'brɪtən/, "jumper' /'dʒʌmpə/, and 'ba'nana' /bə'na:nə/. The stress in these words never changes and so when you learn the word you must learn where the stress is. Then you will probably get the /ə/ sound in the right place.

Exercise 2

Listen to these words and then repeat them.

London, comfortable, wonderful, vegetable, opposite.

Exercise 3

Small words like *a*, *the* and *to* are not usually stressed and so often have the /ə/ sound in them.

Listen to and repeat these short phrases.

a bee, a man, a woman;
an aunt, an aeroplane;
to town, to Sydney, to try;
the boat, the hat, the desk.

Exercise 4

The word 'and' has the /ə/ sound in it if it is not stressed. Listen and repeat. You will also hear that the 'd' is not pronounced.

Jack and Jill.
Bacon and eggs.
Black and white.
Pencils and rulers.
Dogs and cats.

Exercise 5

Some words with stress on the second syllable have an /ə/ sound in the first syllable. Listen and repeat.

alive, away, among, above, alarm.

Exercise 6

Many words of two or more syllables ending in 'or', 'er', 'ure' or 'our' have the /ə/ sound in the final syllable, which is not stressed. Listen and repeat.

better, calculator, colour, furniture, measure.

Exercise 7

Some of the small words like *to*, *from* and *and* that have /ə/ in them when they are not stressed, will change if they are stressed and have a stronger vowel sound. Listen to this short conversation.

A: What time's the train from York?
B: To York?
C: No, from York.

From in *A* has the /ə/ sound in it. *From* in *C* has the /ɒ/ sound in it because it is stressed. Listen to the conversation again and repeat it after the tape.

Exercise 8

Read through this dialogue and look at the questions at the end before you listen to the tape.

Mrs Hinton is moving to a new house and she is being helped by furniture removers.

Mrs Hinton: Put the picture by the window and the books on the table.
Removal man: Yes, madam. Where shall I put this big box?
Mrs Hinton: That's to go in the kitchen. But take care!
Removal man: Can't hear you—just a minute . . .
Mrs Hinton: Oh no! My china was worth a fortune.
Removal man: Sorry madam. What did you say?

Now look at these questions.

1. How many /ə/ sounds are there in the first two lines?
2. Where is the stress in the word *kitchen* (line 4)?
3. Which is the most important word in the sentence *What did you say?* Which tone is used in this sentence?

Exercise 9

Read the part of Mrs Hinton. She's very angry about her china being broken.

Exercise 10
Read the part of the removal man. He's trying to be helpful.

Today's silly sentence

The banana that was on the table was for the girl that Robert met at the ball.

Group activities

1. Look at these pictures. Make up some sentences using the form

   John is better than Susan at . . .

   Remember that the words *better than* and *at* all have the /ə/ sound. (/betə ðən/, /ət/,)

2. Look at this dialogue which has been mixed up. Work with a partner and see if you can sort it out.

   Just opposite, next to the paper shop.
   Do you know where the 22 bus stop is?
   Okay thanks, I must hurry to catch it.
   Yes just round the corner.
   Yes I'd run if I were you; the bus has just gone round . . .
   On the corner or opposite?

3. With your partner work out where all the /ə/ sounds are in this dialogue. Practise the dialogue until you think you have got them all right.

PART 3

THE DIPHTHONGS

Introduction to Diphthongs

In part three of this book we are going to look at English diphthongs. Diphthongs are made up of two vowels pronounced one after the other, *in the same syllable*. For example, the words 'chair' and 'play' have two vowel sounds in one syllable (/εə/ and /eɪ/); these are diphthongs. The word 'seeing' also has two vowel sounds (/iː/ and /ɪ/) but these are not in the same syllable and so this is not a diphthong.

All the diphthongs are made up of the pure vowel sounds that we looked at in Part 2 of this book. Because of this, it is very important for you to master the pure vowels before you move onto the diphthongs.

When you say the two vowel sounds of the diphthong they must be said very closely together and with a smooth movement between them. This movement is called a 'glide'. The glides will be shown on the vowel charts together with the positions of the tongue for the two vowels making up the diphthong.

Let us take for example the diphthong /eɪ/, as in the word 'gate'. This diphthong is made up of the two pure vowels /e/ and /ɪ/ and so we will show it in this way.

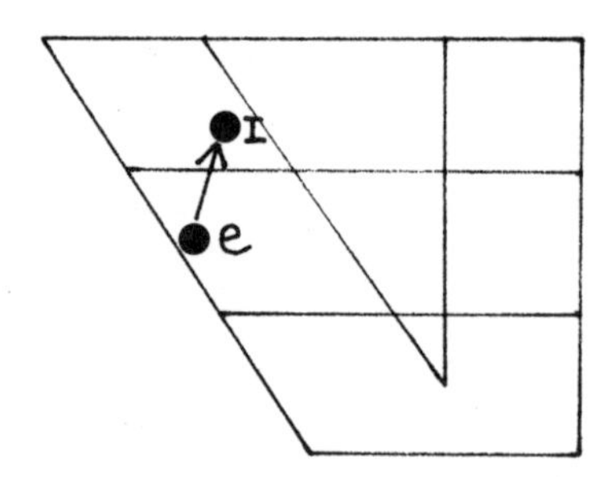

Lip positions
As with the pure vowels the lip positions are very important. As your lip positions change when you say a diphthong we will have two pictures for each.

Move your lips from the first position to the second, and check that you are doing it in the right way by looking in the mirror.

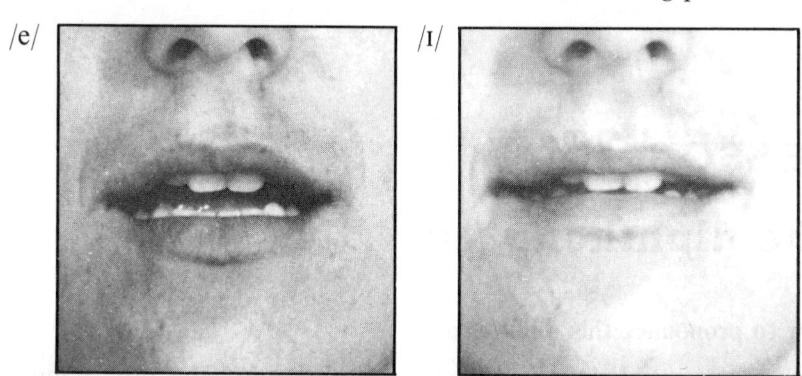

Stress
If you listen carefully to the diphthongs you will hear that the first sound is stressed more than the second sound. For example, when we say /eɪ/ the /e/ sound is pronounced louder and longer than the /ɪ/ sound. Take care to put the right stress on the diphthong because you may make it sound like two vowels if you do it wrongly.

Listening pre-test

Before you begin the lessons on diphthongs, do this listening pre-test. It will help you to find out which diphthongs you should practise most.

You will hear 60 pairs of words. Sometimes the words will be exactly the same, sometimes they will be slightly different. When you hear each pair, write down on a piece of paper S if the words sound the same, D if they sound different. For example, if you hear 'rail, rail' write S; if you hear 'rail, real' write D.

When you have listened to the 60 pairs of words, turn to the back of the book and . . .

1. Check your answers with the key on page 202.
2. Listen to the tape again, and this time, while you listen, read the words printed in the tapescript on page 202.
3. Look at the error identification chart on page 203. This will tell you which lessons you should concentrate on. For example, if you thought the two words in the first pair were the same, you should study lesson 38.

Lesson 33

The diphthong /eɪ/

How to pronounce this diphthong

Look at the vowel chart and the two photographs. This diphthong is made up of the pure vowels /e/ and /ɪ/, which are both front vowels. When you make this sound your tongue moves backwards and upwards from the first sound to the second, but stays high and to the front of your mouth.

The /e/ part of the diphthong is loud and long and the /ɪ/ is lighter and shorter.

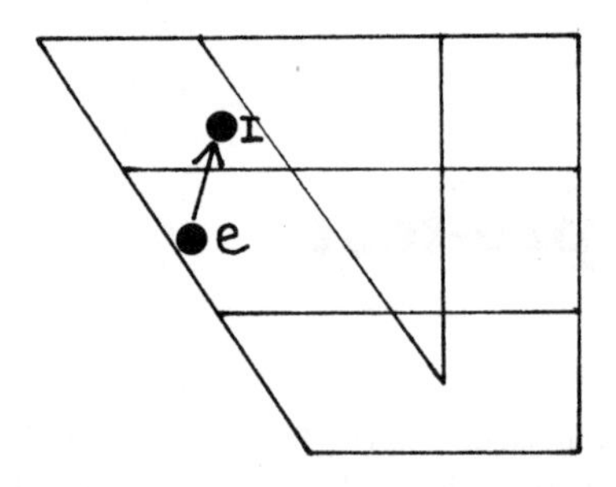

/e/

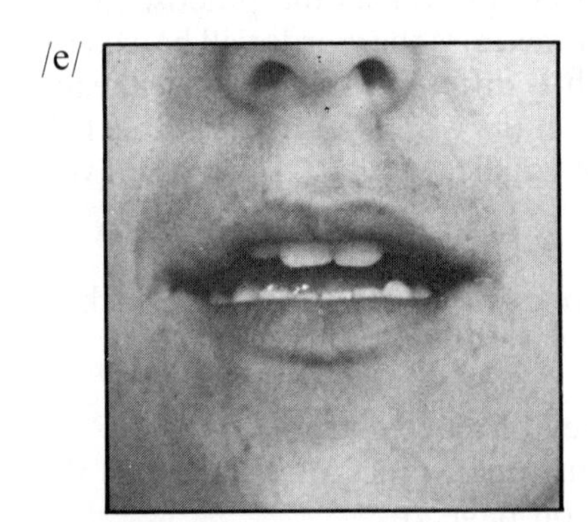

/ɪ/

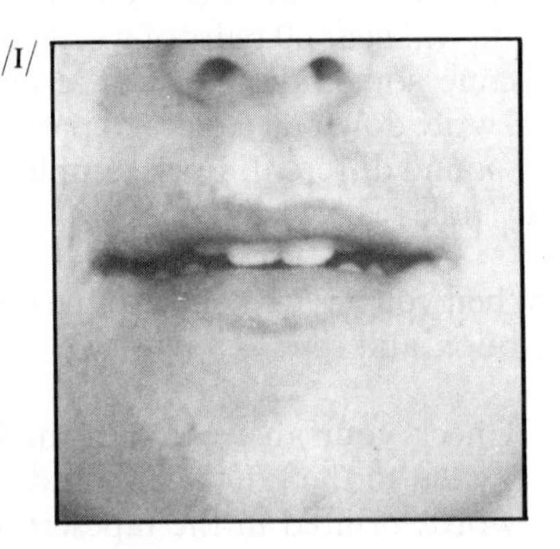

Check the shape of your lips in a mirror when you are practising this sound and take care that they are the same shape as the lips in the photographs.

Exercise 1

1. Repeat the two vowels seperately. /e/ is louder and longer than /ɪ/.

/e/ /ɪ/

2. Now *glide* from /e/ to /ɪ/. Repeat.

/e ɪ/

3. Repeat at normal speed.

/eɪ/

Spelling

/eɪ/ is usually spelt as 'a' followed by a consonant, and then by 'e'. That is: 'a' + consonant + 'e'. (e.g. fade, space, make, late).

It can also be spelt as:
'a' (e.g. lady, tasty, bass),
'ei' or 'ey' (e.g. eight, veil, they, grey),
'ai' or 'ay' (e.g. aim, rain, day, bay),
'ea' (e.g. steak, break).

Exercise 2

Decide whether each word you hear has the pure vowel /e/ or /ɪ/ or the diphthong /eɪ/. The correct answers are underlined in exercise 6 on page 156.

Exercise 3

Repeat these words with /eɪ/ at the beginning.

eight, age, able, ache, aim.

Exercise 4

Repeat these words with /eɪ/ after a consonant or a group of consonants.

break, plate, date, waste, chase.

Exercise 5

Repeat these words that have /l/ after /eɪ/. In these words the /eɪ/ sound becomes /eɪə/.

male, rail, sale, pale, nail.

Exercise 6

Repeat the groups of words. The ones underlined are the ones you heard in exercise 2.

den, din, Dane;
Ken, kin, cane;
wet, wit, wait;
when, win, wane;
well, will, wail;

bet, bit, bait;
led, lid, laid;
met, mit, mate;
pen, pin, pain;
bell, bill, bail.

Exercise 7

Read through this dialogue and look at the questions at the end before you listen to the tape.

Jane and Raymond are friends and they have just bumped into each other at the supermarket. It's Saturday and they're talking about how they are going to spend the rest of the day.

Raymond: Hello Jane, what are you doing today?
Jane: Well, I think it's going to rain so I won't be able to play tennis.
Raymond: How would you like to come and see a play with me?
Jane: That would be nice, but I'm afraid I can't afford it.
Raymond: I'll pay. It was pay-day yesterday.
Jane: Oh, that'll be great. I'll see you later then.
Raymond: O.K. Eight, outside the railway station. See you then.

Now look at these questions.

1. Where are all the stresses in lines 2 and 3?
2. Which is the most important word in the first part of line 5?
3. Where is the stress in the word *yesterday* (line 6)?

Exercise 8

Read the part of Raymond. He likes Jane a lot and would like to take her out.

Exercise 9

Read the part of Jane. She is disappointed because she can't play tennis but would like to go the the theatre with Raymond.

Group activities

1. *The number game*
   Work in pairs for this game. The first person says the number 8.

The next person adds 8 to make 88. Carry on in this way adding eight each time and see how far you can go.

2. Your teacher will say one word in each of these pairs of words. Listen carefully and decide which one it is.

1	2	1	2
met	mate	get	gate
let	late	men	main
fell	fail	edge	age
pen	pain	test	taste

3. Now do the same thing with your partner.

4. *Conversation practice*
   Practise this conversation with a partner.

A: What about a game of [tennis / golf / squash / cards] this afternoon?

B: I'm afraid not. I've got to go to the station to see [Jane / James / Abe / Mabel] off.

A: Well, what about afterwards?

B: O.K. See you later.

Today's silly sentence

Abel and his mate Blake tried to drink their ale in the gale, but failed.

Lesson 34

The diphthong /aɪ/

How to pronounce this diphthong

The /a/ sound at the beginning of this diphthong is a new sound. Look at the vowel chart and the two photographs. /a/ is an open vowel made near the front of the mouth but not as far forward as the /æ/ vowel in Lesson 22. Both the front and the back of the tongue are low in the mouth for this sound. /ɪ/ is a front vowel and for this part of the diphthong the front of the tongue is quite high in the mouth. /a/ is quite long and loud; /ɪ/ is lighter and shorter.

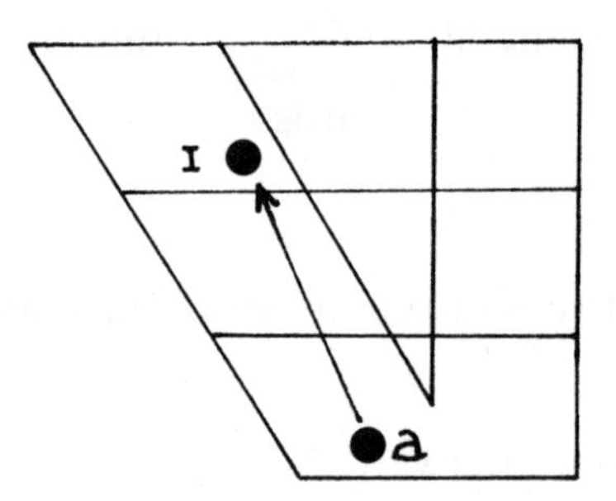

/a/

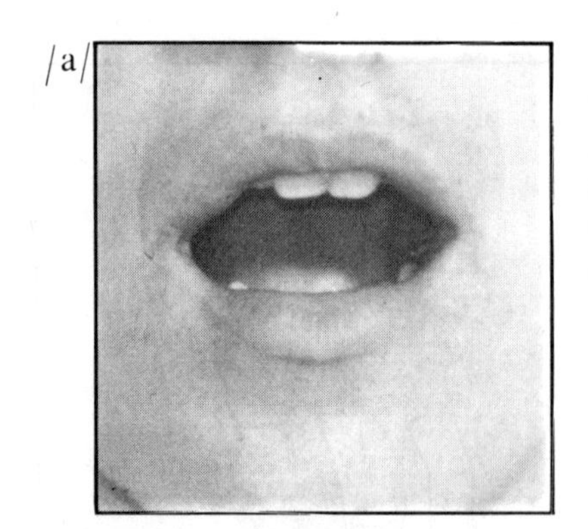

/ɪ/

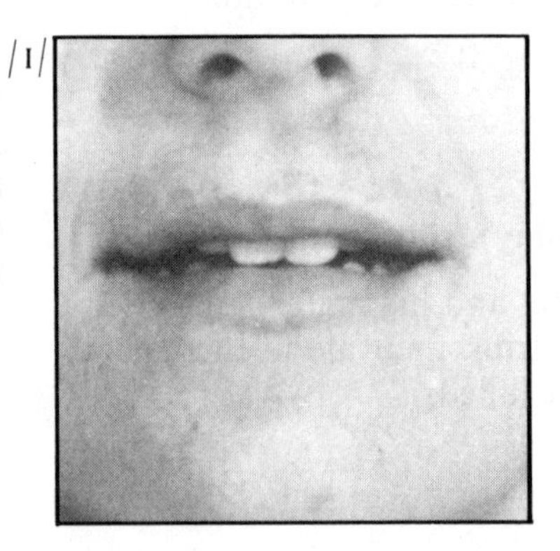

As you can see, the mouth moves from being open to slightly open and the lips are a little more tightly spread for the second part of the diphthong.

Exercise 1

1. Repeat the two vowels separately. /a/ is louder and longer than /ɪ/.

/a/ /ɪ/

2. Now *glide* from /a/ to /ɪ/. Repeat.

/a ɪ/

3. Repeat at normal speed.

/aɪ/

Spelling

The most usual spelling is 'i' + consonant + 'e' (e.g. time, ripe, tide, bite).

/aɪ/ can also be spelt as:
'igh' or 'eigh' (e.g. high, light, height),
'ie' (e.g. lie, die, pie, tried),
'y' (e.g. by, dry, cry).

Exercise 2

Decide whether each word you hear has the pure vowel /ɑː/ or /ɪ/ or the diphthong /aɪ/. The correct answers are underlined in exercise 8 on page 160.

Exercise 3

Decide whether each word you hear has the /eɪ/ or /aɪ/ diphthong. The correct answers are underlined in exercise 9 on page 160.

Exercise 4

Repeat these words with /aɪ/ at the beginning.

either, ice, I'm, I've, item.

Exercise 5

Repeat these words with /aɪ/ after a consonant or group of consonants.

fright, might, tried, flight, fried.

Exercise 6

When the diphthong /aɪ/ is followed by 'r' it becomes /aɪə/. Repeat these words. Note that the 'r' is not pronounced.

tyre, fire, wire, iron, require.

Exercise 7

When /aɪ/ is followed by 'l' it also becomes /aɪə/. Repeat these words.

tile, pile, smile, child, mile.

Exercise 8

Repeat these groups of words. The ones underlined are the ones you heard in exercise 2.

cart,	kit,	<u>kite</u>;	<u>hard</u>,	hid,	hide;
mart,	mit,	<u>might</u>;	heart,	<u>hit</u>,	height;
<u>darn</u>,	din,	dine;	park,	<u>pick</u>,	pike;
lark,	lick,	<u>like</u>;	lard,	lid,	<u>lied</u>;
<u>Mark</u>,	Mick,	Mike;	dark,	<u>Dick</u>,	dyke.

Exercise 9

Repeat these groups of words. The ones underlined are the ones you heard in exercise 3.

<u>Kate</u>,	kite;	<u>lake</u>,	like;
mate,	<u>might</u>;	<u>late</u>,	light;
slayed,	<u>slide</u>;	<u>shade</u>,	shied;
<u>hate</u>,	height;	pain,	<u>pine</u>;
deign,	<u>dine</u>;	lace,	<u>lice</u>.

Exercise 10

Read through this dialogue and look at the questions at the end before you listen to the tape.

Mike is in an electrical shop and wants his hi-fi repaired.

Assistant: Good morning sir. Can I help you?
Mike: Yes, I'm having some trouble with my hi-fi set.
Assistant: I see. I'll take your name and try to get it fixed for you.
Mike: The name's Mike Hines. Do you think it'll be ready by tonight?
Assistant: Well I'll try, but I'm afraid it'll be pricey.
Mike: Oh, never mind. I'll see you tonight then.
Assistant: Yes, I'll try to have it done by then. Goodbye sir.

Now look at these questions.

1. Where are all the stresses in line 2?
2. Where is the stress in the word *afraid* (line 6)?
3. Which tone does Mike use for the first part of line 7?

Exercise 11
Read the part of the Assistant. He's being very helpful.

Exercise 12
Read the part of Mike. He wants his hi-fi repaired quickly and he doesn't mind how much it costs.

Today's silly sentence

Clive hides his fine white wine from Ida.

Group activities

1. Work with a partner for this one. Look at the picture. Ask your partner as many questions as you can, using *why*. Your partner should answer the questions.

2. Your teacher will say one word in each of these pairs of words. Listen carefully and decide which one it is.

1	2	1	2
may	my	day	die
lake	like	whale	while
pay	pie	paint	pint
male	mile	way	why

3. Now make a sentence using one of these words. Read your sentence to the class.

4. *Conversation practice*
   Practise this conversation with a partner.

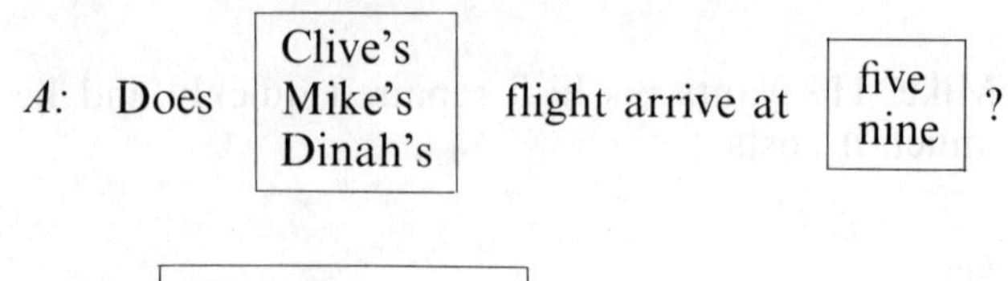

A: Does [Clive's / Mike's / Dinah's] flight arrive at [five / nine] ?

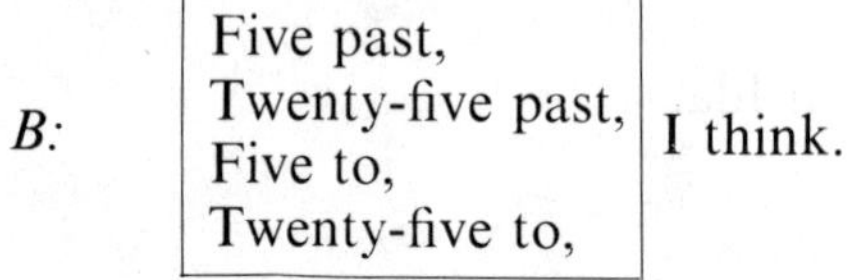

B: [Five past, / Twenty-five past, / Five to, / Twenty-five to,] I think.

A: Fine! I'll try to get out to the airport an hour before.

B: O.K. See you there!

Lesson 35

The diphthong /ɔɪ/

How to pronounce this diphthong

Look at the vowel chart. This sound is made up of the pure vowels /ɔː/ and /ɪ/. /ɔː/ is a back vowel, but both the back and the front of the tongue are low in the mouth for this part of the diphthong. /ɪ/ is made with the front of the tongue quite high in the mouth. The /ɔː/ is quite loud and long and the /ɪ/ is lighter and shorter.

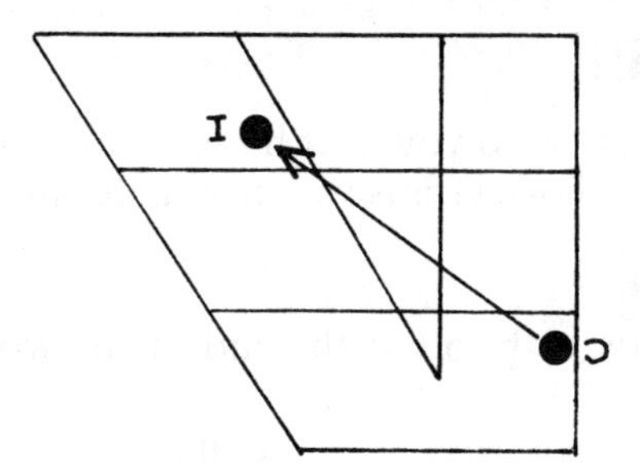

Look at the photographs and you can see the shape of the lips for both parts of this sound. Look in the mirror when you are practising this sound and check that the shape of your lips is the same.

/ɔː/

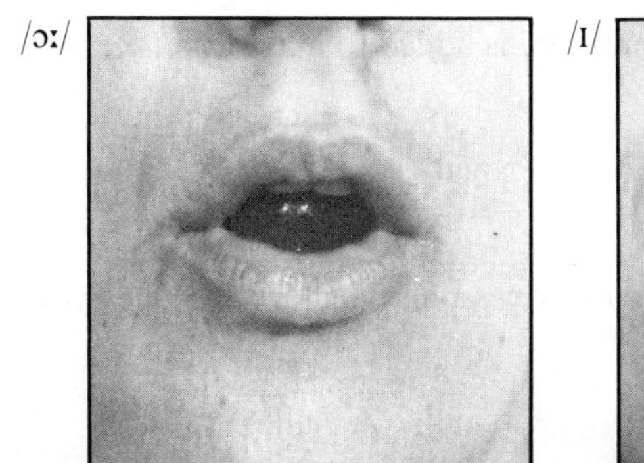

/ɪ/

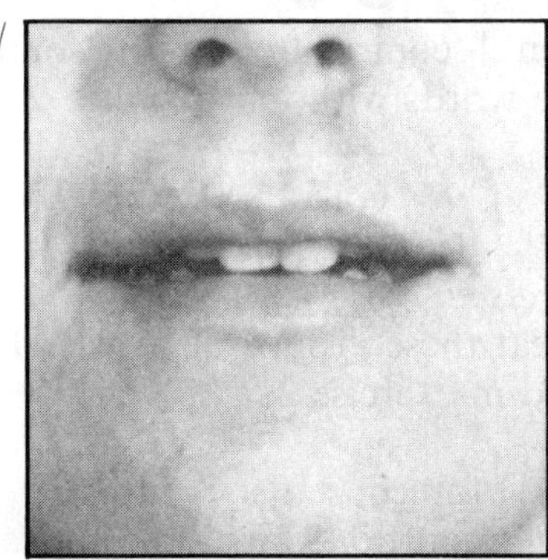

Exercise 1

1. Repeat the two vowels separately. /ɔː/ is louder and longer than /ɪ/.

/ɔː/ /ɪ/

2. Now *glide* from /ɔː/ to /ɪ/. Repeat.

/ɔː ɪ/

3. Repeat at normal speed.

/ɔɪ/

Spelling

/ɔɪ/ is spelt as:
  'oi' (e.g. noise, voice, boil, coil),
  'oy' (e.g. boy, coy, toy).

Exercise 2

Decide whether each word you hear has the pure vowel /ɔː/ or /ɪ/ or the diphthong /ɔɪ/. The correct answers are underlined in exercise 6.

Exercise 3

Repeat these words with /ɔɪ/ at the end of the word.

boy, joy, toy, employ, annoy.

Exercise 4

Repeat these words with /ɔɪ/ between consonants.

choice, point, noise, voice, boys.

Exercise 5

When /l/ comes after /ɔɪ/ the sound /ə/ is added to make /ɔɪə/. Repeat these words with /ɔɪə/ + /l/.

oil, coil, boil, royal, spoil.

Exercise 6

Repeat these groups of words. The ones unerlined are the ones you heard in exercise 2.

forced,	fist,	foist;	fall,	fill,	foil;
courts,	kits,	quoits;	ball,	bill,	boil;

corn,	kin,	<u>coin</u>;	<u>tall</u>,	till,	toil;
all,	ill,	<u>oil</u>;	call,	<u>kill</u>,	coil.

Exercise 7

Read through this dialogue and look at the questions at the end before you listen to the tape.

Joy and Roy are watching a film on television. Roy is not enjoying it.

Roy: What's that noise?
Joy: Sh, I'm enjoying the film.
Roy: But, I heard a noise.
Joy: Sh, you're spoiling the film.
Roy: Ah yes, it's the kettle boiling.
Joy: Well, you'd better make the coffee then.

Now look at the questions.

1. Where is the stress in the word *enjoying* (line 2)?
2. Which tone does Roy use in line 1?
3. Where are the stresses in line 4?

Exercise 8

Read the part of Joy. She's trying to watch television and is getting annoyed with Roy.

Exercise 9

Read the part of Roy. He's bored with television and is annoying Joy.

Today's silly sentence

The noisy boy's voice annoyed Joyce.

Group activities

1. Work in pairs to fill in the words on the right. Each of them has the /ɔɪ/ sound.

   You put this in your car. It's . . .
   When you cook food in water, it is . . .
   A seafood which is in a hard shell is an . . .
   Children play with these. They're . . .
   The opposite of silence is . . .
   You use it when you speak. It's your . . .
   You can have meat or fish. You have the . . .

2. Make up a sentence of your own for each of the words you have just found. Read them out to the class.

Lesson 36

Revision of the /-ɪ/ diphthongs

The three diphthongs we have practised so far have one thing in common—they all end with /ɪ/. Look at the diagram, which will remind you of how the three sounds are made. Remember that the first pure vowel is louder and longer than the /ɪ/.

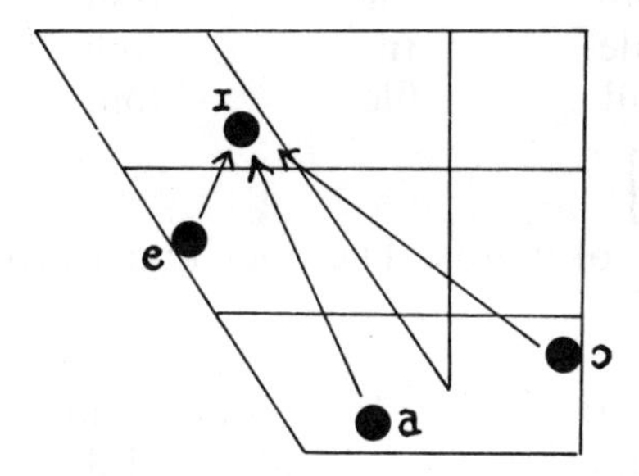

Exercise 1

Practise all three diphthongs.

1. Repeat the vowels separately.

/e/ /ɪ/ /a/ /ɪ/ /ɔː/ /ɪ/

2. Glide the vowels together.

/e ɪ/ /a ɪ/ /ɔː ɪ/

3. At normal speed.

/eɪ/ /aɪ/ /ɔɪ/

Exercise 2

Decide whether each word you hear has the /eɪ/, the /aɪ/ or the /ɔɪ/ diphthong. The correct answers are underlined in exercise 4 on page 168.

Exercise 3 

In each sentence, you will hear *two* of the words from each line. Decide which words you heard and write A, B or C. The correct answers are in exercise 5 below.

	A	B	C
1.	Kate	kite	quoit;
2.	bay	buy	boy;
3.	ray	rye	Roy;
4.	tray	try	Troy;
5.	lane	line	loin;
6.	paint	pint	point;
7.	ale	I'll	oil;
8.	bail	bile	boil;
9.	tale	tile	toil;
10.	fail	file	foil.

Exercise 4 

Repeat the groups of words. The ones underlined are the ones you heard in exercise 2.

Kate,	kite,	quoit;	paint,	pint,	point;
bay,	buy,	boy;	ale,	I'll,	oil;
ray,	rye,	Roy;	bail,	bile,	boil;
tray,	try,	Troy;	tale,	tile,	toil;
lane,	line,	loin;	fail,	file,	foil.

Exercise 5

Repeat these sentences. They are the ones you heard in exercise 3.

1. Kate flew her old kite on a windy day.
2. Send the boy out to buy some milk.
3. Roy's a little ray of sunshine!
4. Try not to drop all the glasses off the tray this time!
5. Only one line of traffic can go down the narrow lane.
6. Be a good lad and buy me a pint of paint, will you?
7. I'll fetch the oil for you, sir.
8. You bail out the water while I boil the kettle.
9. I'll toil all day to tile your roof.
10. This should foil the thieves from stealing the file.

Lesson 37

The diphthong /əʊ/

This diphthong and the one in lesson 38 (/aʊ/) both end in the /ʊ/ vowel.

How to pronounce this diphthong

Look at the vowel chart. You can see that /əʊ/ is made up of the two pure vowels /ə/ and /ʊ/. When you make the sound /ə/, it is the centre of the tongue which is important and it is quite high in the mouth. For /ʊ/ the back of the tongue is moved up. /ə/ is pronounced loud and long, /ʊ/ is lighter and shorter.

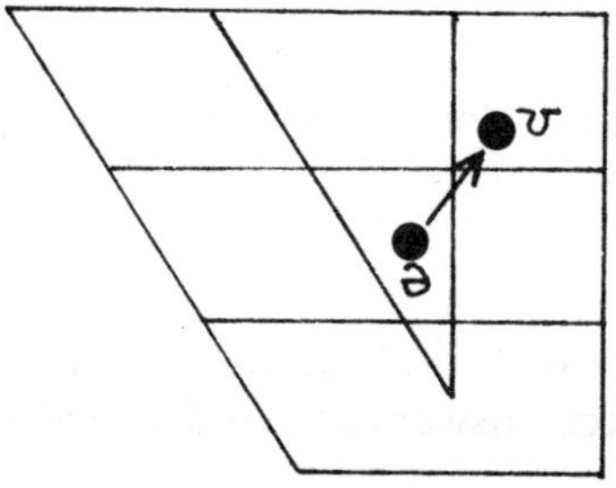

Look at the photographs. You can see that the lips move from being loosely spread to rounded when you make the /əʊ/ diphthong. Check in the mirror when you are practising these sounds and make sure that your lips are the right shape.

/ə/

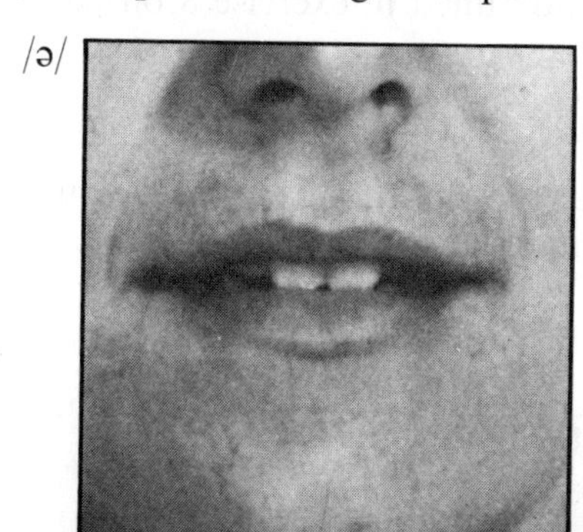

/ʊ/

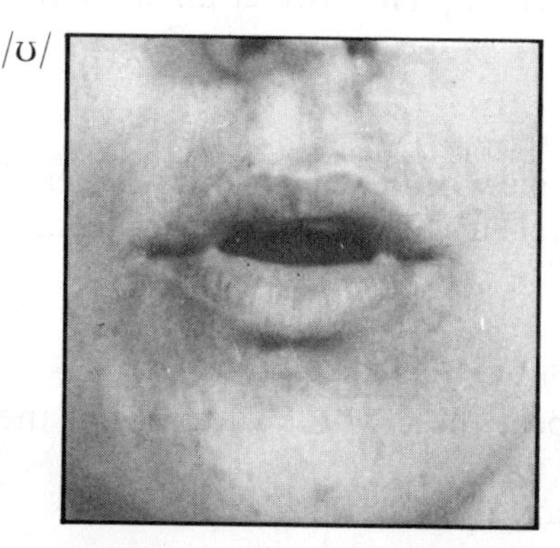

Exercise 1

1. Repeat the two vowels separately. /ə/ is louder and longer than /ʊ/.

/ə/ /ʊ/

2. Now *glide* from /ə/ to /ʊ/. Repeat.

/ə ʊ/

3. Repeat at normal speed.

/əʊ/

Spelling

/əʊ/ can be spelt as:
'o' (e.g. so),
and is often spelt as 'o' + consonant + 'e' (e.g. home, hope, stone). It can also be spelt as:
'oa' (e.g. road, Joan),
'oe' (e.g. hoe, toe),
'ou' (e.g. though),
'ow' (e.g. show, know, slow),
'ew' (e.g. sew).

Exercise 2

Decide whether each word you hear has the diphthong /əʊ/ or the pure vowel /ɔː/. The correct answers are underlined in exercise 7 on page 171.

Exercise 3

Decide whether each word you hear has the diphthong /əʊ/ or the pure vowel /ɜː/. The correct answers are underlined in exercise 8 on page 171.

Exercise 4

Decide whether each word you hear has the diphthong /əʊ/ or the pure vowel /uː/. The correct answers are underlined in exercise 9 on page 171.

Exercise 5

Repeat these words with /əʊ/ at the beginning.

over, oath, oats, own, oak.

Exercise 6

Repeat these words with /əʊ/ after a consonant or a group of consonants.

go, coast, float, slow, throw.

Exercise 7

Repeat these pairs of words. The ones underlined are the ones you heard in exercise 2.

loan,	lawn;	bone,	born;
low,	law;	owning,	awning;
stow,	store;	boat,	bought;
coat,	caught;	folk,	fork;
load,	lord;	stoke,	stalk.

Exercise 8

Repeat these pairs of words. The ones underlined are the ones you heard in exercise 3.

float,	flirt;	dote,	dirt;
goad,	gird;	joke,	jerk;
stow,	stir;	slow,	slur;
loan,	learn;	coast,	cursed;
bone,	burn;	tone,	turn.

Exercise 9

Repeat these pairs of words. The ones underlined are the ones you heard in exercise 4.

cope,	coop;	hope,	hoop;
slow,	slew;	rose,	ruse;
throw,	threw;	boat,	boot;
mode,	mood;	toe,	two;
flow,	flew;	grow,	grew.

Exercise 10

Read through this dialogue and look at the questions at the end before you listen to the tape.

Joe and Rose are standing outside a telephone box waiting to use the telephone. It is a very cold evening in winter.

Rose: It's a bit cold, isn't it. I think it might snow.
Joe: Mm, it's freezing. I don't know what he's doing in there.

Rose: No, I don't. I just want to phone home to let them know I'm okay.
Joe: I wanted to phone my girlfriend, we're supposed to be going to see a show tonight.
Rose: Oh, nice. I hope you enjoy it.
Joe: Thanks. Look, he's finished now. Off you go.

Now look at these questions.

1. Which tone does Rose use for *isn't it* (line 1)?
2. Which is the most important word in the second part of line 2?
3. Where is the stress in the word *supposed* (line 5)?

Exercise 11
Read the part of Rose. She starts talking to Joe to pass the time but she doesn't know him.

Exercise 12
Read the part of Joe. He's getting a bit angry because he's been waiting so long.

Today's silly sentence

Boats float; goats don't.

Group activities

1. Play this word game with all your group. Start off with the word *boat*. The next person changes the first sound to make *coat*. The next person changes the last sound to make *comb* and so on. Carry on round the class in this way. If anybody can't think of a word they drop out. Carry on until only one person is left.

2. Look at Mr Knowles' diary opposite. Make and answer questions about where he is going during the week.

3. *Conversation practice*
   Practise this conversation with a partner.

A: Hey! There's a good show on. Feel like going?

B: Oh, I don't know. I promised to go over and see [Joe. / Flo. / Rose. / the Joneses.]

A: . . .? Do you know [him / her / them] too?

B: How about asking [him / her / them] to come with us?

A: Great idea! I haven't seen . . . for ages!

Lesson 38

The diphthong /aʊ/

How to pronounce this diphthong

Look at the vowel chart. You can see that the diphthong /aʊ/ is made up of the two pure vowels /ɑː/ and /ʊ/. These are both back vowels. For the first part of the diphthong the back of the tongue is low in the mouth and it moves up for the /ʊ/ part of the diphthong. /ɑː/ is pronounced loud and long and /ʊ/ is light and short.

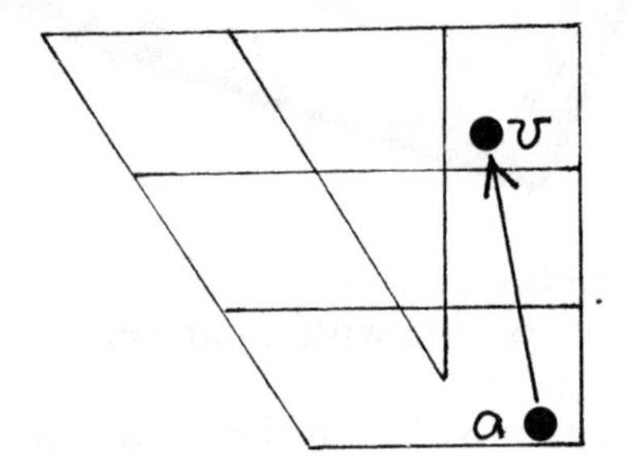

Look at the photographs. For the first part of the diphthong the mouth is open with the lips loosely spread. For the second part the lips are rounded.

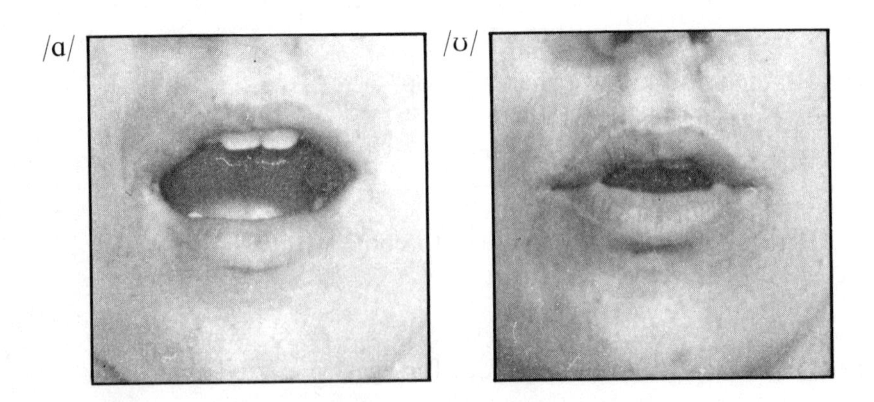

Exercise 1

1. Repeat the two vowels separately. /ɑː/ is louder and longer than /ʊ/.

/ɑː/ /ʊ/

2. Now *glide* from /ɑː/ to /ʊ/. Repeat.

/ɑː ʊ/

3. Repeat at normal speed.

/aʊ/

Spelling

/aʊ/ can be spelt as:
'ou' (e.g. mouse, house, proud, round),
'ow' (e.g. cow, town, crowd, owl).

Exercise 2

Decide whether each word you hear has the /əʊ/ or the /aʊ/ diphthong. The correct answers are underlined in exercise 6 on page 176.

Exercise 3

Repeat these words with /aʊ/ at the beginning.

out, ounce, outside, outlaw, outrage.

Exercise 4

Repeat these words with /aʊ/ after a consonant or a group of consonants.

mountain, frown, shout, ground, proud.

Exercise 5

In some words before 'l' or 'r' /aʊ/ becomes /aʊə/. Repeat these words. Note that the 'r' is not pronounced.

towel, tower, hour, shower, foul.

Exercise 6

Repeat these pairs of words. The ones underlined are the ones you heard in exercise 2.

stoat,	stout;	boat,	bout;
float,	flout;	crone,	crown;
honed,	hound;	dole,	dowel;
told,	towelled;	foal,	foul;
coal,	cowl;	bowl,	bowel.

Exercise 7

Read through this dialogue and look at the questions at the end before you listen to the tape.

Mr Brown has just answered the door to a policeman.

Policeman: Excuse me, I'm looking for a Mr Brown.
Mr Brown: I'm Mr Brown; but I'm just going out. I've got an appointment in town.
Policeman: Well, I've just found your wallet with a thousand pounds in it.
Mr Brown: Oh good, I was so worried; but . . . er . . . I must hurry now.
Policeman: Ah, well I'd just like to know how a thousand pounds . . .

Now look at these questions.

1. Where are all the stresses in line 8?
2. Which tone does Mr Brown use when he says *oh good* (line 6)?
3. Where is the stress in the word *appointment* (line 3)?

Exercise 8

Read the part of the policeman.

Exercise 9

Read the part of Mr Brown. He's trying to get away from the policeman.

Today's silly sentence

How now, brown cow!

Group activities

1. Look at these pictures. They are all words with an /aʊ/ sound in them. See if you can work them out.

2. Make a sentence each using one of these words. Read your sentence to the rest of the class.

3. Your teacher will say one word in each of these pairs of words. Listen carefully and decide which one it is.

1	2	1	2
town	tone	sow	sew
found	phoned	house(v.)	hose
loud	load	now	know
about	a boat	ground	groaned

4. Now try the same thing with a partner.

Lesson 39

The diphthong /ɪə/

There are three diphthongs which end with the central vowel /ə/. These diphthongs are in lessons 39, 40 and 41.

How to pronounce this diphthong

Look at the vowel chart. This diphthong is made up of the pure vowels /ɪ/ and /ə/. /ɪ/ is a high front vowel and /ə/ is a central vowel. The front of the tongue is high for the first part of the diphthong and then moves down as the middle of the tongue moves up for /ə/.

/ɪ/ is loud and long and /ə/ is lighter and shorter.

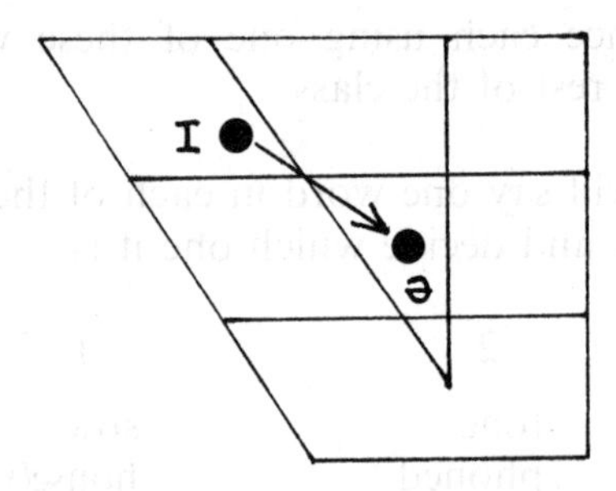

Look at the shape of the lips in the photographs. The lips are spread for both parts of the diphthong but they are spread more widely for /ɪ/.

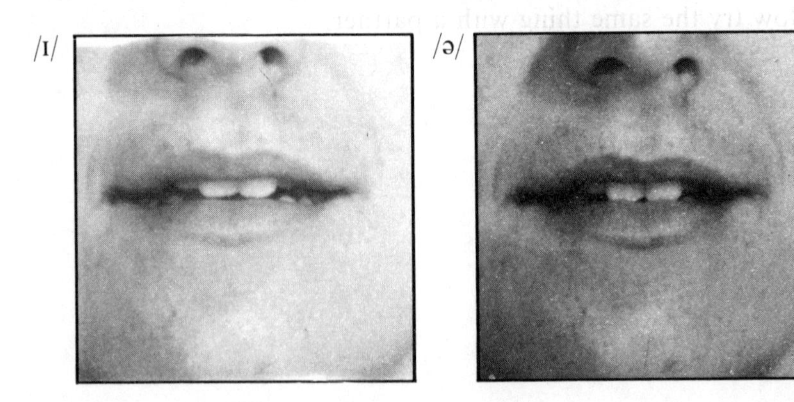

Exercise 1

1. Repeat the two vowels separately. Remember that /ɪ/ is louder and longer.

/ɪ/ /ə/

2. Now *glide* from /ɪ/ to /ə/. Repeat.

/ɪ ə/

3. Repeat at normal speed.

/ɪə/

Spelling

/ɪə/ is usually spelt as:
'eer' (e.g. deer, cheer),
'ear' (e.g. fear, dear, tear).
But it can also be spelt as:
'ere' (e.g. here),
'ea' (e.g. idea),
'ier' (e.g. pierce, fierce).

Exercise 2

Decide whether each word you hear has the vowel /ɪ/ or the diphthong /ɪə/. The correct answers are underlined in exercise 5 below.

Exercise 3

Decide whether each word you hear has the vowel /iː/ or the diphthong /ɪə/. The correct answers are underlined in exercise 6 on page 180.

Exercise 4

Repeat these words with /ɪə/ after a consonant or a group of consonants.

clear, nearly, hear, fierce, cheerful.

Exercise 5

Repeat the pairs of words. The ones underlined are the ones you heard in exercise 2.

lid,	leered;	Sid,	seared;
in,	Ian;	bid,	beard;
rid,	reared;	fizz,	fears.

Exercise 6

Repeat the pairs of words. The ones underlined are the ones you heard in exercise 3.

knee,	near;	bee,	beer;
read,	reared;	sneeze,	sneers;
bead,	beard;	fees,	fears;
fee,	fear;	tea,	tear (n.);
lead,	leered;	pea,	peer.

Exercise 7

Read through this dialogue and look at the questions at the end before you listen to the tape.

Ian and Jane are in their local pub.

Ian: Well my dear, would you like a beer, or something else?
Jane: A beer's a good idea.
Ian: Two beers please.
Jane: Cheers. Thanks for the beer.
Ian: Cheers. I'm glad we're here!

Now look at these questions.

1. Which tone does Ian use in line 3?
2. Where is the stress in the word *idea* (line 2)?
3. Which tone does Jane use for *cheers* in line 4?

Exercise 8

Read the part of Ian.

Exercise 9

Read the part of Jane.

Today's silly sentence

Dear, dear, poor Thea is nearly in tears.

Group activities

1. Work in pairs. Look at the map opposite, and ask and answer questions using *near*. e.g. Is Barnes near Ealing?

Answer: Yes, it is.
No, it's near . . .
No, it's nearer to . . .

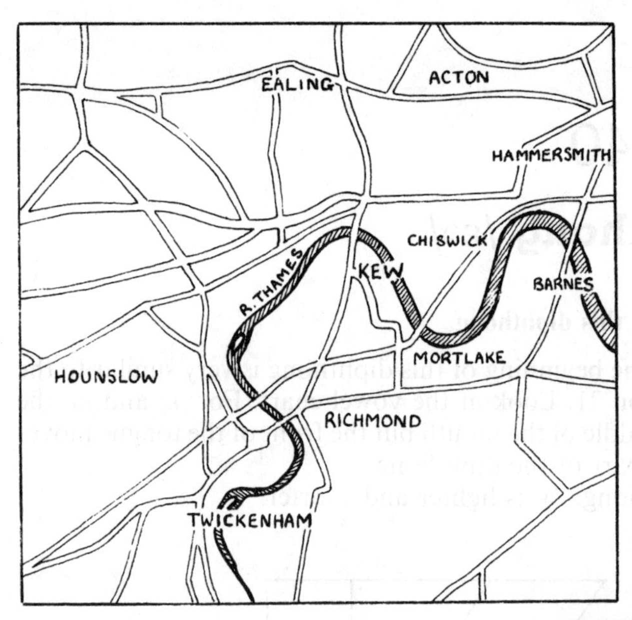

2. Work with a partner and see if you can fill in this crossword. All the words have /ɪə/ in them of course.

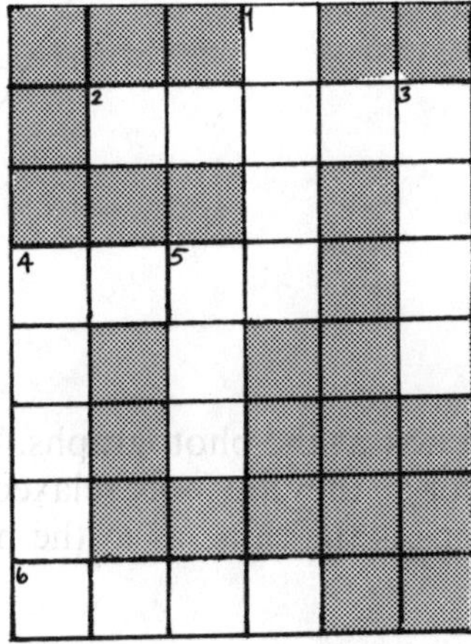

Clues

Down

1. Listen, can you ———— that noise?
3. It's not a copy, it's a ———— Piccasso.
4. He used to have a moustache only, but now he has grown a ———— as well.
5. Let me whisper something in your ———— .

Across

2. At the end of the speech, there was a loud ———— .
4. Would you like wine or ———— ?
6. ———— John,
   Thank you for your letter.

Lesson 40

The diphthong /εə/

How to pronounce this diphthong

The /ε/ sound at the beginning of this diphthong is very similar to the /e/ sound in Lesson 21. Look at the vowel chart. For /ε/ and /ə/ the tongue is in the middle of the mouth but the front of the tongue moves down for the /ə/ part of the diphthong.

/ε/ is loud and long; /ə/ is lighter and shorter.

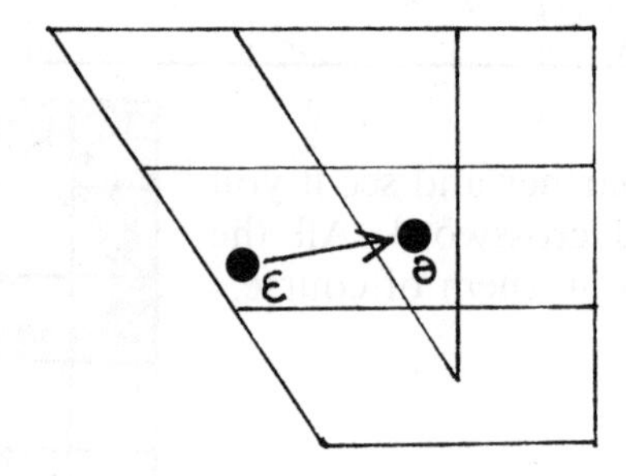

Look at the photographs. The lips are slightly more open for /ε/, but for /ə/ they are more relaxed. Check in the mirror that the shape of your lips is the same as in the photographs.

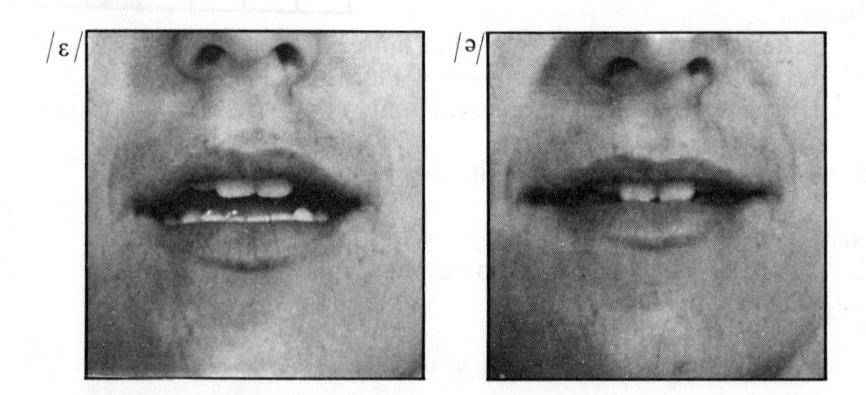

Exercise 1

1. Repeat the vowels separately.

/ɛ/ /ə/

2. Now *glide* from one to the other. Repeat.

/ɛ ə/

3. Repeat at normal speed.

/ɛə/

Spelling

/ɛə/ can be spelt in these ways;
- 'air' (e.g. chair, pair, air),
- 'are' (e.g. dare, care),
- 'ear' (e.g. wear, tear, bear).

Exercise 2

Decide whether each word you hear has the /ɪə/ or the /ɛə/ diphthong. The answers are underlined in exercise 5 below.

Exercise 3

Repeat these words with /ɛə/ at the end. Note that an 'r' at the end of a word is usually not pronounced.

there, mare, swear, fair, spare.

Exercise 4

Repeat these words with /ɛə/ in front of another syllable. Note that when 'r' is followed by another syllable or word beginning with a vowel, then it is pronounced.

Mary, dairy, swearing, staring, sharing.

Exercise 5

Repeat these pairs of words. The ones underlined are the ones you heard in exercise 2.

peer, pair; beer, bear;
dear, dare; spear, spare;
fear, fair; hear, hair;

sneer,	snare;	steer,	stare;
clear,	Clare;	spearing,	sparing.

Exercise 6

Read through this dialogue and look at the questions at the end before you listen to the tape.

Pete is looking for a friend and has knocked on Sue's door.

Pete: Hello, I'm looking for Mary. Do you know her?
Sue: Mary. Has she got fair hair?
Pete: Yes that's right.
Sue: Oh well, she shares a flat upstairs with Claire.
Pete: Is she there at the moment?
Sue: No they're both out, but have a chair and you can wait here.

Now look at these questions.

1. Which tone does Pete use when he asks the question *Do you know her?* (line 1)?
2. Which tone does Sue use when she says *Mary* (line 2)?
3. Where is the stress in the word *upstairs* (line 4)?

Exercise 7

Read the part of Pete.

Exercise 8

Read the part of Sue.

Today's silly sentence

Mary, Mary, quite contrary, how does your garden grow?

Group activities

1. Your teacher will say one word in each of these pairs of words. Listen carefully and decide which one it is.

1	2	1	2
cheer	chair	rear	rare
beer	bare	steer	stare
mere	mare	pier	pear
deer	dare	tear	tear (v.)

Now try the same thing with a partner.

2. Look at the picture. With a partner make and answer questions about the picture using *where*.

Lesson 41

The diphthong /ʊə/

How to pronounce this diphthong

Look at the vowel chart. You can see that this diphthong is made up of the vowels /ʊ/ and /ə/. /ʊ/ is a back vowel and so the back of the tongue is high in the mouth for the first part of the diphthong. It moves down as the middle of the tongue moves up for /ə/.

/ʊ/ is quite loud and long and /ə/ is lighter and shorter.

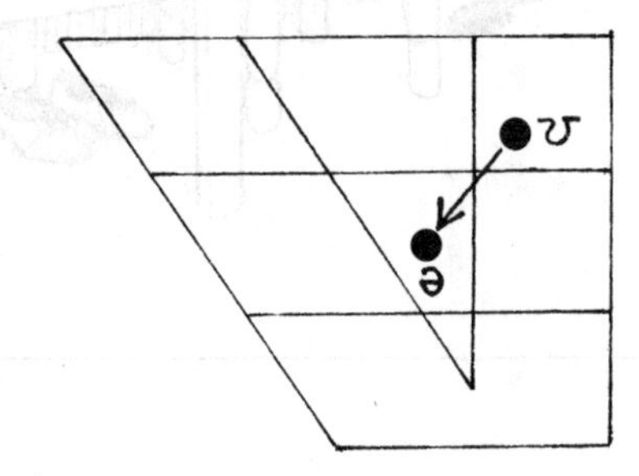

Look at the photographs. The lips are rounded for /ʊ/ and slightly spread for /ə/. Look in the mirror when you are practising this sound and check that the shape of your lips is the same as in the photograph.

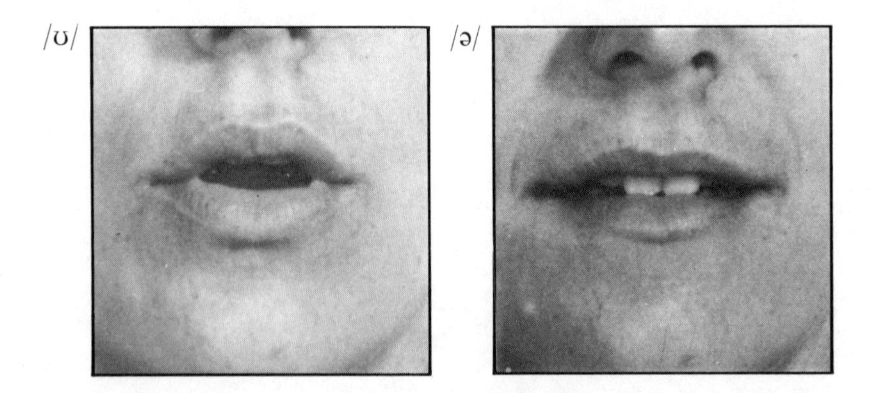

Exercise 1

1. Repeat the two vowels separately. Remember that /ʊ/ is louder and longer than /ə/.

/ʊ/ /ə/

2. Now *glide* from one to the other. Repeat.

/ʊ ə/

3. Repeat at normal speed.

/ʊə/

Spelling

/ʊə/ is spelt as:
'oor' (e.g. poor),
'our' (e.g. tour, gourd),
'ure' (e.g. sure).

Exercise 2 /jʊə/

There are some words where /ʊə/ comes after the semi-vowel /j/; this sounds like a very long vowel. Listen to the difference.

poor pure

Spelling

/jʊə/ is spelt as:
'ure' (e.g. cure, pure, endure),
'ur' (e.g. during, curious, furious),
'ewe' (e.g. fewer, ewer, skewer).

Exercise 3

Decide whether each word you hear has the pure vowel /uː/ or the diphthong /ʊə/ or /jʊə/. The answers are underlined in exercise 6 on page 188.

Exercise 4

Repeat these words with /ʊə/ after a consonant or a group of consonants.

poor, boor, moor, tour, sure.

Exercise 5

Repeat these words with /jʊə/ after a consonant or group of consonants.

pure, endure, during, curious, furious.

Exercise 6

Repeat these pairs of words. The ones underlined are the ones you heard in exercise 3.

<u>who</u>,	hewer;
shoe,	<u>sure</u>;
<u>do</u>,	doer;
few,	<u>fewer</u>;
two,	<u>tour</u>.

Exercise 7

Read through this dialogue and look at the questions at the end before you listen to the tape.

Mr Hall is in court and the judge is talking to him.

Mr Hall: I was touring round rural Wales during my holidays when I ran out of petrol.

Judge: Would the jury please note this.

Mr Hall: Y'see, I was sure there'd be enough.
Judge: Carry on.
Mr Hall: And so I was so furious, I hit this poor tourist.
Judge: I see. Well, I'm sure we can find a good cure for your fury!

Now look at these questions.

1. Which is the most important word in line 4?
2. Where are all the stresses in line 6?
3. Which tone does the Judge use in line 5?

Exercise 8
Read the part of Mr Hall. He's very sorry for what he has done.

Exercise 9
Read the part of the Judge. He speaks very formally.

Today's silly sentence

Muriel was furious with Stewart.

Group activities

1. Fill in the words on the right. They all have /ʊə/ or /jʊə/.
   John was very angry. He was . . .
   Mary was dying to see her present. She was . . .
   Jim was very short of money. He was . . .
   There were not as many. There were . . .
   What a doctor does when he makes a patient better. He . . .
   It is thin and sharp, and you put it through meat. A . . .
   A person who is visiting another country, on holiday. A . . .

2. Now make a sentence of your own using one of these words. Look in the dictionary to check that you know the meaning. Read your sentence to the class.

3. Work with a partner and sort out this dialogue.

   I'd be curious to know who it was.
   Oh, he's furious.
   He's sure somebody stole some jewels from the shop.
   How is Charlie?
   Why is he furious?
   So would Charlie, he's very poor now.

Lesson 42

Revision of /-ə/ diphthongs

Look at the diagram to remind yourself of how these three diphthongs are pronounced.

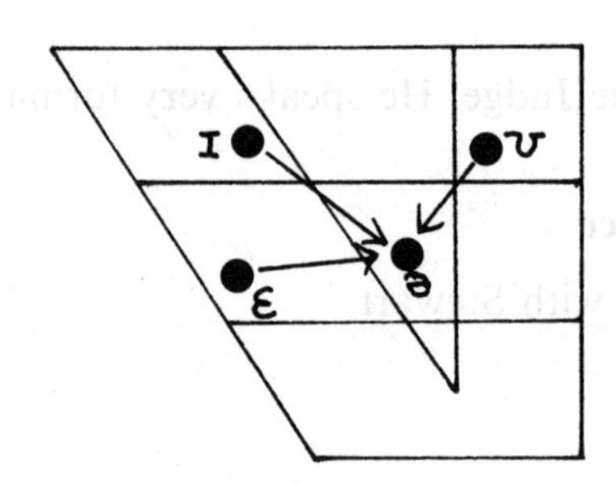

Exercise 1

1. Repeat the vowels separately. Remember the stress!

   /ɪ/ /ə/   /ɛ/ /ə/   /ʊ/ /ə/

2. Now *glide* the vowels together. Repeat.

   /ɪ ə/   /ɛ ə/   /ʊ ə/

3. Repeat at normal speed.

   /ɪə/   /ɛə/   /ʊə/

Exercise 2

Decide which diphthong each word you hear has. The answers are underlined in exercise 4 on page 191.

Exercise 3

In each sentence you will hear one of the words from each line. Decide which word you heard and write down A, B or C. The answers are in exercise 5 below.

	A /ɪə/	B /ɛə/	C /ʊə/
1.	here	hair	hewer
2.	fear	fair	fewer
3.	sheer	share	sure
4.	deer	dare	doer
5.	peer	pair	pure
6.	skier	scare	skewer
7.	tear	tear (v.)	tour

Exercise 4

Repeat the groups of words. The ones underlined are the ones you heard in exercise 2.

here,	**hair,**	hewer;
fear,	fair,	**fewer;**
sheer,	share,	sure;
deer,	dare,	doer;
peer,	pair,	pure;
skier,	**scare,**	skewer;
tear,	tear (v.),	**tour.**

Exercise 5

Repeat the sentences which you heard in exercise 3.

1. Bring it over here, please!
2. I fear you may be too late.
3. What about giving me my share?
4. How dare you disobey me!
5. That's the third pair you've bought this week!
6. Shish kebab is meat on a skewer.
7. Watch out, or Kirsty'll tear it!

The spelling of short vowels and diphthongs

Here are a few tips at the end of the book to help you with spelling. Sometimes it is very difficult to know whether to pronounce a short vowel or a diphthong.

The short vowel /ɪ/ and the diphthong /aɪ/

(a) When you see the letter ‘i’ followed by *one* consonant, you should usually pronounce it as the short vowel /ɪ/.

e.g. bit, mit, spin, knit, pin.

(b) ‘i’ is also pronounced as /ɪ/ when it is followed by a double consonant.

e.g. bitten, mitten, spinner, knitted, pinned.

(c) But, when the letter ‘i’ is followed by one consonant + ‘e’, you should usually pronounce it as /aɪ/.

e.g. bite, mite, spine, pine.

Exercise 1

Repeat these groups of words.

‘i’ + 1 consonant.	‘i’ + 2 consonants.	‘i’ + consonant + ‘e’.
bit	bitten	bite
mit	mitten	mite
spin	spinner	spine
pin	pinned	pine

Exercise 2

Read the following words. Say each word *before* the voice on the tape, and then repeat it.

pillar, pill, pile; bitter, bite, bit;
sitter, site, sit; mite, mit, mitten.

The short vowel /æ/ and the diphthong /eɪ/

There is the same rule with the letter 'a'.

(a) 'a' + one consonant is usually pronounced /æ/.

e.g. mat, rat, glad, fad, can.

(b) 'a' + a double consonant is usually pronounced /æ/.

e.g. canning, fatten, patted, gladden.

(c) 'a' + one consonant + 'e' is usually pronounced /eɪ/.

e.g. cane, rate, mate, pane, lane.

Exercise 3
Repeat these groups of words.

'a' + 1 consonant.	'a' + double consonant.	'a' + consonant + 'e'.
mat	matted	mate
can	canning	cane
glad	gladden	glade
fat	fatten	fate
plan	planned	plane

Exercise 4
Read the words below. Say each word *before* the voice on the tape, and then repeat it.

fade, fad; rat, rate; gladden, glade;
mat, mate, matted; mad, made, madden.

The short vowel /ɒ/ and the diphthong /əʊ/

(a) 'o' + one consonant is usually pronounced /ɒ/.

e.g. pot, sot, god, rod, not.

(b) 'o' + double consonant is usually pronounced /ɒ/.

e.g. potted, rotten, knotted, flogging.

(c) 'o' + one consonant + 'e' is usually pronounced /əʊ/.

e.g. rote, note, mode, smote, code.

Exercise 5

Repeat these groups of words.

'o' + 1 consonant.	'o' + double consonant.	'o' + consonant + 'e'.
rot	rotten	rote
nod	nodded	node
not	knotted	note
con	conned	cone

Exercise 6

Say these words *before* the voice on the tape, then repeat.

spot, spotted, note, spoke, nod, node,
nodding, not, note, mock, smote, rot, rote.

Exercise 7 *Dictation*

Write down the words which you hear on the tape. Each word will be said twice. The answers are on page 205.

Group activity

One student reads out two or three words below in turn, and the others close their books. The others write down the word which has been dictated.

tin,	sob,	sag,	time,	tame,	tinny,
soggy,	sagging,	shin,	shod,	sham,	side,
note,	sake,	silly,	soppy,	flapping.	

Keys to listening pre-tests

Consonants: Part 1

Answers

1.	D	16.	S	31.	D	46.	S
2.	D	17.	D	32.	S	47.	D
3.	D	18.	D	33.	S	48.	D
4.	D	19.	S	34.	S	49.	S
5.	D	20.	D	35.	D	50.	S
6.	S	21.	D	36.	D	51.	D
7.	D	22.	S	37.	S	52.	S
8.	D	23.	S	38.	D	53.	D
9.	D	24.	S	39.	S	54.	S
10.	S	25.	D	40.	D	55.	D
11.	S	26.	D	41.	S	56.	S
12.	S	27.	D	42.	D	57.	S
13.	D	28.	D	43.	D	58.	D
14.	D	29.	S	44.	S	59.	S
15.	S	30.	D	45.	D	60.	D

Tapescript

1.	sick,	sink	24.	veal,	veal
2.	jam,	dam	25.	bays,	beige
3.	beard,	veered	26.	find,	wind
4.	rich,	ridge	27.	sing,	sin
5.	ridge,	rids	28.	choose,	shoes
6.	lion,	lion	29.	zoo,	zoo
7.	hair,	air	30.	rack,	rag
8.	when,	Gwen	31.	chased,	taste
9.	catch,	cats	32.	singer,	singer
10.	tap,	tap	33.	rare,	rare
11.	cake,	cake	34.	pleasure,	pleasure
12.	then,	then	35.	fife,	five
13.	Sue,	zoo	36.	tame,	dame
14.	figure,	finger	37.	bulb,	bulb
15.	den,	den	38.	jam,	yam
16.	chase,	chase	39.	why,	why
17.	ring,	rink	40.	jam,	ham
18.	thank,	sank	41.	gone,	gone
19.	safe,	safe	42.	those,	doze
20.	set,	send	43.	thigh,	thy
21.	pay,	bay	44.	now,	now
22.	yes,	yes	45.	chew,	two
23.	ram,	ram	46.	teat,	teat

47.	thought,	taught	54.	toss,	toss
48.	wine,	vine	55.	shoe,	Sue
49.	hub,	hub	56.	rush,	rush
50.	thick,	thick	57.	sing,	sing
51.	pod,	pond	58.	pays,	paid
52.	rage,	rage	59.	pipe,	pipe
53.	leisure,	ledger	60.	rag,	rack

Error identification

Look at the mistakes you made in the Listening Pre-Test. Beside the number of each question, we have suggested which sounds and which lessons you may need to look at to help you with your mistakes.

	Sounds	*Lessons*		*Sounds*	*Lessons*
1.	/k/, /ŋ/	3, 13	31.	/tʃ/, /t/	9, 2
2.	/dʒ/, /d/	10, 2	32.	/ŋ/	13
3.	/b/, /v/	1, 4	33.	/r/	15
4.	/tʃ/, /dʒ/	9, 10	34.	/l/, /ʒ/	14, 7
5.	/dʒ/, /z/	10, 6	35.	/f/, /v/	4
6.	/l/, /n/	14, 12	36.	/t/, /d/	2
7.	/h/	8	37.	/b/, /l/	1, 14
8.	/w/, /n/	17, 12	38.	/dʒ/, /j/	10, 16
9.	/tʃ/, /s/	9, 6	39.	/w/	17
10.	/t/, /p/	2, 1	40.	/dʒ/, /h/	10, 8
11.	/k/	3	41.	/g/, /n/	3, 12
12.	/ð/, /n/	5, 12	42.	/ð/, /d/	5, 2
13	/s/, /z/	6	43.	/θ/, /ð/	5
14.	/g/, /ŋ/	3, 13	44.	/n/	12
15.	/d/, /n/	2, 12	45.	/tʃ/, /t/	9, 2
16.	/tʃ/, /s/	9, 6	46.	/t/	2
17.	/ŋ/, /k/	13, 3	47.	/θ/, /t/	5, 2
18.	/θ/, /s/	5, 6	48.	/w/, /v/	17, 4
19.	/s/, /f/	6, 4	49.	/h/, /b/	8, 1
20.	/t/, /n/	2, 12	50.	/θ/, /k/	5, 3
21.	/p/, /b/	1	51.	/d/, /n/	2, 12
22.	/j/, /s/	16, 6	52.	/r/, /dʒ/	15, 10
23.	/m/, /r/	11, 15	53.	/ʒ/, /dʒ/	7, 10
24.	/v/, /l/	4, 14	54.	/t/, /s/	2, 6
25.	/z/, /ʒ/	6, 7	55.	/ʃ/, /s/	7, 6
26.	/f/, /w/	4, 17	56.	/r/, /ʃ/	15, 7
27.	/ŋ/, /n/	13, 12	57.	/s/, /ŋ/	6, 13
28.	/tʃ/, /ʃ/	9, 7	58.	/z/, /d/	6, 2
29.	/z/	6	59.	/p/	1
30.	/k/, /g/	3	60.	/g/, /k/	3

Consonants: Part 2

Answers

1.	D	16.	D	31.	D	46.	D
2.	D	17.	D	32.	D	47.	D
3.	D	18.	D	33.	S	48.	S
4.	S	19.	D	34.	D	49.	D
5.	D	20.	S	35.	D	50.	D
6.	S	21.	D	36.	S	51.	S
7.	S	22.	S	37.	D	52.	S
8.	D	23.	S	38.	D	53.	S
9.	D	24.	D	39.	S	54.	D
10.	D	25.	S	40.	D	55.	D
11.	D	26.	S	41.	S	56.	D
12.	D	27.	D	42.	D	57.	D
13.	D	28.	D	43.	S	58.	S
14.	D	29.	S	44.	S	59.	D
15.	S	30.	S	45.	D	60.	D

Tapescript

1.	sick,	thick	23.	make,	make
2.	raise,	race	24.	rove,	rope
3.	lesion,	legion	25.	tooth,	tooth
4.	tyre,	tyre	26.	where,	where
5.	get,	yet	27.	rain,	lane
6.	rife,	rife	28.	rink,	rick
7.	toss,	toss	29.	tight,	tight
8.	leisure,	ledger	30.	stem,	stem
9.	cat,	catch	31.	send,	sent
10.	puss,	push	32.	thy,	thigh
11.	Gwen,	when	33.	rib,	rib
12.	rove,	robe	34.	finger,	figure
13.	when,	fen	35.	raid,	rage
14.	huts,	hutch	36.	ridge,	ridge
15.	posh,	posh	37.	save,	safe
16.	sink,	sing	38.	Bob,	bomb
17.	robe,	rope	39.	your,	your
18.	tease,	teethe	40.	hate,	fate
19.	eat,	heat	41.	dead,	dead
20.	ring,	ring	42.	teat,	teeth
21.	yacht,	jot	43.	wreathe,	wreathe
22.	catch,	catch	44.	noon,	noon

45.	Reg,	wretch	53.	pleasure,	pleasure
46.	ride,	write	54.	cash,	catch
47.	read,	wreathe	55.	bide,	bite
48.	rave,	rave	56.	rag,	rack
49.	vine,	wine	57.	toot,	tooth
50.	sin,	sing	58.	hive,	hive
51.	raise,	raise	59.	eel,	heel
52.	pill,	pill	60.	cash,	catch

Error identification

	Sounds	*Lessons*		*Sounds*	*Lessons*
1.	/s/, /θ/	6, 5	31.	/d/, /t/	2
2.	/z/, /s/	6	32.	/ð/, /θ/	5
3.	/ʒ/, /dʒ/	7, 10	33.	/r/, /b/	15, 1
4.	/t/, /r/	2, 15	34.	/ŋ/, /g/	13, 3
5.	/g/, /j/	3, 16	35.	/d/, /dʒ/	2, 10
6.	/r/, /f/	15, 4	36.	/r/, /dʒ/	15, 10
7.	/t/, /s/	2, 6	37.	/v/, /f/	4
8.	/ʒ/, /dʒ/	7, 10	38.	/b/, /m/	1, 11
9.	/t/, /tʃ/	2, 9	39.	/j/	16
10.	/s/, /ʃ/	6, 7	40.	/h/, /f/	8, 4
11.	/g/, /w/	3, 17	41.	/d/	2
12.	/v/, /b/	4, 1	42.	/t/, /θ/	2, 5
13.	/w/, /f/	17, 4	43.	/r/, /ð/	15, 5
14.	/s/, /tʃ/	6, 9	44.	/n/,	12
15.	/p/, /ʃ/	1, 7	45.	/dʒ/, /tʃ/	10, 9
16.	/k/, /ŋ/	3, 13	46.	/d/, /t/	2
17.	/b/, /p/	1	47.	/d/, /ð/	2, 5
18.	/z/, /ð/	6, 5	48.	/r/, /v/	15, 4
19.	/h/	8	49.	/v/, /w/	4, 17
20.	/ŋ/	13	50.	/n/, /ŋ/	12, 13
21.	/j/, /dʒ/	16, 10	51.	/r/, /z/	15, 6
22.	/k/, /tʃ/	3, 9	52.	/p/, /l/	1, 14
23.	/m/, /k/	11, 3	53.	/ʒ/	7
24.	/v/, /p/	4, 1	54.	/ʃ/, /tʃ/	7, 9
25.	/t/, /θ/	2, 5	55.	/d/, /t/	2
26.	/w/	17	56.	/g/, /k/	3
27.	/r/, /l/	15, 14	57.	/t/,/θ/	2, 5
28.	/ŋ/, /k/	13, 3	58.	/h/, /v/	8, 4
29.	/t/	2	59.	/h/	8
30.	/m/	11	60.	/ʃ/, /tʃ/	7, 9

Pure vowels

Answers

1. D	16. S	31. S	46. D
2. D	17. S	32. S	47. S
3. S	18. D	33. D	48. D
4. S	19. D	34. D	49. D
5. D	20. D	35. D	50. S
6. D	21. D	36. S	51. D
7. D	22. S	37. D	52. S
8. S	23. S	38. S	53. D
9. D	24. D	39. S	54. D
10. S	25. S	40. D	55. S
11. S	26. D	41. D	56. S
12. D	27. D	42. S	57. D
13. D	28. S	43. D	58. D
14. S	29. D	44. S	59. D
15. D	30. D	45. D	60. D

Tapescript

1.	cut,	cart	23.	bit,	bit
2.	soot,	suit	24.	suit,	soot
3.	park,	park	25.	dirt,	dirt
4.	seat,	seat	26.	curd,	card
5.	bat,	bet	27.	cart,	cut
6.	pip,	peep	28.	nought,	nought
7.	short,	shot	29.	peep,	pip
8.	shoot,	shoot	30.	curt,	cut
9.	cap,	carp	31.	sap,	sap
10.	bet,	bet	32.	shoot,	shoot
11.	and /ə/,	and /ə/	33.	cart,	caught
12.	cart,	curt	34.	bet,	bit
13.	bit,	bet	35.	bet,	bat
14.	lock,	lock	36.	cart,	cart
15.	taught,	tart	37.	cut,	cat
16.	put,	put	38.	seat,	seat
17.	back,	back	39.	but /ə/,	but /ə/
18.	cut,	curt	40.	soot,	suit
19.	hat,	hut	41.	cut,	curt
20.	cock,	cork	42.	bought,	bought
21.	carp,	cap	43.	caught,	cot
22.	rut,	rut	44.	bit,	bit

45.	pip,	peep
46.	bat,	bet
47.	cot,	cot
48.	caught,	cart
49.	cut,	cart
50.	bet,	bet
51.	bit,	bet
52.	put,	put
53.	cart,	curt
54.	cat,	cut
55.	cut,	cut
56.	curt,	curt
57.	cat,	cart
58.	peep,	pip
59.	cut,	cat
60.	cot,	caught

Error indentification

	Sounds	*Lessons*
1.	/ʌ/, /ɑː/	23, 25
2.	/ʊ/, /uː/	28, 29
3.	/ɑː/	25
4.	/iː/	18
5.	/æ/, /e/	22, 21
6.	/ɪ/, /iː/	19, 18, 20
7.	/ɔː/, /ɒ/	27, 26
8.	/uː/	29
9.	/æ/, /ɑː/	22, 25
10.	/e/	21
11.	/ə/	32
12.	/ɑː/, /ɜː/	25, 31
13.	/ɪ/, /e/	19, 21
14.	/ɒ/	26
15.	/ɔː/, /ɑː/	27, 25
16.	/ʊ/	28
17.	/æ/	22
18.	/ʌ/, /ɜː/	23, 31
19.	/æ/, /ʌ/	22, 23
20.	/ɒ/, /ɔː/	26, 27
21.	/ɑː/, /æ/	25, 22
22.	/ʌ/	23
23.	/ɪ/	19
24.	/uː/, /ʊ/	29, 28
25.	/ɜː/	31
26.	/ɜː/, /ɑː/	31, 25
27.	/ɑː/, /ʌ/	25, 23
28.	/ɔː/	27
29.	/iː/, /ɪ/	18, 19, 20
30.	/ɜː/, /ʌ/	31, 23
31.	/æ/	22
32.	/uː/	29
33.	/ɑː/, /ɔː/	25, 27
34.	/e/, /ɪ/	21, 19
35	/e/, /æ/	21, 22
36.	/ɑː/	25
37.	/ʌ/, /æ/	23, 22
38.	/iː/	18
39.	/ə/	32
40.	/ʊ/, /uː/	28, 29
41.	/ʌ/, /ɜː/	23, 31
42.	/ɔː/	27
43.	/ɔː/, /ɒ/	27, 26
44.	/ɪ/	19
45.	/ɪ/, /iː/	19, 18, 20
46.	/æ/, /e/	22, 21
47.	/ɒ/	26
48.	/ɔː/, /ɑː/	27, 25
49.	/ʌ/, /ɑː/	23, 25
50.	/e/	21
51.	/ɪ/, /e/	19, 21
52.	/ʊ/	28
53.	/ɑː/, /ɜː/	25, 31
54.	/æ/, /ʌ/	22, 23
55.	/ʌ/	23
56.	/ɜː/	31
57.	/æ/, /ɑː/	22, 25
58.	/iː/, /ɪ/	18, 19, 20
59.	/ʌ/, /æ/	23, 22
60.	/ɒ/, /ɔː/	26, 27

Diphthongs

Answers

1.	D	16.	D	31.	S	46.	D
2.	S	17.	D	32.	D	47.	S
3.	D	18.	D	33.	D	48.	S
4.	D	19.	D	34.	D	49.	S
5.	D	20.	S	35.	D	50.	D
6.	D	21.	D	36.	D	51.	D
7.	S	22.	S	37.	D	52.	D
8.	D	23.	D	38.	S	53.	D
9.	S	24.	S	39.	S	54.	D
10.	D	25.	S	40.	D	55.	D
11.	S	26.	D	41.	D	56.	D
12.	D	27.	D	42.	D	57.	S
13.	S	28.	D	43.	S	58.	D
14.	S	29.	S	44.	S	59.	D
15.	D	30.	D	45.	S	60.	D

Tapescript

1.	now,	nor
2.	gate,	gate
3.	quoits,	cots
4.	no,	now
5.	here,	hair
6.	lie,	lay
7.	near,	near
8.	so,	sir
9.	buy,	buy
10.	blade,	bled
11.	boy,	boy
12.	beard,	bid
13.	share,	share
14.	go,	go
15.	show,	shoe
16.	shown,	shone
17.	oil,	all
18.	buy,	boy
19.	get,	gate
20.	side,	side
21.	caught,	coat
22.	shown,	shown
23.	share,	shear
24.	tour,	tour
25.	care,	care
26.	got,	goat
27.	bore,	boy
28.	toil,	tile
29.	take,	take
30.	cart,	kite
31.	oil,	oil
32.	sir,	so
33.	bid,	beard
34.	knee,	near
35.	now,	no
36.	boot,	boat
37.	gate,	get
38.	no,	no
39.	out,	out
40.	boy,	bore
41.	shown,	shone
42.	sheer,	she
43.	buy,	buy
44.	nail,	nail

45.	point,	point
46.	show,	shoe
47.	near,	near
48.	fair,	fair
49.	tour,	tour
50.	toy,	tie
51.	fear,	fee
52.	peer,	pair
53.	beard,	bid
54.	no,	now
55.	goal,	girl
56.	no,	nor
57.	sigh,	sigh
58.	buy,	bar
59.	buy,	boy
60.	foal,	foul

Error identification

	Sounds	*Lessons*
1.	/ɑʊ/	38
2.	/eɪ/	33
3.	/ɔɪ/	35
4.	/əʊ/, /ɑʊ/	37, 38
5.	/ɪə/, /ɛə/	39, 40
6.	/aɪ/, /eɪ/	34, 33
7.	/ɪə/	39
8.	/əʊ/	37
9.	/aɪ/	34
10.	/eɪ/	33
11.	/ɔɪ/	35
12.	/ɪə/	39
13.	/ɛə/	40
14.	/əʊ/	37
15.	/əʊ/	37
16.	/əʊ/	37
17.	/ɔɪ/	35
18.	/aɪ/, /ɔɪ/	34, 35
19.	/eɪ/	33
20.	/aɪ/	34
21.	/əʊ/	37
22.	/əʊ/	37
23.	/ɛə/, /ɪə/	40, 39
24.	/ʊə/	41
25.	/ɛə/	40
26.	/əʊ/	37
27.	/ɔɪ/	35
28.	/ɔɪ/,/aɪ/	35, 34
29.	/eɪ/	33
30.	/aɪ/	34
31.	/ɔɪ/	35
32.	/əʊ/	37
33.	/ɪə/	39
34.	/ɪə/	39
35.	/ɑʊ/, /əʊ/	38, 37
36.	/əʊ/	37
37.	/eɪ/	33
38.	/əʊ/	37
39.	/ɑʊ/	38
40.	/ɔɪ/	35
41.	/əʊ/	37
42.	/ɪə/	39
43.	/aɪ/	34
44.	/eɪ/	33
45.	/ɔɪ/	35
46.	/əʊ/	37
47.	/ɪə/	39
48.	/ɛə/	40
49.	/ʊə/	41
50.	/ɔɪ/, /aɪ/	35, 34
51.	/ɪə/	39
52.	/ɪə/, /ɛə/	39, 40
53.	/ɪə/	39
54.	/əʊ/, /ɑʊ/	37, 38
55.	/əʊ/	37
56.	/əʊ/	37
57.	/aɪ/	34
58.	/aɪ/	34
59.	/aɪ/, /ɔɪ/	34, 35
60.	/əʊ/, /ɑʊ/	37, 38

Answers to exercises

Page 8 1. a) to check she heard the instructions correctly; b) slowly and deliberately; 2. always; 3. rising.

Page 14 1. Yes, she is polite; 2. rise-fall; 3. '**min**utes.

Page 20 1. rise-fall. She was surprised; 2. to'**mor**row; 3. '**Can** you '**give** her a '**mess**age?

Page 25 1. vege'**tar**ian '**veg**etables. They are not the same. Vegetables has three syllables; 2. fish; 3. falling.

Page 30 1. '**happ**ening; 2. rising; 3. I'm '**not** '**sure** but I '**think** it's a'**bout** '**six**ty '**miles** '**east** of '**Lon**don.

Page 36 1. falling; 2. her; 3. falling.

Page 41 1. '**fash**ionable; 2. falling; 3. But it'll '**match** your '**cham**pagne-'**col**oured '**shirt**.

Page 45 1. falling; 2. falling; 3. '**in**terested. Yes, '**in**terest.

Page 49 1. It is not falling; 2. have; 3. rising.

Page 53 1. jewellery. Falling; 2. Ni'**ger**ia; 3. '**That's** for '**me** to '**judge**.

Page 57 1. '**mar**vellous; 2. falling; 3. '**Would** you '**mind** '**stay**ing for a '**few** more '**hours** to '**fin**ish this '**man**uscript?

Page 61 1. rising; 2. new; 3. '**Can**ada.

Page 66 1. a'**ttract**; 2. rising; 3. '**Oh**, '**stop** being '**si**lly. It's '**no**thing to '**do** with '**me**.

Page 70 1. She is pleading. She really wants to go into the gallery; 2. to'**night**; 3. The '**peo**ple in '**that** '**line** in the '**hall** are '**all** '**wait**ing to '**have** a '**look** as '**well**.

Page 75 1. rise-fall; 2. car of, for ages, river and, car'll; 3. luckier.

Page 79 1. rise-fall; 2. mis'**take**; 3. '**You** '**used** to '**go** '**down** to the '**youth** '**club** in '**Yar**mouth.

Page 83 1. ex'**act**ly; 2. falling; 3. '**I** '**see**, well '**one** of these '**tab**lets after '**meals** will '**do** the '**trick**. '**Next** '**please**!

Page 93 1. falling; 2. will not; 3. You '**see** there's '**been** a '**rob**bery at the '**key** '**fac**tory.

Page 97 1. fall-rise; 2. up'**stairs**; 3. just.

Page 101 1. live; 2. '**Tin**ton for '**three** '**weeks**, '**then** '**Pin**low for '**three**; 3. falling.

Page 104 1. pounds; 2. falling; 3. rising.

Page 108 1. rising; 2. 'accident. No—acci'**den**tal; 3. '**Rea**lly, '**did** they '**catch** the '**man** who '**did** it?

Page 113 1. rising; 2. '**Now** '**don't** for'**get** you must '**shut** up the '**draw**ers and '**put** the '**co**ver on the '**type**writer; 3. cashier.

Page 121 1. falling; 2. dis'**as**ter; 3. '**Charles** '**Carn**forth—'**he**'s in '**all** the dis'**aster** '**films**.

Page 125 1. a'**bout**; 2. falling; 3. snow.

Page 129 1. rising; 2. '**foot**ballers; 3. '**My** '**daugh**ters think the i'**dea**'s '**aw**ful.

Page 133 1. cookery; 2. falling; 3. '**Yes**, I '**on**ly '**want**ed to '**see** '**how** to '**boil** an '**egg**.

Page 137 1. group; 2. rising; 3. '**mur**derer.

Page 144 1. rising; 2. No, the first part is falling; 3. '**Yes**, I '**think** it '**starts** on the '**third**.

Page 148 1. six—Put the picture by the window and the books on the table; 2. '**kit**chen; 3. What. Rising.

Page 156 1. '**Well**, I '**think** it's '**go**ing to '**rain** so I '**won't** be '**able** to '**play** '**ten**nis; 2. nice; 3. '**yes**terday.

Page 160 1. '**Yes**, I'm '**ha**ving some '**troub**le with my '**hifi** '**set**; 2. a'**fraid**; 3. falling.

Page 165 1. en'**joy**ing; 2. falling; 3. '**Sh**, you're '**spoil**ing the '**film**.

Page 172 1. falling; 2. what; 3. sup'**posed**.

Page 176 1. '**Ah**, '**well** I'd '**just** like to '**know** '**how** a '**thous**and '**pounds** . . .; 2. falling; 3. ap'**point**ment.

Page 180 1. falling; 2. i'**dea**; 3. falling.

Page 184 1. rising; 2. falling; 3. up'**stairs**.

Page 189 1. sure; 2. And I was '**so** '**fur**ious I '**hit** '**this** '**poor** '**tour**ist; 3. falling.

Dictation

1. shot	2. note	3. pit	4. pitted
5. cane	6. canned	7. rotten	8. win
9. wine	10. winning	11. ram	12. ramming
13. lame	14. trip	15. tripe	

Chart of phonetic symbols

These are the phonetic symbols used in this book.

Consonants

Symbol	*Example*	*Type of sound*
/p/	pit	Stop
/b/	bit	Stop
/t/	tin	Stop
/d/	done	Stop
/k/	kill	Stop
/g/	gun	Stop
/f/	five	Fricative
/v/	very	Fricative
/θ/	thick	Fricative
/ð/	then	Fricative
/s/	sun	Fricative
/z/	zoo	Fricative
/ʃ/	shut	Fricative
/ʒ/	leisure	Fricative
/h/	hill	Fricative
/tʃ/	charm	Affricate
/dʒ/	judge	Affricate
/m/	man	Nasal
/n/	nun	Nasal
/ŋ/	sing	Nasal
/l/	lion	Lateral
/r/	right	Continuant
/j/	yet	Semi-vowel
/w/	wet	Semi-vowel

Pure vowels

Symbol	*Example*
/iː/	feet
/ɪ/	fit
/e/	bet
/æ/	bat
/ʌ/	but
/ɑː/	cart
/ɒ/	cot
/ɔː/	cord
/ʊ/	put
/uː/	mood
/ə/	the
/ɜː/	bird

Diphthongs

Symbol	*Example*
/eɪ/	day
/aɪ/	side
/ɔɪ/	boy
/əʊ/	so
/ɑʊ/	found
/ɪə/	fear
/ɛə/	share
/ʊə/	sure

Foreign Language Notes

Italian Notes

by David Hart

Consonanti

Lezione 1: /p/ /b/
La pronuncia di queste due consonanti è molto simile in inglese ed in italiano.

/p/ come in 'pepper', 'stop'. Il suono in inglese, che sia iniziale, mediano o finale, è accompagnato da una più forte aspirazione. Quando invece è preceduto da /s/, come nella parola 'sport', corrisponde esattamente all'italiano.

/b/ come in 'bob', 'bubble'. Il suono inglese è assai vicino alla /b/ italiana.

Lezione 2: /t/ /d/
Per ambedue queste consonanti vi sono due differenze rispetto alla pronuncia italiana:

(i) mentre in italiano, nella maggior parte dei casi, si pronunciano con la lingua dietro i denti, in inglese vanno pronunciate con la lingua puntata contro gli alveoli (l'interno delle gengive);
(ii) vi è lo stesso fenomeno dell'aspirazione descritta sopra per il suono /p/, più marcato nel caso della /t/.

Lezione 3: /k/ /g/
La pronuncia inglese di questi due suoni è assai vicina a quella italiana.

Lezione 4: /f/ /v/
La pronuncia inglese corrisponde esattamente a quella italiana.

Lezione 5: /θ/ /ð/
Questi due suoni inglesi non esistono in italiano.

/θ/ suono sordo, come in 'think' o 'theme'. Per pronunciarlo bisogna mettere la punta della lingua tra i denti ed espellere l'aria tra la lingua e i denti superiori, senza ritirare la lingua. Fare attenzione a spingere sufficientemente la lingua in avanti, per evitare di produrre il suono /f/; e lasciare la punta della lingua dietro i denti superiori, per non produrre il suono /t/.

/ð/ suono sonoro, come in 'this' o 'there'. La posizione della lingua è come quella descritta sopra per il suono /θ/. La differenza consiste nel fatto che la laringe vibra quando si produce questo suono. Fare attenzione a spingere sufficientemente la lingua in avanti, per evitare di produrre il suono /v/; e a non lasciare la punta della lingua contro gli alveoli, per evitare di produrre il suono /d/.

Lezione 6: /s/ /z/

/s/ suono sordo, come in 'sun'. Corrisponde all' /s/ italiana in principio di parola ('sono').

/z/ suono sonoro, come in 'zoo' o 'rose'.

Corrisponde all' /s/ italiano di parole come 'rosa' e perciò non corrisponde alla pronuncia della lettera 'z' in italiano.

Lezione 7: /ʃ/ /ʒ/

/ʃ/ suono sordo, come in 'she'. Corrisponde al suono iniziale della parola italiana 'scena'.

/ʒ/ suono sonoro, come in 'measure', 'television'. E' un suono piuttosto raro in inglese, inesistente in italiano, e corrisponde alla pronuncia del pronome francese 'je'.

Lezione 8: /h/

Consonante sorda, come in 'how', 'who'. Davanti ad una vocale è quasi sempre aspirata ('who', 'whom', 'whose'); per le pochissime eccezioni, vedere gli esercizi.

Lezioni 9 e 10: /tʃ/, /dʒ/

Questi due suoni consonantici esistono anche in italiano, ma la loro rappresentazione ortografica è diversa.

/tʃ/ come in 'chip'. Corrisponde esattamente alla 'c' dolce di 'cena'.

/dʒ/ come in 'John'. Corrisponde esattamente alla 'g' dolce di 'erge'.

Lezioni 11, 12 e 13: /m/, /n/, /ŋ/

/m/ come in 'make', 'common', 'ham'. Il suono corrisponde esattamente alla /m/ italiana quando si trova in posizione iniziale o mediana; in posizione finale, invece, bisogna fare attenzione a chiudere fermamente le labbra, soprattutto quando la /m/ è preceduta da un suono vocalico breve.

/n/ come in 'not', 'cannot', 'ran'. Il suono corrisponde esattamente alla /n/ italiana quando si trova in posizione iniziale o mediana; in posizione finale bisogna fare attenzione a spingere la lingua fino agli alveoli, soprattutto quando la /n/ è preceduta da un suono vocalico breve.

/ŋ/ come in 'sing', 'singer', 'think'. Bisogna ricordare che
(i) quando 'ng' si trova in posizione finale in inglese ('sing') abbiamo un suono dorso-velare: per produrlo, la parte posteriore della lingua deve essere alzata contro la parte posteriore del palato per produrre un suono nasale;
(ii) quando 'ng' si trova in posizione mediana la pronuncia può essere come descritta sopra ('singer'), ma vi può essere invece una corrispondenza alla pronuncia italiana (cf. 'longer' e 'lungo').

Lezioni 14 e 15: /l/, /r/

/l/ come in 'let'. In posizione iniziale corrisponde esattamente al suono italiano, il quale non varia mai ('letto', 'mela'); è la cosidetta /l/ chiara.

come in 'tell', 'metal', 'table'. Quando la /l/ inglese è preceduta da un suono vocalico, si discosta dal suono italiano. Viene pronunciata sollevando il dorso della lingua mentre la punta tocca gli alveoli.

/r/ come in 'rat', 'carry', 'caring'. Non corrisponde all' /r/ italiana. La pronuncia inglese si avvicina a quella siciliana in parole come 'Trapani': si piega la punta della lingua verso gli alveoli, senza toccarli, e senza farla vibrare. L'aria respirata passa sopra la lingua.

come in 'car', 'cart', 'more', 'burned'. Quando l' /r/ si trova in posizione finale, davanti ad una 'e' muta, o davanti ad una consonante, perde il suo valore di consonante per funzionare invece da *continuant*, influenzando il suono vocalico che la precede.

Lezioni 16 e 17: /j/, /w/

/j/ come in 'you' o 'yes'. Rispetto all' /i/ iniziale in italiano ('ieri'), è più breve e leggera. Si pronuncia con le labbra allargate e la lingua nella posizione della /i/, ritraendola poi rapidamente per formare il suono vocalico.

/w/ come in 'will' o 'twice'. Rispetto all' /u/ iniziale in italiano ('uomo'), è più breve e leggera. In principio di parola o di sillaba si pronuncia con le labbra arrotondate e più chiuse che non in italiano.

Vocali

Lezioni 18 e 19: /iː/, /ɪ/

/iː/ come in 'feet', 'read'. Suono vocalico anteriore chiuso e lungo, è molto vicino all'italiano di 'filo', o communque laddove la 'i' italiana è seguita da una sola consonante. Rispetto alla posizione fissurale delle labbra per produrre il suono italiano, in inglese le labbra sono un po' più allentate.

/ɪ/ come in 'fit', 'rid'. Suono vocalico anteriore molto breve, non trova corrispondenza in italiano. Si può paragonarlo alla 'i' italiana che si trova davanti alle consonanti doppie di parole come 'affitto'. Da notare che la posizione della lingua è più bassa e indietro di quanto non lo sia in italiano.

Lezione 21: /e/
Come in 'let', 'head'. E' un suono vocalico anteriore, più vicino alla 'e' di 'gente' di non a quella di 'mente'; la posizione della lingua è leggermente più bassa di quanto non lo sia in italiano.

Lezioni 22 e 23: /æ/, /ʌ/
/æ/ come in 'cap'. Non trova corrispondenza in italiano. Suono vocalico breve, anteriore e aperto. La posizione della lingua è bassa, dietro i denti inferiori. E' tra la 'e' di 'leva' e la 'a' di 'lava'. Attenzione a non trasformarlo in un suono di 'e' aperta.

/ʌ/ come in 'cup'. Non trova corrispondenza in italiano. E' un suono leggermente più aperto di quanto non lo sia l' /æ/ inglese: il punto della lingua è ritirato e ulteriormente abbassato.

Lezione 25: /ɑː/
Come in 'fast','part'. E' una vocale posteriore ed aperta assai vicino alla 'a' italiana di 'vano', ma è importante notare che il suono inglese è più lungo. La posizione della lingua è più indietro di quanto non lo sia in italiano.

Lezioni 26 e 27: /ɒ/, /ɔː/
/ɒ/ come in 'not', 'want'. E' una vocale breve e posteriore, simile alla 'o' italiana di 'notte', ma più aperta; per produrre il suono inglese le labbra sono leggermente più allentate, meno arrotondate.

/ɔː/ come in 'port'. 'all'. Vocale lunga, posteriore e meno aperta di /ɒ/, non trova corrispondenza in italiano. Va pronunciata con le labbra più arrotondate rispetto alla 'o' italiana, ed è notevolmente più lunga.

Lezioni 28 e 29: /ʊ/, /uː/
/ʊ/ come in 'book', 'full'. Vocale breve, posteriore e chiusa, non ha corrispondenza esatta in italiano. Le labbra sono meno arrotondate rispetto alla pronuncia della 'a' italiana quando viene seguita dalle consonanti doppie, come in 'buttare'.

/uː/ come in 'fool', 'rule'. Vocale lunga, è ancora più posteriore e chiusa dell' /ʊ/ inglese, e non trova corrispondenza esatta in italiano. Per quanto riguarda la posizione della lingua può essere paragonata alla 'u' italiana di parole come 'mulo', ma le labbra sono meno arrotondate in inglese.

Lezioni 31 e 32: /ɜː/, /ə/

/ɜː/ come in 'first', 'word'. Vocale lunga e centrale, non trova corrispondenza in italiano. Le labbra sono allentate e un po' allargate.

/ə/ come in 'the', 'away'. Vocale centrale con suono molto breve, non trova corrispondenza in italiano. Può essere paragonato al suono francese in parole come 'le' e 'que'.

Dittonghi

N.B. Il dittongo, l'unione di due vocali in una sola sillaba, è assai comune in inglese. In alcuni casi esistono in italiano dei suoni molto simili a quelli inglesi. La differenza principale è che i due elementi di un dittongo inglese risultano più fusi l'un a l'altro che non in italiano, e vanno pronunciati insieme e piuttosto rapidamente.

Lezioni 33, 34 e 35: /eɪ/, /aɪ/, /ɔɪ/

/eɪ/ come in 'fail'. 'late'. Questo suono è vicino all'italiano di 'sei', 'lei'.

/aɪ/ come in 'quite', 'lie'. Questo suono è vicino all'italiano di 'assai', 'stai'.

/ɔɪ/ come in 'boy', 'oil'. Questo suono è vicino all'italiano di 'poi'.

Lezione 37: /əʊ/

Come in 'home', 'told'. Non c'è nessuna corrispondenza in italiano in quanto non esiste la vocale breve /ə/ che è la prima di questo dittongo. (Ved. la lezione 32 della sezione precedente). Le labbra sono inizialmente allentate e poco aperte, per essere poi arrotondate, come se si stesse per pronunciare una /w/ inglese.

Lezione 38: /ɑʊ/

Come in 'pound', 'cows'. Questo suono è vicino all'italiano di 'causa'. Vi è lo stesso accenno al suono /w/ che si trova con il dittongo /əʊ/ (Lezione 37).

Lezioni 39, 40 e 41: /ɪə/, /ɛə/, /ʊə/

N.B. In questi tre dittonghi inglesi le prime vocali sono /ɪ/, /ɛ/ e /ʊ/, ma l'ultima è la /ə/ inglese (ved. Lezione 32 della sezione precendente), inesistente in italiano.

/ɪə/ come in 'here', 'dear'. Bisogna formare prima l' /ɪ/ e passare molto rapidamente all' /ə/; nel passaggio dalla prima alla seconda vocale la lingua si metterà nella posizione atta a formare una /j/; questo suono deve essere però appena accennato. La prominenza della prima vocale è abbastanza evidente. L' /r/ finale non viene pronunciata. Il suono più vicino in italiano sarebbe rappresentato dalla seguenza 'ia' in 'chiamare'.

/ɛə/ come in 'chair', 'there'. Non c'è nessuna corrispondenza con l'italiano. In questo dittongo le vocali /ɛ/ e /ə/ vanno pronunciate praticamente insieme, e vi è lo stesso accenno al suono /j/ che si trova con il dittongo /ɪə/.

/ʊə/ come in 'poor'. Il suono più vicino in italiano sarebbe rappresentato dalla seguenza 'ua' in, per esempio, 'effettua', ricordando che l'inglese ha la vocale breve /ə/ al posto della /a/ in italiano. Nel passaggio veloce tra le due vocali, vi sarà un accenno al suono /w/.

Portuguese Notes

by Roger Jones

Consoantes

Lição 1: /p/, /b/

Trata-se de duas consoantes oclusivas bilabiais com valor muito semelhante às das mesmas consoantes em Português. Mas é importante notar que o /p/ inicial, como em 'poor', 'Paul', etc., é mais forte que a consoante correspondente em Português, e se articula com uma *explosão* de ar (aspiração). Para obter esta aspiração, pratique a palavra com um fósforo acendido perto à boca: ao explotar a sílaba inicial a chama se vacila ou se apaga, o qual não é o caso em Português. Quando o /p/ inicial em Inglês está precedido de 's' (como em 'sport') ou quando está em posição medial ou final em uma palavra (por exemplo, em 'happy', 'lip') a articulação corresponde ao /p/ português—isso é, não há aspiração.

O /b/ inglês também é mais forte que a consoante correspondente em Português. Aproxima-se do /b/ português no início de palavra (isto é, ao primeiro 'b' de 'beber', por exemplo), e se articula com uma ligeira vibração das cordas vocais. Em posição medial ou final se articula com menos força e sem vibração.

Lição 2: /t/, /d/

O /t/ (mudo—sem vibração das cordas vocais) e o /d/ (sonoro—com vibração das cordas) se pronunciam em Portugûes com a língua atrás dos dentes, mas em Inglês se pronunciam com a língua a bater nos alvéolos (interior das gengivas). Isto é, em Português, a articulação é dental, em Inglês alveolar. Além disso, o /t/ ingles inicial articula-se com aspiração (igual que no caso do /p/), enquanto em posição medial ou final, ou quando está precedido por um 's' o /t/ é mais semelhante ao /t/ português—isto é, não há aspiração.

Lição 3: /k/, /g/

Trata-se de duas consoantes oclusivas velares de valor semelhante ao das correspondentes portuguesas. O /k/ é mudo e o /g/ é sonoro. Como no caso do /p/ e do /t/, o /k/ em Inglês, em posição inicial se articula com aspiração.

/k/ como em 'car', 'keep', 'queue', 'according', pronúncia-se como o 'c' (+a, o, u) ou 'qu' (+e, i) portuguêses de 'casa', 'quero'.

/g/ como em 'garden', 'guilty', se pronúncia como o 'g' (+a, o, u) ou 'gu' (+e, i) portuguêses de 'gasto', 'guincho'.

Lição 4: /f/, /v/

Estas duas consoantes fricativas labio-dentais tem o mesmo valor nas duas línguas.

/f/ como em 'fast', 'effort', 'laugh' pronúncia-se como o /f/ português em 'feira', 'farofa'.

/v/ como em 'very', 'every', 'above', se pronúncia em todas as posições como a 'v' português de 'vila'.

Lição 5: /θ/, /ð/

Duas consonantes fricativas palato-alveolares que não existem em Português e cuja pronúncia tem de ser cuidadosamente praticada. Para pronunciar estas consoantes é preciso colocar a língua bem (mas ligeiramente) entre os dentes, com a ponta de fora, e expelir o ar entre a língua e os dentes (mas sem trocar a posição da língua durante a articulação.)

/θ/ como em 'thick'. 'thin', 'myth' pronúncia-se com muita aspiração (a prova do fósforo, de novo!) mas sem vibração das cordas vocais, enquanto—

/ð/ articula-se com vibração das cordas vocais. Em posição intervocálica o /ð/ (como em 'mother') será quase o mesmo do que o /d/ português na mesma posição: isto é, para practicar esta consoante em Inglês, ha de pronunciar uma palavra portuguesa como 'cada' com a língua entre os dentes para o /d/, e expelir o are com bastante vibração das cordas vocais.

Lição 6: /s/, /z/

Estas duas consoantes existem em Português com o mesmo valor.

/s/ como em 'Saturday' ou 'salt', equivale ao /s/ português em início de palavra (ortograficamente 's'—'sala', 'ss'—'assar', 'ç'—'açucar' ou 'c' + e/i—'cedo'. 'ciclo').

/z/ como em 'zoo' ou 'rose'. Equivale ao 'z' ortográfico português, ('zoológico', por example, ou ao 's' intervocálico ('rosa'), isto é, a articulação é a mesma do o /s/, mas com vibração das cordas vocais.

Lição 7: /ʃ/, /ʒ/

Estas consoantes palato-alveolares também tem equivalentes em Português.

/ʃ/ como em 'should'. Em Inglês esta consoante representa-se ortograficamente por 'sh', enquanto em Português por 'ch'. Porém, o som é o mesmo nas duas línguas. Português—'churrasco', 'chapeu', 'acho'. Inglês—'should', 'ashes', 'wish'.

/ʒ/ como em 'decision', 'garage', 'measure'. O som equivalente em Português é aquel representado por o 'j' ortogáfico de 'jarra' ou o 'g' de 'gelo'. Em geral o /ʒ/ inglês só encontra-se em palavras emprestadas originalmente da língua francesa. A articulação desta consoante é a mesma do que o /ʃ/, mas com vibração das cordas vocais.

Lição 8: /h/
Consoate fricativa glotal sorda. Não existe em Português como consoante independente, mas em Inglês o 'h' ortográfico indica geralmente que a vogal seguinte é pronunciada com aspiração anterior: isto é, é preciso expelir grande quantidade de ar (com a garganta muito aberta—como para um suspiro de cansaço) antes de pronunciar a vogal

Lições 9 e 10: /tʃ/, /dʒ/
Estas consoantes (africatas palato-alveolares) não existem independentemente em Português, ao menos no Português do Portugal. Porém, no Português do Brasil encontra-se o som equivalente.

/tʃ/ como em 'chair', 'merchant', 'each'. O 'ch' (ortográfico) do Português é diferente desta consoante inglesa, que se pronúncia como se houvesse um 't' muito rápido anterior ao 'ch'. No Português brasileiro, este som tem equivalente em palavras como 'tio', 'leite',—isto é, um som africato (um 't' rápido, e após um 'ch': /t/ + /ʃ/) sem vibração das cordas vocais. Existe também em Português a palavra infantil 'atchim!' (para espirro) onde ocorre esta africata, igual que na palavra inglesa 'atchoo!'

/dʒ/ como em 'jacket', 'magic', 'badge'. Este som é composto de um 'd' muito rápido seguido de um /ʒ/ como na palavra 'jarra'. O som vai acompanhado de vibração das cordas vocais. Em Português brasileiro este som tem equivalente em palavras como 'de' 'sede', 'faculdade'.

Lições 11, 12, 13: /m/, /n/, /ŋ/
Trata-se de três consoantes nasais que existem em Português com o mesmo valor.

/m/ como em 'make, 'hammer', 'am'. Consoante nasal-labiodental que se pronúncia exatamente como o 'm' português no início de palavra ou intervocálico: 'mapa', 'amar'. No entanto, o 'm' português quando precedido por uma vogal ou seguido por uma consoante ou quando em final de palavra nasaliza a vogal anterior, o que *não* acontece em Inglês, onde a vogal e o 'm' conservam os seus respetivos valores (isto é, os lábios devem fechar-se para pronunciar o 'm'). Pode comparar-se 'simples' em Português com 'simple' em Inglês, ou 'bem' com 'I'm' para notar esta diferença.

/n/ nasal alveolar. Em Português a articulação é geralmente dental, com a língua atrás dos dentes, enquanto em Inglês pronúncia-se com a língua a bater nos alvéolos (pode comparar-se neste sentido com o /t/ inglês, que também tem geralmente uma articulação alveolar). Como no caso do 'm', o elemento de nasalização da vogal anterior que se encontra em Português, *não* comparece em Inglês: compare 'tanto' em Português com 'tantrum' em Inglês.

/ŋ/ nasal velar. Como em 'sing', 'link', 'longer'. Pronúncia-se exatamente como o 'n' seguido de /k/ ou /g/ em Português, em palavras como 'cinco', 'longo', 'sangue'. Em Português, este som [ŋ] é alófono do fonema /n/ enquanto em Inglês é fonema, e por essa razão é muito importante distinguir o /n/ do /ŋ/. Compare-se 'sin' ([sɪn]) com 'sing' ([sɪŋ]).

Lição 14: /l/

Trata-se em Inglês de uma consoante lateral dental ou alveolar cujo valor em Português é, em geral, muito mais *escuro* ou recuado, particularmente em posição final de palavra. Em Inglês tem um som muito *claro* no princípio da sílaba (mais claro do que em Portuguêes, onde o 'l' sempre tem mais tensão muscular e mais retroflexão: compare-se 'letter' em Inglês com 'letra' em Português); e um som mais escuro (mas não tanto como em Português) quando precedido de vogal em final de sílaba, por exemplo em 'salt', 'sell'!

Em geral, o 'l' portugues é sempre mais escuro, particularmente quando precede consoantes e em posição final, onde as vezes se converte num som semelhante ao /ʊ/ ('Brasil', 'sal' = [bræ'ziʊ] ['saʊ]. Um som tão escuro não existe em Inglês (ao menos em Standard English) e há de evitarse. Para reduzir ao mínimo um acento português ao pronunciar este som em Inglês, particularmente em posição final, é importante manter contato entre a ponta da língua e os alvéolos. Além disso, sempre há menos tensão muscular da língua em Inglês do que em Português.

Lição 15: /r/

Como em 'really, 'arrive', 'every', 'car'. Em Português, há dos tipos de /r/: o de, por exemplo, 'carro' ou 'Rio', e o de 'caro'; o primeiro—o /r/ do início de palavra ou o /r/ duplo medial—articula-se ou como consoante dental 'vibrada' (come se fosse [rrrrrr]) ou como uma fricativa velar (esta última pronunciação sendo muito geral no Português do Brasil)—[x]; e o segundo com a língua batendo ligeiramente—e somente uma vez—nos alvéolos. Estas duas formas de articulação do /r/ português devem evitar-se sempre: para pronunciar o /r/ inglês a ponta da língua approxima-se muito dos alvéolos mas não chega a tocar neles, e os lados da língua tambén se elevam um pouco para tocar nos dentes laterais, e o ar passa então por cima da língua. Comparem-se: real (Inglês), real (Português); rest (Inglês), resto (Português).

E importante notar que o 'r' inglês no final de palavra ('car', 'rather', 'war') não se pronúncia, ao menos em muitas variedades do Inglês britânico, mas alonga-se a vogal anterior (isto é, 'car' = [kɑː]). Porém, em geral, no Inglês americano, esta 'r' final se articula fortemente da maneira acimamencionada.

Lições 16 e 17: /j/, /w/
Trata-se de duas semivogais que também existem em Português, com o mesmo valor.

/j/ como em 'you', 'yes', 'young' (ao início de palavra representada ortograficamente por a letra 'y' frequentemente); 'accuse'; 'suit' (['sjuːt] em Inglês britânico, mas ['suːt] em Inglês americano); beauty. Corresponde exatamente ao valor do 'i' intervocálico português em palavras como 'maio', 'génio', 'iodo'.

/w/ como em 'wood', 'wear', 'twelve', 'quick'. Corresponde exatamente ao valor do 'u' semivocálico em palavras portuguesas como 'tranquilo', 'sanguíneo' (Vale a pena de notar-se que as palavras inglesas iniciando-se com as letras 'wh—' se pronúnciam as vezes [hw—] em lugar de [w—]).

Vogais

Lição 18: /iː/
Como em 'leak', 'cheese', 'be', 'these', 'piece', 'peace'. Corresponde aproximadamente ao 'i' acentuado em Português em palavras como 'filho', 'tio', isso é, é uma vogal dianteira muito fechada e articulada com os lábios muito extendidos (como se fosse um sorriso!). Contudo, o /iː/ inglês articula-se com maior duração do que o /iː/ português, e além disso esta vogal é um pouco menos fechada do que a portuguesa. Um detalhe muito importante: se corta-se a duração da vogal em Inglês, o ouvinte ouve um [ɪ] em vez do [iː]—isso é, uma palavra como 'beat' (['biːt]) percebe-se como 'bit' (['bɪt]).

Lição 19: /ɪ/
Como em 'little', 'big' (acentuado); 'city' 'whisky' (sem acentuação). Corresponde ao /ɪ/ não acentuado em Português, em palavras como 'leite', 'frente'. Em Inglês, o /ɪ/ pode ser ou acentuado ou átono, enquanto em Português é sempre átono. Átono e em final de palavra, a

articulação é sempre mais forte em Inglês do que em Português, onde o /ɪ/ quase desaparece: compare-se 'whisky' em Inglês (['wɪskɪ]) com a mesma palavra em Português (['wiːsk(ɪ)])—ao pronunciar a palavra à maneira portuguesa obter-se-á um som semelhante a 'whisk' em Inglês.

Lição 21: /e/
Como em 'better', 'bed'. Enquanto a língua portuguesa tem um /e/ muito fechado ('vermelho') e um /ɛ/ muito aberto ('amarelo', 'pé'), o Inglês só tem um /e/ situado entre as duas formas portuguesas, mas aproximando-se mais à versão aberta. O /e/ inglês também é bastante mais corto do que o /e/ ou o /ɛ/ portugueses.

Lição 22: /æ/
Como em 'back', 'can', 'have'. Não existe vogal correspondente em Português. Há que pronunciar um som intermédio entre o /e/ aberto de 'pé' e o /a/ também muito aberto de 'pá', mas com muito mais tensão muscular da garganta, com os lados da língua batendo ligeiramente nos dentes laterais superiores, e com os lábios bem extendidos. O que tem que resultar, ao menos em sua forma exagerada, é um som bastante *estrangulado*, no qual se nota muita tensão faríngea.

Lição 23: /ʌ/
Como em 'buck', 'hut', 'bud'. Esta vogel tambén não tem correspondente em Português. Aproxima-se ao /a/ de 'cá', embora é um pouco mais céntrico em Inglês. Articula-se com menos tensão muscular do que o /æ/ da lição anterior.

Lição 25: /ɑː/
Como em 'aunt', 'can't'. Esta vogal corresponde aproximadamente ao 'a' longo e aberto que encontra-se em palavras como 'mar' ou 'tirar'. E uma vogal muito aberta mas traseira, com a língua bastante retirada na boca.

Lições 26 e 27: /ɒ/, /ɔː/
/ɒ/ como em 'off', 'cough'. Esta vogal equivale aproximadamente ao 'o' aberto português em palavras como 'pote', 'avó', 'só', mas realmente a sua articulação é a de uma /aː/ com os lábios bastante mais redondos.

/ɔː/ como em 'port', 'caught', 'or'. Em Português existe um 'o' aberto, /ɔ/, em palavras como 'avó', e um 'o' fechado, /o/, como em 'avô'. O som inglês se situa entre as duas variedades portuguesas, aproximando-se mais do /o/ fechado, mas articulado de uma maneira muito mais longa (como se pronunciasse-se 'avô' como 'avôôô').

Lições 28 e 29: /ʊ/, /uː/

/ʊ/ como em 'look', 'put'. Esta vogal corresponde em forma traseira ao /ɪ/ dianteiro da lição 19. Isso é, trata-se de um 'u' breve, tónico, cujo som correspondente português é átono é encontra-se em palavras como 'lutar' ou 'morder'. Porém, como no caso do /ɪ/ inglês, a pronunciação do /ʊ/ em Ingles é sempre mais forte ou acentuada do que em Português.

/uː/ como em 'food', 'group', 'rude', 'juice'. Esta vogal corresponde em forma traseira ao /iː/ dianteiro da lição 18. Trata-se de um 'u' um pouco menos fechado do que o 'u' acentuado em palavras portuguesas como 'murmúrio' ou 'cru', mas de maior duração na articulação, e com os lábios ligeiramente arredondadas (embora um pouco menos do que em Português).

Lições 31 e 32: /ɜː/, /ə/

/ɜː/ como em 'girl', 'heard', 'burn'. Trata-se de uma vogal tônica, muito céntrica, com a língua em posição *neutra* (isto é, nem alta nem baixa). Aproxima-se ao 'a' português de 'cano' ou 'vamos', mas sem nasalização.

/ə/ como em 'the', 'a', 'other'. Trata-se de uma vogal *sempre átona* semlhante em Inglês ao /ɜː/ tónico acimamencionado, articulado de uma maneira muito reduzido ou fraco. Assemelha-se ao 'e' átono português em palavras como 'rude' ou 'padre' (embora o 'e' átono destas palavras inclinam-se geralmente à pronunciação de [ɪ], particularmente no Português do Brasil). Em Inglês, é preciso exagerar um pouco a sua pronúncia comparado com o Português, porque nesta língua há tendencia para *engolir* este som.

Ditongos

Lição 33: /eɪ/

Como em 'they'. 'weigh', 'hate'. Este ditongo existe em Português em palavras como 'deixar', 'lei'.

Em Inglês este ditongo pronúncia-se como emissão de um 'e' meio-fechado e de um 'i', e com o primeiro elemento mais acentuado do que o segundo.

Lição 34: /aɪ/

Como em 'die', 'buy', 'bright'. Este ditongo tem correspondente exato em palavras portuguesas como 'pai', 'gaita', 'paisagem'.

Lição 35: /ɔɪ/

Como em 'oil', 'boy'. Este ditongo tem correspondente exato em Português em palavras como 'comboio', ou 'dezoito'.

Lição 37: /əʊ/
Como em 'though', 'so'. Este ditongo não tem correspondente em Português. No entanto a pronúncia de 'ao' e 'au' em sílabas não acentuadas, com o primeiro elemento muito central e neutro ([ə]), em palavras como 'ao pé', 'causou' ([əʊ'pɛ], [kəʊ'zoʊ]) é muito semelhante à do ditongo inglês.

Lição 38: /ɑʊ/
Como em 'how', 'bough'. Este ditongo tem correspondente exato em Português, em sílabas acentuadas, em palavras como 'mau', 'carapau'.

Lição 39: /ɪə/
Como em 'hear', 'here', 'beer'. Este ditongo assemelha-sa ao ditongo português 'ia' em palavras como 'mania', 'permitia'. Não entanto, é preciso notar que o elmento final deste ditongo em Português é um pouco mais longo que o do ditongo inglês, onde o *schwa* final é muito fraco.

Lição 40: /ɛə/
Como em 'hair', 'bare', 'there'. Este ditongo inglês nao tem correspondente exato em Português, mas encontra-se um som semelhante no nome próprio de origem estrangeira 'Léa', mas começando com um 'e' relativamente aberto ([ɛ]).

Lição 41: /ʊə/
Como em 'poor', 'sure'. O ditongo português que mais se aproxima deste ditongo em Inglês aparece em palavras portuguesas como 'lua' ou 'tua'. Porém, é preciso notar que en Inglês o *schwa* final é mais breve e mais fraco do que o elemento final em Português.

Spanish Notes

by Roger Jones

Consonantes

Lección 1: /p/, /b/

/p/ una consonante bilabial, oclusiva, sorda, muy parecida en su manera de articulación a la /p/ castellana, pero con la diferencia de que en inglés cuando está en posición inicial de palabra, por ejemplo en 'pot', se articula acompañada por una ligera *explosión* de aire (= aspiración). Para lograr este efecto, téngase una cerilla encendida cerca de la boca y al articular la 'p' con aspiración se notará que la llama se vacila o se apaga del todo.

En cualquier otra posición, e inclusive en el grupo consonantal inicial 'sp-', la aspiración no ocurre.

En posición final de palabra la /p/ se articula de una manera bastante floja, aunque no tan floja como en castellano, donde el hablante pone sus labios en posición para articular el sonido, pero resulta que éste no se suelta. Téngase en cuenta que el fenómeno de la aspiración también se encuentra en el caso de la /t/ y de la /k/, en posición inicial; y que lo que se ha dicho sobre la articulación de la /p/ en posición final es aplicable a las demás consonantes oclusivas, sordas y sonoras.

/b/ oclusiva, bilabial, sonora. La /b/ inglesa se pronuncia como la /b/ castellana en palabras como 'bomba', 'boda', 'ambos', 'enviar', o sea, como consonante oclusiva y no fricativa. Hay que evitar la articulación de la fricativa bilabial [β] la cual se representa también por la letra 'b' o por la 'v'—este último sonido realmente no figura en la fonología inglesa.

Lección 2: /t/, /d/

Estas dos consonantes oclusivas (la /t/ sorda, la /d/ sonora) tienen una articulación dental en castellano, con la punta de la lengua apoyada contra los incisivos superiores. En cambio la /t/ y la /d/ inglesas no son dentales sino alveolares y se articulan con la punta de la lengua apoyada más bien contra los alvéolos.

En el caso de la /t/, hay aspiración en posición inicial (véase la nota sobre la lección 1).

En el caso de la /d/, hay que tener cuidado de no pronunciarla en inglés con el valor que tiene en castellano en palabras como 'lado', 'adscrito', 'cada' en las cuales la /d/ se realiza alofónicamente en forma de una dental fricativa ([ð]).

Lección 3: /k/, /g/

/k/ velar, oclusiva, sorda, y teniéndo prácticamente el mismo valor que la /k/ castellana.

/g/ velar, oclusiva, sonora. La /g/ inglesa tiene el mismo valor que la /g/ castellana en palabras como 'gloria', 'rango', 'gobierno'. Sin embargo la /g/ castellana frecuentemente se realiza como velar fricativa ([ɣ]) sonora—en palabras como 'agua', 'lago', 'agosto', por ejemplo—y este alófono del fonema /g/ no se encuentra en inglés.

Lección 4: /f/, /v/

/f/ labiodental, fricativa, sorda. Esta consonante tiene el mismo valor en los dos idiomas.

/v/ labiodental, fricativa, sonora. Esta consonante se parece en inglés a la anterior /f/, salvo que la /v/ es sonora.

En castellano, la 'v' ortográfica pertenece al fonema /b/, y como tal se realiza fonéticamente como una oclusiva bilabial sonora ([b]) o como una fricativa bilabial sonora ([β]). Ninguna de estas dos realizaciones corresponde a la 'v' inglesa, la cual siempre se articula con los incisivos superiores en muy ligero contacto con la parte interior del labio inferior, y con vibración de las cuerdas vocales.

Lección 5: /θ/, /ð/

/θ/ interdental, fricativa, sorda. En su punto de articulación se aproxima a la del fonema /d/ castellano en palabras como 'escudo', 'madera'. Sin embargo, la articulación de la /θ/ inglesa es más interdental. La mayoría de hispanohablantes españoles no tendrán el menor problema con este sonido, como corresponde exactamente a la 'zeta' ([θ]) ibérica en palabras como 'cinco' (['θiːŋko]). Para los demás hispanohablantes cuya variedad de castellano no tiene este sonido, basta o con imitar el modelo ibérico o con hacer la tentativa del punto de vista inglés, sacando la punta de la lengua entre los dientes superiores e inferiores.

/ð/ interdental, fricativa, sonora. Esta consonante se parece en inglés a la anterior /θ/, salvo que la /ð/ es sonora. Se aproxima al valor del alófono [ð] del fonema /d/ en palabras castellanas como 'madera', 'adquirir', 'perdón' (véase lección 2), pero la articulación es más interdental, y el sonido se emite con más fuerza.

Lección 6: /s/, /z/

/s/ alveolar, fricativa, sorda. La /s/ inglesa en todas sus posiciones se parece en su manera y punto de articulación a la /s/ inicial de hispanohablantes latinoamericanos (el mejor modelo para comparación quizá sea el argentino o el uruguayo). En España la /s/—sobre todo la /s/ inicial—tiene una cualidad apico-alveolar (o sea, cierto elemento de retroflexión y de tensión muscular) que casi la convierte en [ʃ] (por lo menos para el anglófono nativo), y este tipo de articulación tiene que evitarse lo más posible.

En ciertas regiones de España y en la mayor parte de América Latina hispanohablante la /s/ en posición final de palabra se realiza como una fricativa laríngea ([h])—en 'las madres', por ejemplo—y es muy importante tratar de evitar tal articulación y conformarse con la pronunciación correcta sobredicha.

En castellano la /s/ nunca se encuentra en posición inicial seguida por otra consonante y sólo se encuentra en grupo consonántico precedida por /e/ en palabras como 'escuela', 'eslavo', 'esmero', 'esnob', 'España'. Por eso, al pronunciar palabras inglesas que empiezan por /s/ seguida de consonante—por ejemplo, palabras como 'school', 'Slav', 'smear', 'snob', 'Spain', el hispanohablante debe prestar mucha atención para no pronunciar la /s/ con una /e/ antepuesta, pronunciando la palabra 'station' erróneamente como *[eˈsteiʃən].

/z/ alveolar, fricativa, sonora. Esta consonante se parece en su articulación a la anterior /s/, pero esta vez se trata de una consonante sonora. Aparece esporádicamente en castellano como alófono del fonema /s/ en palabras como 'mismo', 'asno', 'esbelto', donde el fonema /s/ se realiza como [z] al preceder otra consonante sonora. Sin embargo, en inglés la diferencia entre la /s/ y la /z/ es fonémica y por eso es de suma importancia distinguir los dos sonidos. Compárese, por ejemplo, 'precedent' [s], con 'president' [z].

Lección 7: /ʃ/, /ʒ/

/ʃ/ palato-alveolar, fricativa, sorda. Esta consonante inglesa no tiene equivalente exacto en castellano. Su punto de articulación es esencialmente el mismo del de la /tʃ/ castellana en 'chorizo', siendo parecida su manera de articulación. La diferencia esencial está en que en vez de ser una africada breve como la /tʃ/ castellana es una consonante fricativa articulada en inglés de un manera más prolongada y más violenta.

/ʒ/ palato-alveolar, fricativa, sonora. Corresponde a la anterior /ʃ/ pero la /ʒ/ es sonora. En general, sólo se encuentra en ciertas palabras prestadas del francés, por ejemplo 'beige, 'azure', 'leisure'. Es precisamente el sonido que se encuentra en el pronombre francés 'je' ('yo'). Aunque este sonido no existe en el castellano ibérico, se encuentra corrientemente en la pronunciación latinoamericana de la 'll' ortográfica, en posición inicial y medial, en palabras como 'llegar', 'calle' ([ʒe'gar], ['kaʒe]), y este es el modelo exacto que hay que imitar para lograr lo que se oye en inglés.

Lección 8: /h/
Se trata de una consonante laríngea, ligeramente fricativa, sorda, que se emite con una aspiración considerable. Esta consonante inglesa no tiene equivalente en castellano, salvo en el caso de la realización del fonema /s/ en posición final de palabra como [h]—alófono que se encuentra corrientemente en algunas regiones de España (señaladamente en Andalucía y Extremadura) y aún más extensamente en América Latina hispanohablante, en palabras como 'las madres' por ejemplo, donde la 's' final se realiza como dicha [h].
Hay que tener mucho cuidado de no sustituir la fricativa velar castellana /x/ (como en la palabra 'José'), por la /h/ inicial inglesa.

Lección 9: /tʃ/
Esta consonante es una africada palato-alveolar sorda. Corresponde esencialmente a la 'ch' ortográfica en castellano en palabras como 'chico', 'macho', o sea, tiene aproximadament el mismo valor en los dos idiomas. Sin embargo en inglés, el lugar de articulación es bastante más anteriór.

Lección 10: /dʒ/
Se parece a la anterior /tʃ/ en su punto y manera de articulación, la única diferencia siendo que la /dʒ/ es sonora. Se encuentra en palabras como 'just' y 'hedge'. Hay que tener mucho cuidado para no pronunciar esta africada, sobre todo en posición inicial de palabra, como si fuese una fricativa palatal sonora /ɟ/, la cual se encuentra a menudo en castellano en posición inicial en palabras como 'hielo', 'yerno', 'hierro' (['ɟɛlo], ['ɟɛrno], ['ɟɛrro]).

Lección 11: /m/
Consonante bilabial nasal, con la misma manera y el mismo punto de articulación en inglés y en castellano.

Lección 12: /n/
Consonante nasal alveolar que tiene el mismo valor en inglés y en castellano.

Lección 13: /ŋ/
Consonante nasal velar. Se encuentra en palabras como 'wrong', 'sing', 'single', 'ankle'. Esta consonante existe en castellano, como alófono del fonema /n/, ante las consonantes velares, como por ejemplo en las palabras 'banco', 'cinco', fingir'; y también en habla popular, en

posición final, en palabras como 'pan' (['paŋ]). Sin embargo, en inglés la /ŋ/ no sólo se encuentra ante consonante velar, como en 'single', sino también entre vocales (en 'singer', por ejemplo) y en posición final de palabra como por ejemplo en 'singing' (['sɪŋɪŋ]).

La /ŋ/ existe en inglés como fonema distinto de la /n/, y por eso el hispanohablante debe tener mucho cuidado de no sustituir /n/ por /ŋ/, o vice-versa, para evitar cualquier confusión posible de sentido: 'singer', por ejemplo (['sɪŋə]) = 'cantante', mientras 'sinner'(['sɪnə]) = 'pecador'!

Lección 14: /l/

Consonante lateral. En términos generales la /l/ inglesa corresponde en su pronunciación a la /l/ castellana. Sin embargo se diferencian en que mientras en los dos idiomas en posición inicial o medial de palabra se articula de una manera *clara* (the *clear* /l/), en posición final de sílaba o palabra en inglés la /l/ suele tomar un matiz velar, con más tensión muscular y con la raiz de la lengua retirada hacia atrás y hacia abajo (the *dark* /l/). Este alófono *oscuro*—que se nota aún más señaladamente en inglés americano—no tiene forma correspondiente en castellano, salvo que se nota en España en la /l/ final de los Catalanes hispanoparlantes.

Lección 15: /r/

Continuant, o continuante sin fricción, sonora. Este sonido no tiene ni equivalente ni aproximación en castellano. La /r/ castellana tiene dos realizaciones principales: la vibrante alveolar multiple, representada ortográficamente por 'r' en posición inicial de palabra y por 'rr' en posición medial; y la vibrante simple (una breve oclusión del ápice de la lengua contra los alvéolos), representada ortográficamente por 'r' en posición medial o final. En contraste, la /r/ inglesa es una consonante *continuante* sonora que se articula elevando la punta de la lengua hasta muy cerca de los alvéolos; los bordes de la lengua también se elevan, tocando ligeramente los molares superiores posteriores. De este modo, la lengua toma la forma de un plato pequeño formado por la punta de la lengua y los bordes. El aire pasa por encima de la lengua y es canalizado por el *pequeño plato* con una obstrucción mínima antes de salir de la cavidad bucal. Advertencia: Hay que tener cuidado de no sustituir la /r/ castellana, sobre todo la [rr] vibrante múltiple, por la /r/ inglesa.

Lección 16: /j/

Semi-vocal. Tiene su equivalente en castellano en palabras como 'nieto', 'tierno', 'piedra'. En inglés este sonido se representa frecuentemente por la 'y' ortográfica ('yes', 'yellow', 'youth, etc.).

Las semi-vocales españolas tienen un grado de cerrazón que a menudo lleva a una realización fricativa de este sonido: en castellano, palabras como 'hierro', 'ayer', 'mayo' a menudo van acompañadas de cierto elemento de fricción (['ʝɛrro], ['aʝɛr], ['maʝo]) y si esta fricción se transfiere a la semi-vocal inglesa, resultará una pronunciación inaceptable ('youth' saldrá como *[ʝu:θ], por ejemplo, en vez de la forma correcta [ju:θ]).

Lección 17: /w/
Semi-vocal, frecuentemente representada ortográficamente por 'wh-'. Este sonido tiene equivalente en castellano en palabras como 'puerta', 'cuatro', 'huevo'. Hay que evitar de pronunciar la /w/ inglesa reforzándola con una /g/ labializada o una /b/ velarizada, como ocurre a veces en castellano (pronunciando 'hueso', por ejemplo, como ['gweso] o ['bweso]). Pronunciar la palabra inglesa 'woman' como *['gwʊmən] en vez de su forma correcta (['wʊmən]) es completamente inaceptable.

Vocales

Lección 18: /i:/
Esta vocal corresponde bastante a la /i:/ castellana, pero se nota que en inglés la vocal es un poco menos cerrada y menos tensa que la castellana, y—sobre todo—que tiene una duración más larga. Si se pronuncia, por ejemplo, una palabra como 'beat' (/bi:t/) dándole a la vocal un valor castellano, se oirá más bien *['bit] o inclusive *['bɪt]. Por eso, es de suma importancia notar que la /i:/ inglesa no sólo es menos cerrada comparada con la equivalente castellana, sino que también la duración es más prolongada.

Lección 19: /ɪ/
Esta vocal no tiene equivalente exacta en castellano. Se trata de una vocal más abierta y más corta que la /i:/, aunque hay que tener en cuenta que una /ɪ/ seguida por una consonante sonora será más larga que una /i:/ seguida por una consonante sorda (o sea, la 'i' [ɪ] de 'bid' se alarga más que la 'ea' [i:] de 'beat', por ejemplo).

En castellano, la /ɪ/ se encuentra de modo intermitente (y como alófono) en habla rápida, en palabras como 'rico' (['rrɪko]), 'hijo' (['ɪxo]), donde el fonema /i:/ se manifiesta en forma alofónica con la lengua un poco más retractada.

Lección 21: /e/
La /e/ castellana se encuentra en casi todas sus realizaciones entre la vocal cardinal 2 /e/ y la cardinal 3 /ɛ/ pero con una tendencia hacia

aquélla. Lo contrario ocurre en el caso de la /e/ inglesa. Sin embargo, en castellano la /e/ tiene una realización más abierta en palabras como 'perro', 'guerra' ([ɛ] y es ésa la que corresponde más bien a la /e/ inglesa.

Lección 22: /æ/
Como en 'back', 'can', 'have'. No existe equivalente en castellano. Hay que realizar un sonido intermedio entre la /e/ relativamente abierta ([ɛ]) de 'perro' y la /a/ también muy abierta de 'casa', pero con bastante más fuerza laríngea y con los lados de la lengua en contacto muy ligero con los molares superiores, y con los labios muy extendidas. Lo que tiene que resultar, si se realiza bien, es un sonido algo *estrangulado* (por lo menos en su forma más exagerada), en que se registra bastante tensión muscular en la garganta.

Lección 23: /ʌ/
Como en 'buck', 'hut', 'bud'. Esta vocal tampoco tiene equivalente en castellano, pero se aproxima a la /a/ de palabras como 'mal' o 'prado', pero con una duración bastante más corta en inglés y también con un punto de articulación más céntrica. Se articula con bastante menos tensión laríngea que la /æ/ de la lección anterior.

Lección 25: /ɑː/
Esta vocal posterior abierta es de duración larga, con la lengua bastante retractada. Su valor se aproxima a la pronunciación de 'madre' como 'maaadre', por ejemplo, y también se parece al sonido 'aaaaah—' que emite un enfermo cuando un médico le está examinando el interior de la boca con un palito presionado contra la parte superior de la lengua.

Lección 26: /ɒ/
Esta vocal inglesa es realmente una /aː/ de la lección anterior, realizada con los labios bien redondos. Per también se puede afirmar que se aproxima a la 'o' castellana en palabras como 'dogma', 'dote', 'arroz', pero pronunciada en inglés con la boca un poco más abierta y con la lengua menos elevada y más posterior que en castellano.

Lección 27: /ɔː/
Vocal de larga duración que se aproxima a la del las palabras castellanas 'hora', 'amor'. Se encuentra en inglés con varias representaciones ortográficas, en palabras como 'bought', 'taught', 'taut', 'sort', 'awful'.

Lección 28: /ʊ/
Como vocal posterior, ésta tiene algunos rasgos en común con su equivalente anterior, la /ɪ/ de la lección 2. Es un fonema distino e independiente de la /uː/ (véase la lección 12), y como tal tiene que distinguirse de ella, como también fúe el caso de la /iː/ y la /ɪ/. Se pronuncia con menos duración que la /uː/, con la lengua menos elevada, y con menos tensión muscular. No existe como fonema independiente en castellano, pero sí se encuentra como alófono del fonema /uː/ en palabras como 'turrón', 'junto', 'condujo', 'mundo' ([tʊ'rrɔn], ['xʊnto], [kɔn'dʊxo], ['mʊndo]).

Lección 29: /uː/
Así como la /iː/ inglesa tiene ciertas características en común con la /iː/ castellana, sin que estos fonemas sean totalmente iguales en los dos idiomas, se puede decir que la /uː/ inglesa y la /uː/ castellana también comparten rasgos similares. En inglés la /uː/ se pronuncia de una manera menos cerrada que la castellana, con menos tensión muscular (aunque no carece del todo de esta característica) y con una duración más alargada. (Tiene esto en común con la /iː/ inglesa, y si no se permite suficiente duración es muy posible que el oyente perciba una /ʊ/ en vez de una /uː/).

Lecciones 31 y 32: /ɜː/, /ə/
/ɜː/ como en 'bird', 'hurt', 'pearl', es una vocal céntrica que no tiene equivalente en castellano. Se pronuncia con la lengua en posición *neutra* en la boca, o sea, ni elevada ni rebajada, y más o menos plana.
/ə/ tampoco tiene equivalente en castellano. Su punto y manera de articulación es esencialmente el mismo que para la /ɜː/, aunque un poquito más abierto a menudo. Hay que tener en cuenta que ésta es siempre una vocal *inacentuada* o *átona*. Se encuentra en palabras como 'the', 'father', 'picture'.

Diptongos

Lección 33: /eɪ/
Como en 'they', 'weigh', 'hate'. Este diptongo tiene un valor parecido al diptongo 'ei' en palabras com 'peine', 'reino', 'Teide'.

Lección 34: /aɪ/
Como en 'die', 'buy', 'bright'. Este diptongo corresponde al diptongo 'ai' en palabras castellanas como 'baile', 'gaita', 'fraile'.

Lección 35: /ɔɪ/
Como en 'oil', 'boy'. Este diptongo es de valor semejante al diptongo castellano en palabras como 'hoy', 'doy'.

Lección 37: /əʊ/
Como en 'though', 'so'. Como este diptongo no existe en castellano, y los valores de las vocales individuales tampoco, este sonido puede causar problemas para los hispanohablantes. Véase primero las lecciones 32 y 28 de las sección de vocales, para fijarse bien en la articulación de los dos elementos. Le lengua tiene que empezar relativamente alta en la parte central de la boca, para pronunciar la /ə/, y con los labios entreabiertos; a continuación, los labios se cierran un poco mas, en posicion redonda, para articular la /ʊ/. El elemento acentuado es el primero.

Lección 38: /ɑʊ/
Como en 'how', 'bough', 'house'. Este diptongo se pronuncia como el de las palabras castellanas 'causa', 'jaula', o el nombre feminino 'Laura'.

Lección 39: /ɪə/
Este diptongo no tiene correspondiente en castellano. Véanse los capítulos 19 y 32 de la sección de vocales, para la articulación en inglés de los elementos individuales de este diptongo. Hay que tener en cuenta que el elemento más acentuado del diptongo es el primero (o sea, la /ɪ/), y que la schwa se pronuncia, como siempre, de una manera muy floja. El diptongo se aproxima *algo* al sonido final de palabras como 'permitia', pero el /ə/ se pronunica en inglés con la boca mucho menos abierta y mas relajada o *floja* que para la 'a' castellana.
El diptongo aparece en palabras como 'fear', 'here', 'beer'.

Lección 40: /ɛə/
Como en 'pear', 'fairly'. No tieno equivalente en castellano. Se aproxima algo al sonido de las vocales de 'vea' o 'lea', pero—igual que con los diptongos /ɪə/ y /ʊə/— no hay que olvidarse de que el /ə/ ingles es mucho menos abierto y *neutro* (central) que la 'a' castellana; y también hay que pronunciar las dos vocales como un diptongo—una sola emisión de voz—y no como dos vocales individuales.

Lección 41: /ʊə/
Como en 'poor', 'sure'. Las dos vocales finales de las palabras castellanas 'falúa' y 'charrúa' se aproximan a este diptongo inglés, pero una vez más la Schwa final en inglés es mucho menos abierta, mas central y mas *floja* que la 'a' final castellana. Igual que en el caso de los diptongos /ɪə/ y /ɛə/, el elemento acentuado es el primero.

French Notes

by Che Viccars

Consonnes

Leçons 1–3: /p/ /b/, /t/ /d/, /k/ /g/
Le français, tout comme l'anglais, possède trois paires de consonnes explosives: /p/, /b/, (consonnes labiales—leçon 1); /t/, /d/ (consonnes alvéolaires—leçon 2); et /k/, /g/ (consonnes palatales-vélaires—leçon 3). /p/, /t/, /k/ sont des consonnes sourdes, i.e. prononcées sans vibration des cordes vocales (voiceless). /b/, /d/, /g/ sont des consonnes sonores; i.e. les cordes vocales sont mises en vibration (voiced). (Voir Introduction p. 2).

Cependant les consonnes explosives de l'anglais sont presque toujours accompagnées d'un souffle d'air plus ou moins fort (explosion ou aspiration). Prononcez, devant une allumette ou la flamme d'une bougie, le mot français 'pour'. La flamme reste presque immobile. Maintenant prononcez le mot anglais 'pond'. Si la flamme vacille, vous avez bien prononcé la consonne anglaise /p/. On voit cette même différence d'aspiration, à un moindre degré, entre le mot français 'cave' et le mot anglais 'cave'. N'oubliez jamais l'aspiration qui distingue les consonnes anglaises des consonnes françaises.

Pour les consonnes explosives /t/, /d/, la différence entre l'anglais et le français réside non seulement dans le degré de l'aspiration, mais aussi dans la position de la langue. En français, on appuie la pointe de la langue contre les dents supérieures, tandis qu'en anglais, il faut appuyer la pointe de la langue contre les gencives d'en haut.

Leçons 4–8: /f/ /v/, /θ/ /ð/, /s/ /z/, /ʃ/ /ʒ/, /h/
La prononciation des consonnes explosives nécessite la fermeture de la bouche, ou plus precisément du canal buccal, soit par les lèvres, soit par la langue. Quand le souffle n'est pas tout à fait interrompu, et qu'il se produit une impression de frottement, la consonne est dite *fricative*. Le français a trois paires de consonnes fricatives: /f/, /v/, consonnes labio-dentales (leçon 4); /s/, /z/, consonnes alvéolaires (leçon 6), et /ʃ/, /ʒ/, consonnes palatales (leçon 7). /f/, /s/, /ʃ/ sont des consonnes sourdes. /v/, /z/, /ʒ/ sont des consonnes sonores. Ces trois paires de consonnes se trouvent aussi en anglais, et sont prononcées comme en français.

Notez, cependant, que le son /ʒ/ n'est trouvé qu'entre deux voyelles en anglais, dans des mots tels que 'measure', 'leisure', (La lettre 'j' représente en anglais un autre son /dʒ/—voir leçon 10).

A ces six consonnes communes aux deux langues s'ajoutent en anglais la paire /θ/, /ð/ (leçon 5) et /h/, sons qui n'existent pas en français.

Pour prononcer /θ/ (consonne sourde) ou /ð/ (consonne sonore), regardez bien le schéma à la page 27. Imaginez alors que vous tirez la langue à quelqu'un, puis soufflez. Evitez surtout de prononcer /s/ ou /z/ au lieu de /θ/ ou /ð/.

En général, la lettre 'h' n'a plus aucune valeur phonétique en français; c'est-à-dire qu'elle ne représente aucun son. Si le 'h' dit aspiré ne change jamais la prononciation d'un mot, mais empêche toute liaison ou toute élision ('le héros', 'une honte'), le 'h' anglais est en réalite *aspiré*, n'étant en effet qu'une expiration d'air, comme un soupir ou l'halètement de quelqu'un qui est essoufflé. Il est très important de ne pas omettre de prononcer cette consonne.

Leçons 9 et 10: /tʃ/, /dʒ/

Les consonnes affriquées /tʃ/, consonne sourde (leçon 9) et /dʒ/, consonne sonore (leçon 10), sont en effet des phonèmes doubles, très rares en français. On trouve des exemples de /tʃ/ dans des mots d'origine étrangère tels que 'chulo', 'chistera', 'caoutchouc', 'match', 'catch'. On trouve /dʒ/ dans 'Cambodge', 'djellaba', 'djinn', 'jazz'.

N.B. La lettre 'j' se prononce uniformément /dʒ/ en anglais.

Leçons 11–13: /m/, /n/, /ŋ/

Le français, comme l'anglais, a trois consonnes nasales. Les deux langues partagent les consonnes /m/ (labiale) et /n/ (linguale), mais tandis que le français possède une consonne palatale /ɲ/ ('ignore', 'signe') l'anglais possède une consonne vélaire /ŋ/ ('sing', 'rang'). Ce son n'existe pas en français sauf dans des mots empruntés à l'anglais, tels que 'le smoking', 'le parking', 'le pressing'. Il se rapproche très approximativement à une voyelle nasale suivie dans certains mots de /g/, par example, dans 'dingue', 'en garde', 'une longue main'. Il y a certains mots en anglais dans lesquels le 'g' est prononcé ('finger', 'ingot'); tandis que dans beaucoup d'autres, le 'g' est muet ('singer', 'flinging').

Leçons 14 et 15: /l/, /r/

Il y a deux consonnes liquides en français; /l/, consonne latérale, et /r/, consonne roulée.

/l/ Pour prononcer le /l/, la pointe de la langue touche les alvéoles des dents supérieures ('lit', 'mal', 'couleur'). Le /l/ anglais en position initiale (*clear* l) est articulé de cette manière, mais avec la langue un peu plus en arrière. A la fin d'une syllabe, cependant, le /l/ anglais change de qualité, devenant plus vélaire (*dark* l). Cette consonne latérale vélaire n'existe pas en français standard. De plus, il y a des différences sensibles d'articulation parmi les anglophones. Imitez alors la prononciation de ceux autour de vous.

/r/ La consonne palatale vélaire /r/, appelée dorsale ou *parisienne*, s'oppose en français à la consonne roulée dite *apicale* et plus courante en province. Le /r/ anglais est aussi prononcé différemment selon le pays ou la région d'origine du locuteur. Il n'y a pas d'équivalent en français.

Leçons 16 et 17: /j/, /w/

Il y a deux semi-consonnes (ou semi-voyelles) en anglais, /j/ et /w/. Elles sont prononcées exactement comme les semi-consonnes françaises /j/, consonne fricative palatale (le yod), et /w/, consonne latérale postérieure.

Le /j/ se trouve en français dans des mots tels que 'yacht', 'nièce', 'moyen', 'grenouille'.

Le /w/ se trouve en français dans des mots tels que 'oui', 'fouet', 'soir', 'ouest'. Notez qu'en anglais des mots qui commencent par les lettres 'wh' sont parfois prononcés /hw/ au lieu de /w/.

Voyelles

Leçons 18–20: /iː/, /ɪ/

En français il y a une voyelle /i/ ('si', 'style'), antérieure et fermée (la langue est avancée et se rapproche du palais pour que le passage de l'air expiré soit étroit). En anglais il y a deux voyelles antérieures: /iː/ ('seat'), fermée et longue, et /ɪ/ ('sit'), un peu moins fermée que /iː/ et brève. Le /i/ français se situe entre les deux voyelles anglaises. La position de la langue pour le /iː/ anglais long, prononcé les lèvres écartées, est plus avancée que pour le /i/ français; pour le /ɪ/ anglais bref, elle est moins avancée.

Leçon 21: /e/

L'anglais n'a qu'une voyelle /e/ ('let'), antérieure, moins fermée que /ɪ/. Le français a deux voyelles qui y ressemblent: le /e/ fermée de 'les', 'thé', 'j'ai', et le /ɛ/ ouvert de 'pêche', 'terre', 'j'aime'. Le /e/ anglais se situe entre les deux voyelles françaises, se rapprochant de la voyelle ouverte /ɛ/, sauf qu'il est plus bref, et qu'il faut le prononcer les lèvres écartées.

Leçons 22 et 23: /æ/, /ʌ/

/æ/ La voyelle anglaise /æ/ ('cat'), brève, antérieure et ouverte (la langue est moins avancée pour que le passage de l'air expiré soit plus ouvert) ressemble aussi à la voyelle française /ɛ/, mais la bouche est un peu plus ouverte.

/ʌ/ Le /ʌ/ anglais ('cut', 'pup'), antérieur, plus ouvert que /æ/ ressemble de près à la voyelle français /a/ de 'pape', 'arabe', sauf que la bouche s'ouvre un peu moins pour la voyelle anglaise, qui est aussi plus brève.

Leçon 25: /ɑː/
Le /ɑː/ anglais, postérieur (la langue est reculée) et ouvert, est plus long que /ʌ/ (distinguez entre 'part' et 'putt'). Il ressemble beaucoup à la voyelle française /a/ ('patte'), mais allongée. La voyelle française /ɑ/ ('pâte') n'a pas d'équivalent en anglais.

Leçons 26 et 27: /ɒ/, /ɔː/
/ɒ/ La voyelle anglaise /ɒ/ ('boss', 'what'), brève, postérieure, ouverte, est prononcée avec la langue plus reculée et les lèvres un peu moins arrondies que pour la voyelle française /ɔ/ ('bosse', 'col').

/ɔː/ Le /ɔː/ anglais ('or', 'port'), long, postérieur, moins ouvert que /ɒ/, n'est ni le /ɔ/ français de 'porte', ni le /o/ français de 'pose'. Prononcé avec les lèvres bien arrondies, il est plus ouvert et plus long que tous les deux.

Leçons 28 et 29: /ʊ/, /uː/
/ʊ/ La voyelle anglaise /ʊ/ ('wood', 'cook'), brève, postérieure et fermée, se rapproche de la voyelle française /u/ ('ou', 'boule'). Les lèvres sont arrondies, mais la langue est un peu moins avancée que pour le son anglais.

/uː/ La voyelle anglaise /uː/ ('fool', 'hoop'), plus longue, plus postérieure et plus fermée que /ʊ/, n'a pas d'équivalent en français. Attention: ce n'est pas simplement /ʊ/ allongé.

Leçons 31 et 32: /ɜː/, /ə/
Ces deux voyelles moyennes, /ɜː/ dans 'purr' et /ə/ dans 'the', correspondent à peu près aux voyelles françaises /œ/ longue ('fleur', 'peur') et /ə/ breve ('le', 'que'), sauf que le /ə/ et le /ɜː/ anglais sont un peu plus ouverts.

Diphtongues

Toutes les voyelles étudiées jusqu'ici sont des voyelles pures. Mais quand deux sons vocaliques se réunissent dans une même syllabe, ils font une diphtongue. Les diphtongues sont nombreuses en anglais. Les comparaisons données ci-dessous ne sont que des approximations.

N'oubliez pas de prononcer bien mais rapidement les deux éléments de chaque diphtongue.

Leçons 33, 34, 35: /eɪ/, /aɪ/, /ɔɪ/

Ces trois diphtongues sont formées d'une voyelle pure (/e/, /a/, /ɔ/—voir leçons 21, 25 et 27) suivie de la voyelle pure /ɪ/, qui ressemble ici au yod français /j/ dans 'fille', 'plier', 'abeille'.

/eɪ/ comme dans 'bay' ressemble au son final du mot français 'abeille'.

/aɪ/ comme dans 'buy' ressemble à la voyelle plus yod du mot français 'bail'.

/ɔɪ/ comme dans 'boy' n'a pas d'equivalent en français. En français il y a le mot 'oïl' (langue d'oïl) qui ressemble un peu à cette diphtongue anglais; mais il faudrait prononcer le /ə/ et le /i/ beaucoup plus vite et ensemble (formant une diphtongue).

Leçons 37 et 38: /əʊ/, /ɑʊ/

Ces diphtongues sont formées d'une voyelle pure (/ə/, /ɑ/—voir leçons 32 et 25) suivie de la voyelle pure /ʊ/, qui ressemble ici à là semi-consonne /w/ en français comme dans 'oui', 'oiseau', 'moins'. Cependant le /w/ français n'apparaît jamais en position finale.

/əʊ/ comme dans 'low', ressemble un peu à la voyelle française /o/ ('eau') plus /w/.

/ɑʊ/ comme dans 'cow', ressemble à un son très rare en français—celui de 'caoutchouc' ou 'yaourt'.

Leçons 39, 40, 41: /ɪə/, /ɛə/, /ʊə/

Ces trois diphtongues sont formées d'une voyelle pure plus la voyelle moyenne /ə/ (/ə/ caduc ou muet en français).

/ɪə/ comme dans 'fear'—ressemble au deuxième son vocalique du mot 'amie' lorsque le 'e' muet est prononcé, comme dans une chanson.

/ɛə/ comme dans 'pair'—imaginez le mot 'père' sans prononcer la consonne intermédiaire.

/ʊə/ comme dans 'sewer'—ressemble à 'boue' lorsque le 'e' muet est prononcé. En certains cas /ʊə/ est précédé de /j/. Le son /jʊə/, comme dans 'ewer' ou 'manure', n'a pas d'équivalent en français.

Greek Notes

by Irene Warburton

Φωνήεντα

Μαθήματα 1–3: /p/ /b/, /t/ /d/, /k/ /g/
Τά στιγμικά ἄφωνα σύμφωνα /p/, /t/, /k/ *καί τά ἠχηρά* /b/, /d/, /g/ *τῆς Ἀγγλικῆς δέν προφέρονται ἀκριβῶς ὅπως τά ἀντίστοιχα* /p/, /t/, /k/ *καί* /b/, /d/, /g/ *τῆς Ἑλληνικῆς. Ὑπάρχουν ὁρισμένες σημαντικές διαφορές:*

Τά Ἀγγλικά /p/, /t/, /k/ *ὅταν βρίσκονται στήν ἀρχή τῆς λέξης καί ἀκολουθοῦνται ἀπό φωνῆεν,συνοδεύονται ἀπό δασύτητα (ἀπό ἕνα σύντομο* /h/).Αὐτό *δέν συμβαίνει στά Ἑλληνικά,κι ὁ μαθητής θά πρέπει νά συνηθίσει νά μή παραλείπει τή δασύτητα, γιατί λέξεις ὅπως* 'pot', 'tip', *καί* 'cot' *μπορεῖ νά ἀκουστοῦν σάν* 'bought', 'dip' *καί* 'got'.

Στά Ἑλληνικά τά /b/, /d/, /g/ *προφέρονται συνήθως μέ ἐρρινοποίηση, σάν* /mb/, /nd/ *καί* /ŋg/. *Γι' αὐτό οἱ Ἕλληνες προφέρουν πολύ συχνά λέξεις ὅπως οἱ* 'book', 'door', *κλπ. σάν* /mbʊk/, /ndɔːr/, *κλπ. Ὁ μαθητής λοιπόν πρέπει νά προσέξει νά κρατᾶ κλειστή τή δίοδο πρός τή ρινική κοιλότητα, ὅταν προφέρει τούς φθόγγους αὐτούς ὥστε ὁ ἀέρας νά βγαίνει μόνο ἀπό τό στόμα, καί νά εἶναι ἀδύνατη ἡ ἐρρινοποίηση.*

Ἐπειδή στά Ἑλληνικά δέν ὑπάρχει βασικός διαχωρισμός (contrast) *ἀνάμεσα στά* /b/, /mp/ *καί* /mb/, *οἱ Ἕλληνες ἔχουν τήν τάση νά προφέρουν λέξεις ὅπως* 'lab', 'lamp' *καί* 'lamb' *μέ τόν ἴδιο τρόπο, σάν* /læmb/. *Ὁ μαθητής λοιπόν πρέπει νά μάθει α) νά μή βάζει ρινικότητα στά* /b/, /d/, /g/, *β) νά μήν ἠχηροποιεῖ τά* /p/, /t/, /k/ *μετά τά ρινικά* /m/, /n/, /ŋ/, *καί γ) νά μήν ἀφαιρεῖ τή ρινικότητα στά* /mb/, /nd/ *καί* /ŋg/.

Μαθήματα 4–8: /f/ /v/, /θ/ /ð/, /s/ /z/, /ʃ/ /ʒ/, /h/
/f/ /v/ *Τά χειλικά τριβόμενα σύμφωνα* /f/ *καί* /v/ *τῆς Ἀγγλικῆς προφέρονται ὅπως τά ἀντίστοιχα* /f/ *καί* /v/ *τῆς Ἑλληνικῆς.* Παραδείγματα:

'far'	'*φάρος*'	/f'aros/
'vase'	'*βάζο*'	/v'azo/

/θ/ /ð/ *Τά ὀδοντικά τριβόμενα σύμφωνα* /θ/ *καί* /ð/ *προφέρονται ὅπως τά 'Ελληνικά* /θ/ *καί* /ð/ Παραδείγματα:

'theme'	'*θυμάρι*'	/θim'ari/
'those'	'*δάσος*'	/ð'asos/

/s/ /z/ *Τά συριστικά σύμφωνα, δηλαδή τό ἄηχο* /s/ *καί τό ἠχηρό* /z/, *τῆς 'Αγγλικῆς δέ διαφέρουν ἀπό τά ἀντίστοιχα τῆς 'Ελληνικῆς. 'Αλλά ἐπειδή στά 'Ελληνικά τό* /s/ *ἠχηροποιεῖται πρίν ἀπό* /m/, *οἱ "Ελληνες ἔχουν τήν τάση νά προφέρουν λέξεις ὅπως οἱ* 'small', 'smart', *λανθασμένα σάν* /zmɔːl/, /zmaːt/. *Στό 'Αγγλικό σύμπλεγμα* /s/ + /m/ *τό* /s/ *παραμένει ἄηχο.*

/ʃ/ /ʒ/ *Τά ὑπερωικά τριβόμενα συριστικά* /ʃ/ *καί* /ʒ/ *τῆς 'Αγγλικῆς δέν ὑπάρχουν στά 'Ελληνικά. Ὁ μαθητής πρέπει νά προσπαθήσει νά τραβήξει τή γλώσσα του λίγο πιό μέσα ἀπ' ὅ,τι γιά τήν προφορά τῶν* /s/ *καί* /z/ *καί νά ἀνασηκώσει τό πάνω μέρος της,ἔτσι ὥστε νά ἀγγίζει τήν ὑπερώα·τά χείλη νά εἶναι λίγο πιό στρογγυλεμένα.*

/h/ *Τό γλωσσιδικό τριβόμενο* /h/ *(δασύ σύμφωνο) τῆς 'Αγγλικῆς δέν ὑπάρχει ἐπίσης στά Νέα 'Ελληνικά.Οἱ "Ελληνες ἔχουν τήν τάση νά χρησιμοποιοῦν τό 'Ελληνικό* /x/ *στή θέση του,κι ἔτσι προφέρουν λέξεις ὅπως οἱ* 'ham' *(*/hæm/*)*, 'him' *(*/hɪm/*) κλπ., σάν* /xæm/, /xɪm/ *κλπ.Γιά νά προφέρει σωστά τό* /h/ *ὁ μαθητής πρέπει νά προσπαθήσει νά ἀρθρώσει τό 'Ελληνικό* /x/ *χωρίς νά ἀνασηκώσει τή γλώσσα πρός τήν ὑπερώα·ὁ φθόγγος* 'h' *θυμίζει τόν ἦχο τοῦ ἀναστεναγμοῦ.*

Μαθήματα 9 καί 10: /tʃ/, /dʒ/
Τά προστριβόμενα /tʃ/ *καί* /dʒ/ *δέν ὑπάρχουν στά 'Ελληνικά. 'Αποτελοῦν ὅμως συνδυασμούς τῶν* /t/ + /ʃ/ *καί* /d/ + /ʒ/, *κι ἔτσι, ὅταν ὁ μαθητής ἀρχίσει νά προφέρει σωστά τά* /ʃ/ *καί* /ʒ/, *δέ θά ἔχει δυσκολία καί μέ τά* /tʒ/ *καί* /dʒ/.

Μαθήματα 11–13: /m/, /n/, /ŋ/
Τό χειλικό ἔρρινο /m/ *δέ διαφέρει καθόλου στά 'Αγγλικά καί τά 'Ελληνικά:*

'mother'	'*μαμά*'	/mam'a/

Τό ὀδοντικό /n/ *ὅμως τῆς 'Αγγλικῆς διαφέρει λίγο ἀπό τό ἀντίστοιχο* /n/ *τῆς'Ελληνικῆς.Γιά τό 'Ελληνικό* /n/ *ἡ ἄκρη τῆς γλώσσας ἀκουμπᾶ στό πίσω μέρος τῶν πάνω δοντιῶν,ἐνῶ γιά τό 'Αγγλικό* /n/ *ἡ ἄκρη τῆς γλώσσας ἀκουμπᾶ πιό πάνω,στά φατνία (δηλαδή στά οὖλα πού καλύπτουν τίς ρίζες τῶν δοντιῶν).*

Τό οὐρανικό /ŋ/ *γενικά μπορεῖ νά ἐμφανιστεῖ μόνο πρίν ἀπ' τό* /g/ *στά 'Ελληνιλά,κι ἔτσι πολύ συχνά οἱ "Ελληνες προφέρουν τό 'Αγγλικό* /ŋ/ *σάν* /ŋg/.*Γιά νά τό πραγματώσουν σωστά,οἱ μαθητές πρέπει νά τοποθετήσουν τή γλώσσα στό ἴδιο σημεῖο ὅπως καί γιά τήν προφορά τοῦ* /g/,*ἀλλά μέ τή δίοδο πρός τή ρινική κοιλότητα ἀνοιχτή,ὥστε ὁ ἀέρας νά βγαίνει ἀπό τή μύτη,κι ὄχι ἀπό τό στόμα.*

Μαθήματα 14 καί 15: /l/, /r/

Τό ὑγρό /l/ *τῆς Ἀγγλικῆς σχηματίζεται μέ τή μύτη τῆς γλώσσας νά ἀκουμπᾶ πάνω στά φατνία,κι ὄχι πάνω στά δόντια (ὅπως στήν περίπτωση τοῦ Ἑλληνικοῦ* /l/).

Τό ὑγρό /r/ *τῆς Ἀγγλικῆς διαφέρει πολύ ἀπό τό Ἑλληνικό* /r/: *στό Ἑλληνικό ἡ μύτη τῆς γλώσσας χτυπᾶ μιά ἤ δυό φορές στά φατνία· ἀντίθετα,γιά τό Ἀγγλικό* /r/ *ἡ ἄκρη τῆς γλώσσας εἶναι στραμμένη λίγο πρός τά μέσα καί ἀνασηκωμένη λίγο πρός τά φατνία χωρίς νά τά ἀγγίζει,ἐνῶ τό σῶμα της εἶναι τραβηγμένο πιό μέσα ἀπ'ὅ,τι γιά τό Ἑλληνικό* /r/.

Μαθήματα 16 καί 17: /j/, /w/

Τό ἡμίφωνο /j/ *δέν ὑπάρχει στά Ἑλληνικά,ἀλλά προφέρεται σχεδόν ὅμοια μέ τή συλλαβή* /γi/, *ὅταν αὐτή εἶναι στήν ἀρχή τῆς λέξης καί ἀκολουθεῖ φωνῆεν· π.χ.*

'yacht' 'γιός' /jos/

Γιά νά προφέρει σωστά τό /j/ *ὁ μαθητής πρέπει νά προσπαθήσει νά πραγματώσει τό Ἑλληνικό* /γi/ + *φωνῆεν πολύ μαλακά, μέ λιγότερη τριβή στόν οὐρανίσκο.*

Τό ἡμίφωνο /w/ *δέν ὑπάρχει στά Νέα Ἑλληνικά.*Π*ροφέρεται ὅμως ὅπως περίπου ἡ συλλαβή* /u/ *τῆς Ἑλληνικῆς ὅταν ἀκολουθεῖται ἀπό φωνῆεν,γι 'αὐτό κι οἱ Ἕλληνες συνήθως προφέρουν τή λέξη* 'water' *σάν* /γuɔːtə/. *Ὁ μαθητής πρέπει νά προσπαθήσει νά πραγματώσει τό Ἑλληνικό ἀντίστοιχο* /γu/ + *φωνῆεν μέ τόν πρῶτο φθόγγο πολύ πιό μαλακά·ἡ γλώσσα δηλαδή δέν πρέπει νά ἀγγίζει τήν ὑπερώα· τά χείλη νά εἶναι στρογγυλά,σχεδόν κλειστά.*

Σύμφωνα

Μάθημα 18: /iː/

Τό Ἀγγλικό φωνῆεν /iː/ *εἶναι ἀρκετά ὅμοιο μέ τό Ἑλληνικό* /i/, *ἰδίως ὅταν αὐτό τονίζεται,ὅπως στίς λέξεις 'μή'* /miː/ (don't), *'πίνω'* /piːno/ (I drink), *κλπ. Ἡ μόνη διαφορά εἶναι ὅτι γιά τό Ἀγγλικό* /iː/ *ἡ γλώσσα τοποθετεῖται λίγο πιό ψηλά καί τά χείλη εἶναι πιό κλειστά καί πιό τραβηγμένα στίς ἄκρες.*

Μάθημα 19: /ɪ/

Τό Ἀγγλικό φωνῆεν /ɪ/ *δέν ὑπάρχει στά Ἑλληνικά. Ἡ προφορά του βρίσκεται ἀνάμεσα στήν προφορά τῶν Ἑλληνικῶν φωνηέντων* /i/ *καί* /e/.*Οἱ Ἕλληνες ἔχουν μεγάλη δυσκολία μέ τό φθόγγο αὐτό καί κατά κανόνα τόν ἀντικαθιστοῦν μέ τό οἰκεῖο τους* /i/. *Ἔτσι λέξεις ὅπως οἱ* 'hip', 'sin', *κλπ.,ἀκούγονται σάν* 'heap', 'seen' *κλπ. Ὁ μαθητής πρέπει νά συνηθίσει νά τοποθετεῖ τό πάνω μέρος τῆς γλώσσας του λίγο πιό ψηλά ἀπ' ὅ,τι γιά τό Ἑλληνικό* /e/, *μέ τά χείλη πιό κλειστά,ὄχι ὅμως τόσο κλειστά ὅσο γιά τό* /i/.

Μάθημα 21: /e/
Τό Ἀγγλικό φωνῆεν /e/ *εἶναι ὅμοιο μέ τό ἀντίστοιχο Ἑλληνικό.Παραδείγματα:*

'net'	'*νερό*'	/ner'o/
'met'	'*μετά*'	/met'a/
'bed'	'*μπαίνω*'	/b'eno/

Μαθήματα 22 καί 23: /æ/, /ʌ/
Τό φωνῆεν /æ/ *δέν ὑπάρχει στά Ἑλληνικά. Ἡ προφορά του βρίσκεται ἀνάμεσα στήν προφορά τῶν* /e/ *καί* /a/ *τῆς Ἑλληνικῆς.Γι'αὐτό ἡ λέξη* 'bad'*π.χ. συχνά ἀκούγεται ἀπό Ἕλληνες σάν* 'bed' *καί καμιά φορά σάν* 'bud'.*Γιά τήν ὀρθή προφορά τοῦ* /æ/ *τά χείλη πρέπει νά εἶναι πιό ἀνοιχτά καί τραβηγμένα πρός τίς ἄκρες ἀπ' ὅ,τι γιά τό Ἑλληνικό* /a/ *καί ἡ γλώσσα νά μήν εἶναι οὔτε τόσο ψηλά,ὅσο γιά τήν προφορά τοῦ* /e/, *οὔτε τόσο χαμηλά,ὅσο γιά τήν προφορά τοῦ* /a/ *τῆς Ἑλληνικῆς.*

Τό φωνῆεν /ʌ/ *δέν ὑπάρχει στά Ἑλληνικά.Μοιάζει ὡστόσο ἀρκετά μέ τό Ἑλληνικό* /a/, *ὅπως αὐτό προφέρεται στή λέξη 'κάποτε'* /k'apote/.*Γιά τήν προφορά τοῦ* /ʌ/ *ἡ γλώσσα εἶναι πιό τραβηγμένη πρός τά μέσα καί τό σῶμα της ἀνασηκώνεται λίγο ψηλότερα ἀπ'ὅ,τι γιά τό Ἑλληνικό* /a/.

Μάθημα 25: /ɑː/
Τό φωνῆεν /ɑː/ *δέν ὑπάρχει στά Ἑλληνικά.Μοιάζει μέ τό Ἑλληνικό* /a/ *ὅμως,ὅταν αὐτό προφέρεται τονισμένο,ὅπως στό ἐπιφώνημα 'ἄ.' καί τό 'μά.'* /mɑː/ (but), *μέ τή διαφορά ὅτι γιά τό Ἀγγλικό* /ɑː/ *ἡ γλώσσα εἶναι πιό χαμηλά καί πιό πίσω στή στοματική κοιλότητα. Ἐπίσης τό Ἀγγλικό* /ɑː/ *εἶναι πιό μακρό στήν προφορά του ἀπ' τό τονισμένο Ἑλληνικό,ἄν ἀκολουθεῖ ἠχηρό σύμφωνο.*

Μάθημα 26: /ɒ/
Τό φωνῆεν /ɒ/ *τῆς Ἀγγλικῆς δέν ὑπάρχει στά Ἑλληνικά. Ἡ θέση τῆς ἄρθρωσής του εἶναι ἀνάμεσα στίς θέσεις τῶν Ἑλληνικῶν φωνηέντων* /o/ *καί* /a/.*Τό σῶμα τῆς γλώσσας εἶναι πιό πίσω ἀπ'ὅ,τι στό Ἑλληνικό* /o/ *καί τό πίσω μέρος της εἶναι πιό ψηλά ἀπ'ὅ,τι στό* /a/,*ἀλλά ὄχι τόσο ψηλά ὅσο γιά τό* /o/ *τῆς Ἑλληνικῆς.Τά χείλη εἶναι λιγότερο στρογγυλεμένα ἀπ' ὅ,τι στό Ἑλληνικό* /o/.

Μάθημα 27: /ɔː/
Τό φωνῆεν /ɔː/ *εἶναι πιό μακρό στήν προφορά του ἀπό τό Ἑλληνικό* /o/,*ἡ γλῶσσα εἶναι πιό ψηλά καί τά χείλη πιό στρογγυλεμένα.*

Μαθήματα 28 καί 29: /ʊ/, /uː/
Τό φωνῆεν /ʊ/ *σχηματίζεται ἀνάμεσα στά Ἑλληνικά φωνήεντα* /o/ *καί* /u/.*Τά χείλη εἶναι λιγότερο στρογγυλεμένα ἀπ'ὅ,τι στό Ἑλληνικό* /u/ *καί τό πίσω μέρος τῆς γλώσσας εἶναι πιό ψηλά ἀπ'ὅ,τι γιά τό* /o/,*ἀλλ' ὄχι τόσο ψηλά ὅσο γιά τό* /u/ *τῆς Ἑλληνικῆς. Ὁ μαθητής πρέπει νά συνηθίσει νά μή χρησιμοποιεῖ τό Ἑλληνικό* /u/ *στή θέση τοῦ Ἀγγλικοῦ* /ʊ/.
Τό φωνῆεν /uː/ *στά Ἀγγλικά εἶναι πολύ ὅμοιο μέ τό Ἑλληνικό* /u/,*ἰδίως ὅταν αὐτό εἶναι τονισμένο·π.χ.*

'suit' '*σούστα*' /s'usta/

Τό Ἀγγλικό /uː/ *εἶναι λίγο πιό μακρό καί τά χείλη εἶναι λίγο πιό κλειστά κατά τήν προφορά του.*

Μαθήματα 31 καί 32: /ɜː/, /ə/
Τό φωνῆεν /ɜː/ *δέν ὑπάρχει στά Ἑλληνικά,καί πολλές φορές οἱ Ἕλληνες τό ἀντικαθιστοῦν μέ τό οἰκεῖο τους* /e/.*Γιά νά προφέρει σωστά τό φωνῆεν,ὁ μαθητής πρέπει νά προσέξει νά μήν κρατᾶ τή γλώσσα του μπροστά,ὅπως γιά τό* /e/,*ἀλλά νά τήν ἀφήνει στήν κεντρική της θέση·τό μέσο τῆς γλώσσας νά ἀνασηκώνεται λίγο πρός τήν ὑπερώα,ἐνῶ τά χείλη νά εἶναι ἀνοιγμένα ἐλαφρά καί χαλαρά.*
Τό φωνῆεν /ə/ *ἀρθρώνεται παρόμοια μέ τό* /ɜː/,*μόνο πού εἶναι πιό σύντομο,ἀφοῦ προφέρεται πάντα χωρίς τόνο,καί τό μέσο τῆς γλώσσας εἶναι τοποθετημένο λίγο πιό χαμηλά.*

Δ*ίφθογγοι*

Ὅταν δύο φωνήεντα συμπροφέρονται πολύ στενά,ἔτσι ὥστε νά ἀποτελοῦν μία συλλαβή,τότε λέμε ὅτι σχηματίζουν δίφθογγο. Ἐπειδή στά Ἑλληνικά οἱ δίφθογγοι εἶναι σπάνιοι,οἱ Ἕλληνες ἔχουν τήν τάση νά προφέρουν τά δύο φωνήεντα τῶν διφθόγγων ἄλλων γλωσσῶν σάν δύο χωριστές συλλαβές.Οἱ μαθητές πρέπει νά προσέξουν γιά νά ἀποφύγουν αὐτό τό σφάλμα στήν προφορά τῶν διφθόγγων τῆς Ἀγγλικῆς.

Μαθήματα 33–35: /eɪ/, /aɪ/, /ɔɪ/
/eɪ/, *ὅπως στή λέξη* 'lay'. Π*ροφέρεται ὅμοια μέ τό Ἑλληνικό* /ei/ *στή λέξη 'λέει'* (he says)*π.χ.,μόνο πού τό* /i/ *εἶναι πολύ πιό σύντομο,καί τά δύο φωνήεντα ἀποτελοῦν μιά συλλαβή.*
/aɪ/,*ὅπως στή λέξη* 'buy'.*Μοιάζει μέ τό Ἑλληνικό* /'ai/ *στή λέξη 'πάει'* (he goes) *π.χ.,ἄν τά δύο φωνήεντα δοθοῦν σέ μιά συλλαβή,μέ τό* /i/ *πολύ πιό σύντομο.*

/ɔɪ/,*ὅπως στή λέξη* 'boy'. *Ἡ προφορά του μοιάζει μέ τό Ἑλληνικό* /'oi/ *στή λέξη 'χλόη'* (grass) *π.χ.,ἀλλά μέ τά δύο φωνήεντα σέ μιά συλλαβή καί τό* /i/ *πολύ πιό σύντομο.*

Μαθήματα 37 καί 38: /əʊ/, /aʊ/
/əʊ/,*ὅπως στή λέξη* 'low'.*Μοιάζει μέ τό Ἑλληνικό* /ou/,*ἀλλά στόν Ἀγγλικό δίφθογγο τό πρῶτο εἶναι πιό ἀνοιχτό ἀπό τό Ἑλληνικό* /o/,*καί ἡ γλῶσσα εἶναι τοποθετημένη πιό χαμηλά·τό δεύτερο φωνῆεν εἶναι πιό σύντομο καί πιό κλειστό ἀπό τό Ἑλληνικό* /u/ *καί τά δύο φωνήετα προφέρονται σέ μιά συλλαβή.*
/aʊ/,*ὅπως στή λέξη* 'house'. *Ἡ προφορά του πλησιάζει τό Ἑλληνικό* /au/ *στή λέξη 'μιάου'* /mi'au/ *π.χ.,ὅταν τό* /aʊ/ *ἀκούγεται σάν μιά συλλαβή,μέ τό* /u/ *πιό σύντομο καί πιό κλειστό.*

Μαθήματα 39–41: /ɪə/, /εə/, /ʊə/
/ɪə/,*ὅπως στή λέξη* 'fear'.*Μοιάζει μέ τόν Ἑλληνικό συνδυασμό* /ia/ *στή λέξη 'μία'* (one) *π.χ.,ἀλλά καί πάλι τά δυό μέρη τοῦ Ἀγγλικοῦ διφθόγγου συμπροφέρονται στενά,σέ μιά συλλαβή,μέ τό δεύτερο ἀπό τά δυό συντομευμένο.*
/εə/,*ὅπως στή λέξη* 'pear'. Π*ροφέρεται σχεδόν ὅμοια μέ τό Ἑλληνικό* /ea/ *στή λέξη 'νέα'* (news) *π.χ.,μέ τά δυό φωνήεντα ὅμως ἑνωμένα σέ μιά συλλαβή.*
/ʊə/,*ὅπως στή λέξη* 'poor'.*Πλησιάζει τό Ἑλληνικό* /ua/ *στή λέξη 'ἄκουα'* (I was listening) *π.χ.,μόνο πού τά δυό του φωνήεντα ἀποτελοῦν μιά μόνο συλλαβή.*

German Notes

by Margaret and David Wright

Die folgende Erklärungen für Deutschsprechende gehen von der Standardaussprache laut Duden 1974 aus, da es unmöglich ist, im Deutschen wie im Englischen auf regionalen Varianten einzugehen.

Konsonanten

Lektion 1–3: /p/ /b/, /t/ /d/, /k/ /g/

Am Anfang des Wortes gibt es keinen Unterschied zwischen den deutschen und den englischen Plosiven. In beiden Sprachen sind die Stimmlosen /p,t,k,/ von einem starken Stoß Luft, ähnlich einem /h/ gefolgt (Behauchung).

Am Ende der Silbe aber sieht es ganz anders aus. Im Deutschen gibt es keinen Unterschied zwischen /b/ und /p/, /d/ und /t/, /g/ und /k/. Im Englischen gibt es große Unterschiede, nämlich: /p/, /t/, /k/ bleiben stimmlos, sind kurz und haben keinen Einfluß auf dem vorhergehenden Laut. Am Ende der Aussage—vor einer Pause—*kann* es eine Behauchung geben.

/b/, /d/, /g/ sind schwach stimmhaft, aber wichtiger, sind lang und verlängern auch den vorhergehenden Laut—Vokal oder Konsonant. Am Ende einer Aussage kann es auch eine leichte Behauchung geben.

Artikulationsstelle

/p/, /b/ werden in beiden Sprachen auf ähnlicher Weise mit den Lippen gebildet.

/t/, /d/ Auf Deutsch sind /t/ und /d/ öfters mit der Zungenspitze gegen die oberen Schneidezähnen gebildet. Auf Englisch sind beide Laute mit der Zungenspitze gegen die Alveolen gebildet.

/k/, /g/ Wie auf Deutsch.

Lektion 4–8: /f/ /v/, /θ/ /ð/, /s/ /z/, /ʃ/ /ʒ/, /h/

Gemeinsam haben Deutsch und Englisch /f/ und /v/, /s/ und /z/ /ʃ/ und /ʒ/, und /h/. Dazu hat Deutsch /ç/ und /x/, Englisch /θ/ und /ð/. Im Gegenteil zum Deutschen sind alle stimmhaften Konsonanten—hier /v/, /z/, /ʒ/ und /ð/—länger als die Stimmlosen—/f/, /s/, /ʃ/ und /θ/.

/f/, /v/ werden in beiden Sprachen gleich ausgesprochen. Nur muß der Deutschsprechende beachten, daß geschriebenes 'v' auch /v/ und nicht /f/ wie auf Deutsch ausgesprochen wird.

/θ/, /ð/ Diese Laute sind unter den schwierigsten für den Deutschsprechenden. Die Zungenspitze muß die oberen Schneidezähne leicht berühren, und zwar von hinten an der unteren Kante. Die Luft muß dann zwischen Zungenspitze und Zähne gedrückt werden. Ein häufiger Fehler hier liegt darin, daß die Zungenspitze die Alveolen berührt, was ein /s/ oder /z/ verursacht. Auch sollte man die Zunge nicht zwischen obere und untere Zähne hinausstrecken, obwohl dies ein gewißes Übungsmittel sein könnte.

/s/, /z/ Diese Laute sind im Englischen und im Deutschen gleich. Nur muß der Deutschsprechende beachten, daß geschriebenes 'z' nur /z/ sein kann, und nie /ts/. Auch werden geschriebene 'st', 'sp' usw. nie /ʃt/, /ʃp/ ausgesprochen, sondern nur /st/, /sp/ usw.

/ʃ/, /ʒ/ /ʃ/ wird wie im Deutschen ausgesprochen. /ʒ/ hat dieselbe Artikulationsstelle, ist aber stimmhaft und länger. Im Deutschen gibt es dieser Laut in 'Journalist', 'Jalousie' usw.

/h/ Wie im Deutschen ist dieser Laut eine stimmlose Variant des folgenden Vokals. Die Lage der Sprechwerkzeuge entspricht die des folgenden Vokals, wird aber ohne Stimme ausgesprochen.

Lektion 9–10: /tʃ/, /dʒ/

Gemeinsam haben Englisch und Deutsch /tʃ/ und /dʒ/, dazu hat Deutsch /pf/ und /ts/, die im Englischen nicht vorkommen.

Wie auf Deutsch /d/ und /t/ öfters durch Berührung der Schneidezähne mit der Zungenspitze, auf Englisch aber nur durch Berührung der Alveolen gebildet werden, so werden /tʃ/ und /dʒ/ in beiden Sprachen unterschiedlich gemacht. Im Englischen muß der erste Teil dieser Laute—/t/ bzw /d/—mit Zungenspitze und Alveolen gebildet werden. Nach den /t/ kommt ein normales /ʃ/. /dʒ/ wird mit derselben Artikulationsstelle gemacht, ist aber stimmhaft und etwas länger. Theoretisch gibt es diesen Laut in Wörter wie 'Dschungel', 'Manager' usw., aber in der Praxis werden diese oft mit /tʃ/ ausgesprochen. Der Deutschsprechende muß hier besonders aufpassen, daß der englische /dʒ/ wirklich stimmhaft ist.

Lektion 11–13: /m/, /n/, /ŋ/

Beide Sprachen haben alle drei nasale Konsonanten /m/, /n/ und /ŋ/.

/m/ ganz wie auf Deutsch.

/n/ Auf Englisch gibt es nur eine Möglichkeit (gegenüber verschiedene Varianten auf Deutsch). Die Zungenspitze muß gegen die Alveolen gedrückt werden, so daß die Luft durch den Nasenraum geht.

/ŋ/ Dieser Laut ist der, den man in Wörter wie 'Ding', 'singen' usw. findet. Vorsicht: es gibt ja kein /g/ in diesen Wörten. Im Englischen aber *kann* dieser Laut von einem /g/ gefolgt werden, z.B. finger = /fɪŋgə/, aber singer = /sɪŋə/.

Lektion 14–15: /l/, /r/

/l/ und /r/: Beide Laute werden im Englischen anders als im Deutschen gebildet.

/l/ Im Englischen gibt es zwei Formen:

Clear /l/, das vor Vokalen gefunden wird. Die Zunge soll zuerst eine /d/-Stelle mit der Spitze gegen die Alveolen nehmen. Die Zungenseiten werden dann von den Backenzähnen zurückgezogen, so daß Kontakt zwischen Zungenspitze und Alveolen bleibt. Der vordere Zungenrücken bleibt oben, im Gegenteil zum deutschen /l/, wo es eher nach unten liegt. Die Luft strömt rechts und links hinaus.

Dark /l/, das vor Konsonanten—z.B. in 'Field'—und am Ende eines Wortes, wo das folgende Wort nicht mit einem Vokal anfängt, gefunden wird. Die Zunge bildet ein /d/ mit der Spitze gegen die Alveolen. Die Zungenseiten werden von den Backenzähnen zurückgezogen, so daß Kontakt mit den Alveolen bleibt. Der vordere Zungenrücken liegt dieses Mal sehr tief, wobei der hintere Zungenrücken nach oben kommt.

/r/ Ausgesprochen wird /r/ nur vor Vokalen. Die Zunge bildet ein /d/ mit der Spitze gegen die Alveolen. Die Zungenspitze wird zurückgezogen, indem die Zungenseiten gegen den Backenzähnen gedrückt werden. Die Mitte der Zunge bildet eine Rille, die Spitze wird auch leicht nach oben gedreht. Es ist wichtig, daß die Zungenspitze den Gaumen *nicht* berührt.

Lektion 16–17: /j/, /w/

/j/ und /w/: Beide sind stimmhafte Laute.

/j/ gibt es auf Deutsch, wird aber als 'j' geschrieben, Auf Englisch ist /j/ meistens als 'y' geschreiben.

/w/ Hier muß der Deutschsprechende besonders aufpassen. Im Deutschen wird geschriebenes 'w' /v/ ausgesprochen, was nie im Englischen der Fall ist. Ein anderer häufiger Fehler besteht in der Verwechslung von /v/ und /w/. Geschriebenes 'v' soll nur als /v/ und nie als /w/ ausgesprochen werden.

Am besten nehmen die Lippen und die Zunge die /u/ Stellung, und gehen sofort nach Einsetzen der Stimme in die Stellung des folgenden Vokals. Der /u/-Teil darf nur sehr kurz sein, jedenfalls viel kürzer als ein normales /u/.

Vokale

Englisch und Deutsch haben gemeinsam die folgenden Vokale:

/iː/, /ɪ/, /e/, /ɑː/, /ɒ/, /ʊ/, /uː/ und /ə/, die aber doch nicht gleich ausgesprochen werden. Im allgemeinen werden englische Vokale viel lockerer als deutsche Vokale ausgesprochen.

Dazu hat Englisch noch /æ/, /ʌ/, /ɔː/, und /ɜː/, die im Deutschen nicht vorkommen. Deutsch hat noch /eː/, /o/, /y/ und /ø/, die im Englischen nicht vorkommen.

Alle Vokale werden länger, wenn sie von stimmhaften Konsonanten gefolgt werden, und kürzer, wenn sie von stimmlosen Konsonanten gefolgt werden.

Lektion 18–20: /iː/, /ɪ/

/iː/ Deutsch hat einen ähnlichen (zB in 'viel'), der leider nicht ganz wie im Englischen ausgesprochen wird. Beim deutschen /iː/ sind die Lippen breit und etwas gestrafft; im Englischen dagegen sind die Lippen viel lockerer und etwas runder und nehmen eine Stellung wie im 'i' des deutschen 'Wind'. Die Zunge aber nimmt die gleiche Stellung wie im deutschen 'Dieb.' so daß der Unterschied zwischen deutschen 'Dieb' und englischen 'deep' in der Lippenstellung liegt.

/ɪ/ Hat derselben Wert wie /i/ in deutschen 'Wind,' 'Kind' usw., die Lippen aber sind im Englischen lockerer und nicht so breit. /ɪ/ ist auch viel kürzer als das englische /iː/.

Lektion 21: /e/

Dieser Laut hat dieselbe Zungenstellung wie das deutsche /ɛ/ in 'Teller.' Die Lippen beim englischen /e/ sind aber weniger breit und etwas lockerer als beim deutschen /ɛ/.

Lektion 22–23: /æ/, /ʌ/

/æ/ Diesen Laut gibt es nur auf Englisch. Um ihn zu erreichen, fangen wir beim englischen /e/ an. Der ganze Mund wird weiter geöffnet, so daß die Zunge niedriger liegt und die Lippen offener sind. Der Deutschsprechende muß hier besonders beachten, daß er einen Unterschied zwischen /e/ und /æ/ macht, da die deutsche Sprache Wörter wie 'Camping' übernommen hat, die falscherweise als 'Cämping' ausgesprochen werden. Dieses sollte man auf Englisch nicht tun, sondern ein deutlicher Unterschied zwischen /e/ und /æ/ gelten lassen.

/ʌ/ Dieser Laut erreicht man am besten durch das deutsche /a/ in 'Wasser'. Die Lippen sind im Englischen weniger breit (sogenannte neutrale Stellung). Die Zunge wird in der Mitte ein bißchen gehoben.

Lektion 25: /ɑː/

Dieser Laut ist ähnlich dem deutschen /aː/ in 'Jahr' und ist ebenso lang wie dieses. Man muß aber auf die unterschiedliche Aussprache achten:

Wir fangen mit dem deutschen /aː/ in 'Jahr' an. Der Mund wird weiter geöffnet, die Lippen werden etwas gerundet, und die Zunge geht ein bißchen nach hinten. Die Muskulatur ist auch beim englischen /ɑː/ lockerer als beim deutschen.

Lektion 26–27: /ɒ/, /ɔː/
/ɒ/ Wie das deutsche /ɒ/ in 'offen.'
/ɔː/ Im Vergleich zum /ɒ/ ist der Mund enger geschlossen, die Lippen stärker gerundet und etwas gespitzt (wie beim Pfeifen), und die Zunge etwas höher. Der Laut ist auch länger.

Lektion 28–29: /ʊ/, /uː/
/ʊ/ Wie das deutsche /ʊ/ in 'Mutter.'
/uː/ Unterscheidet sich vom deutschen /uː/ in 'Mut' durch lockerere Lippen; im Deutschen sind die Lippen gespitzt, im Englischen ist dies nicht der Fall.

Lektion 31–32: /ɜː/, /ə/
/ə/ Wie das deutsche /ə/ in 'gesagt.'
/ɜː/ Dieser Laut ist fast ein langes /ə/. Nur ist die Zunge etwas höher. Der Deutschsprechende sollte auch darauf achten, daß /ɜː/ nicht das /øː/ oder /ø/ wie in 'mögen' oder 'Götter' ist.

Diphthonge

Deutsch hat /aɪ/, /ɔɪ/, /ɑʊ/, die in Englisch auch vorkommen, aber die wieder nicht gleich ausgesprochen werden. Englisch hat dazu noch /eɪ/, /əʊ/, /ɪə/, /ɛə/ und /ʊə/.

Lektion 33–35: /eɪ/, /aɪ/, /ɔɪ/
Diese Diphthonge bestehen aus dem englischen /e/, /a/ oder /ɔ/ (siehe Lektion 21, 25, und 27) und dem englischen /ɪ/ (siehe Lektion 19).

/eɪ/ Um diesen Laut auszusprechen sollte der Deutschsprechende mit dem englischen /e/ anfangen, und mit dem /ɪ/ enden, wobei das /ɪ/ nur sehr kurz und leise ist, das /e/ aber etwas länger und lauter. Die Lippen bleiben locker in einer neutralen Stellung.

/aɪ/ ist dem deutschen 'ei' oder 'ai' wie in 'Reise' ähnlich, nur ist beim /ɪ/-Teil die Zunge nicht so hoch wie im Deutschen—es ist immer das englische /ɪ/,—und die Lippen bleiben lockerer, nicht gebreitet wie im Deutschen. Das /ɪ/-Teil ist auch kürzer und leiser als das /a/-Teil.

/ɔɪ/ Mit dem englischen /ɔ/ (kürzere Form von /ɔː/) anfangen, dabei aber die Zunge etwas nach unten halten. Dann folgt ein leiseres kürzeres /ɪ/, das ganze nicht so hoch oder vorn wie im deutschen 'Leute'.

Lektion 37–38: /əʊ/, /ɑʊ/

/əʊ/ Fangen wir mit dem englischen /ə/ an. Es folgt ein englisches /ʊ/. Dabei werden Lippen gerundet und Zunge höher gestellt. Der /ə/-Teil ist länger und lauter als der /ʊ/-Teil.

/ɑʊ/ Vorsicht: dieser Laut ist nicht das deutsche 'au' wie in 'Haus'. Das Englische fängt mit dem englischen /ɑ/ an (kürzere Form von /ɑː/, siehe Lektion 25 im vorhergehenden Teil), also hinter dem deutschen /a/ im /au/ von 'Haus'. Der /ʊ/-Teil ist das englische /ʊ/. Die Lippen gehen vom leicht gebreiteten /ɑ/ zum runden /ʊ/. Der /ɑ/-Teil ist länger und lauter als das /ʊ/-Teil.

Lektion 39–41:/ɪə/, /ɛə/, /ʊə/

/ɪə/ Dieser Diphthong besteht aus englischen /ɪ/ und /ə/, wobei das /ɪ/ länger und lauter als das /ə/ ist. Einen ähnlichen Laut gibt es im deutschen 'ziehen', nur sind im Deutschen beide Teile des Diphthongs länger als im Englischen.

/ɛə/ Um diesen Diphthong zu erreichen, fangen wir am besten mit deutschem /ɛ/ wie in 'hätte' an. Diesem folgt ein englisches /ə/. Der /ɛ/-Teil ist länger und lauter als der /ə/-Teil. Vorsicht: dieser Laut ist jener im deutschen 'Ehe'—das erste 'e' hier ist geschlossener als im englischen /ɛə/.

/ʊə/ Wir fangen am besten mit dem deutschen Wort 'Ruhe' an. Der /ʊ/-Teil des englischen /ʊə/ hat dieselbe Zungenstellung, die Lippen aber sind nur leicht gerundet. Der /ə/-Teil in beiden Sprachen ist dasselbe. Der ganze Laut ist aber im Englischen kürzer, wobei das /ʊ/ länger und lauter als das /ə/ ist.